# THE JAPANESE
# Saké
# BIBLE

## BRIAN ASHCRAFT

WITH TASTING NOTES BY **TAKASHI EGUCHI**
FOREWORD BY **RICHIE HAWTIN**

**TUTTLE** Publishing
Tokyo | Rutland, Vermont | Singapore

# SHARING SAKE WITH THE WORLD

**The *Sake Bible* launches at a crucial moment for sake as top chefs, sommeliers and enthusiasts alike are discovering this beautifully handcrafted beverage. Sake has been part of Japanese culture for over a thousand years and until recently you had to be an expert and make frequent visits to Japan to study and unravel the mysteries that are gathered together in this book.**

As a longtime sake enthusiast, reading this book brings me back to my first trip to Japan. I soon realized that the sake I had tasted growing up in Canada had been very basic and rough. In Tokyo, strange oversized 1.8-liter (4-pint) *isshobin* bottles lined the windows and shelves of the local restaurants we visited, each decorated with beautiful labels covered with exotic motifs and unrecognizable characters. With every new bottle I realized no two sake were alike, discovering a surprising range of deep and refined flavors accompanied by fragrant aromas and subtle varying textures. Served in hand-crafted vessels, the sake gently supported the food, and the ritual of pouring for one another created a warm and communal feeling.

Those early experiences kindled my deep curiosity in sake, and as I returned to Japan each year for my DJ concerts, I visited breweries, talked with brewers, tasted local styles and learned as much about sake as I could. I started to fully appreciate the fine balance of tradition and modern technology that forms the basis of this refined, handcrafted and creative process.

As a musician who balances human intuition alongside electronic synthesizers and drum machines to write music, I found a wonderful parallel to the creative process of artisan sake. The attention to technical detail, the restricted ingredients and the astonishing resulting complexity, along with its heady intoxicating feeling, all reminded me of qualities that I strove to instill in my own productions. I was hooked, and just as I share my passion for music in my DJ performances, I set in motion a series of ideas that would allow me to spread my passion for sake to my fans and friends around the world.

This is where my intentions align with this book's creators, in our mission to share our love and knowledge of Japanese sake with an international audience. In this book you'll meet the men and women behind the sake: the families, brewery owners, master brewers and

the staff, whose ingenuity, perseverance and dedication have continued the tradition and development of sake over generations. And you will learn how relatively simple ingredients become such a magic combination, creating the complexity and variety of flavors, textures and aromas that we all find so alluring in sake.

One of the most beautiful, and important, characteristics of sake is that it quietly enhances the flavors of food and actually pairs incredibly well with international cuisine. At tasting events around the world, I marry sake with regional specialties using local ingredients. From pasta and fresh cheeses in Italy, to seafood paella in Spain and delicate farm-to-table dishes at Michelin-starred restaurants, the versatility of sake is unparalleled and something I recommend everyone experiment with!

I remember one particular dinner in Lebanon where guests were astonished and excited how well this foreign beverage paired with their flavorful and hearty cuisine. In combination with the sake, they were tasting their favorite traditional dishes in a refreshing new light. Imagine a creamy lentil pasta with spicy tamarind and juicy pomegranate served with a silky junmai ginjo. Delicious!

Sake already finds itself on the beverage list of fine restaurants around the world and is appreciated by their most discerning customers. And with no additives, premium sake is a natural fit for today's health-conscious consumer. Sake really can be enjoyed everywhere and fits all social situations. Enjoy a rich junmai at your summer BBQ, sip a hearty genshu at a music festival, celebrate your birthday with a bottle of sparkling sake, or savor a delicate junmai daiginjo with your favorite dessert.

Whether you're an enthusiast, an educator, a sommelier, a chef or simply enjoy the unique, warm feeling that sake delivers, *The Sake Bible* will take you deeper into the intoxicating world of Japanese sake.

—Richie Hawtin
Musician, DJ, Sake Samurai, and Sommelier
entersake.com/sake36.com

# A WONDERFUL TIME TO BE A SAKE DRINKER

The morning sun shines on the waves in the harbor as seagulls wail. I look out across the bay to Hokkaido, where I spent time exploring Japan's rich whisky tradition for my book *Japanese Whisky*. This pier in Aomori Prefecture is the farthest north I've been on the main island of Honshu, where I've lived since 2001. It was on this isle that sake as we know it was born.

Snow won't fall for a few weeks, but the brewing season is in full swing. I've ridden train after train, all over Honshu, spending morning after morning in sake breweries and evenings with some of the best sake in Japan—which is, of course, the best in the world.

I often think of the first time I stepped into a sake brewery. It was in 2005, on a crisp fall morning like this in Nara, Japan's ancient capital. I remember the elegant fermented smells hitting my nose as I walked up the dirt road toward the white-walled brewery. I remember marveling that rice, water, yeast and the seemingly magical *koji* microorganisms could create one of the most amazing brews I'd ever imbibed.

This is an interesting time for sake, even as number of breweries continues to decline.

During the late 1800s there were 30,000 breweries in Japan, a number that was halved due to new taxes, increased national competition and brewery consolidation. During the 20th century, through the chaos of war and Japan's economic miracle, that number continued to drop. There are currently some 1,500 sake breweries in Japan. Not all of those are operational, but the best put their own spin on a process that turns rice and water into ambrosia.

As the number of breweries dropped, so did sake sales. After a post–World War II peak in 1975, sake consumption in Japan began to slide. In the Japanese liquor business, sake's prevalence has fallen from a dominant 80 percent during the pre–World War II years to less than 7 percent as of 2017. Beer, by comparison, accounts for around 32 percent of sales, and shochu approximately 10 percent. Liquor taxes, which were powered by sake sales and helped fund Japanese modernization and imperialism during the 20th century, comprised over 30 percent of the nation's taxes in the early 1900s. In 2017, liquor taxes barely amounted to 2 percent, with sake outsold by shochu, liqueurs, and beer. Yet,

according to the Japanese National Tax Agency, sake exports have increased from 1.8 million gallons in 2001 to 6.8 million gallons in 2018, with export sales up 113 percent from the previous year. That increase far surpasses those of Japanese beer, wine and whisky.

People around the world are starting to get into sake like never before, not only opening up new markets for Japanese sake but also giving rise to a new generation of breweries born on foreign soil. Best of all, brewers in Japan and abroad are making some delicious stuff. This is a great time to be a sake drinker. It couldn't happen to a better beverage.

Sake is one of the few Japanese industries that is larger than any one company or any single individual. Even if the biggest sake makers went under tomorrow, its importance and production would still continue across the country. The oldest Japanese texts mention sake (albeit a very different iteration of the modern drink). Sake is used in religious ceremonies and celebrations. It is Japan's gift to the world of drinks. During Prime Minister Masayoshi Ohira's first cabinet meeting on January 5, 1980, he said, "Sake is our national beverage." The word he used was *kokushu*, literally meaning "national alcohol." Ohira wanted the Japanese government to serve sake to visiting officials and heads of state, expressing the fact that sake does not just reflect Japanese culture; it *is* Japanese culture.

This book, although it contains technical information, is not a technical guide. It's a dive into the drink's deep culture and long history, peppered with vignettes that tell a larger story. I visited breweries, drank and geeked out about sake with my coauthor, sake sommelier and blogger Takashi Eguchi. Between us we visited over 150 breweries. Eguchi traveled around the world, visiting breweries in Taiwan, Mexico and Brazil. Our research showed us that great things are happening—a new generation of brewers has arrived.

So here I am, standing on this pier in far northern Japan, looking out at the bay. Tugboats putt-putt by. Waves crash. Seagulls wail. In less than an hour, I'm due at a nearby brewery.

This has been quite the journey.

—Brian Ashcraft

7

新制 姿見酒盃

今様 美人 合

In the wide-mouthed *sakazuki* cup is the reflection of a kabuki actor. Seeing reflections in sake vessels was a popular visual trope in the Edo period (1603–1868).

豊国画

# **SAKE:** JAPAN'S NATIONAL BEVERAGE

## DEFINING SAKE

Japan's earliest written records, dating back to the 8th century, used the imported Chinese kanji character 酒 for sake. In Japanese, the way this character is read can change. Alone, it's simply "sake." When added to the end of words it is read as *-zake* or *-shu*.

For 1,000 years, "sake" has referred to booze brewed from (usually) rice. The word "sake" is thought to be related to the Japanese word *sakaeru*, meaning "to flourish" or "to prosper." The theory is that sake was *sakae mizu*, or "glorious water," and that, over time, simply became "sake." Another theory is that *sa* referred to the rice deity Sanaburi, while *ke* was an ancient reference to food.

In the late 16th century the Portuguese, the first Westerners in Japan, first documented the drink for the Western world, with an entry for *saqe* in a 1603 Japanese-Portuguese dictionary. The Dutch dubbed it *sacki*. In English, the drink has been incorrectly written "saki." It's also been written "saké" to differentiate it from the English word. Increasingly, it's just "sake."

By the late 19th century, when Japan was rapidly Westernizing, the word *nihonshu* (or *nipponshu*), which literally means "Japanese alcohol," was used to distinguish the domestic drink from imported *yoshu* or "Western alcohol." "Sake" typically means liquor in general. In spoken Japanese, nihonshu is commonly used for the drink that we call "sake," thus avoiding any confusion. Abroad, "sake" or "Japanese sake" is fine. In 2015, the terms "nihonshu" and "Japanese sake" were given official geographical indications to separate products brewed in Japan from those not.

Sake is legally defined as being filtered from fermented rice, *koji* and water. Brewer's alcohol is among the permitted additives; total additives cannot exceed 50 percent of the rice. The legal term *seishu* 清酒 (refined sake) is the modern term for filtered sake; this refers to all retail sake, even the cloudy stuff. *Seishu* is used in writing—on bottles, for example—but people don't really use it in spoken Japanese.

This book uses the terms "sake" and, when necessary, "nihonshu" to refer to the drink.

## The Difference between Sake, Wine and Beer

Throughout history, sake has been compared to both wine and beer, as well as with other varieties of alcohol. Westerners have always had a difficult time trying to characterize sake,

because it truly is unlike anything in the West.

In the late 16th century, the Portuguese defined sake as *vinho*, or "wine." In *Historia de Iapam* (History of Japan), Jesuit missionary Luís Fróis recounted how sake was used in church services in Japan when wine was difficult to import. For the Portuguese, no doubt there were intrinsic similarities between wine and sake.

Wine associations continue to this day. The International Wine Challenge now has a sake category, and American wine critic Robert Parker reviews and scores sake. Wine terms, such as *terroir*, have been adopted into Japanese

RIGHT This late 18th century print is from a series pairing famous courtesans with sake brands.
BELOW This jug is Nagasaki's traditional Hasami-ware porcelain from the mid-19th century.

sake lingo (*terowaaru*). In some ways sake is like wine—both are enjoyed with food, both have a similar mouthfeel—though sake isn't as acidic and dry as wine. But in how they are made, sake and wine could not be more different. In the winemaking process, grapes or other fruits are crushed to produce a naturally sugary juice. Yeast, whether wild or added, consumes the sugars and converts them to alcohol. Voilà: wine. Obviously, the quality of the grapes, as well as factors like maturation and the winemaker's skill, determine the quality. Sake brewers often say that 80 percent of wine is the grapes, but 80 percent of sake is the brewer. For whisky, though, between 70 and 80 percent of the flavor is from the cask influence during maturation. (Ranald MacDonald, one of the first Americans to arrive in Japan in the 1840s, compared sake to whisky, but this is inaccurate because sake is not distilled—a misapprehension that still persists.)

Since sake isn't made from juice, it's not a wine

A line-up of Niigata sakes. The prefecture has over 80 breweries, the largest number of any prefecture in Japan. Niigata is the country's third largest sake-producing region after Kyoto and Hyogo.

in the traditional sense. It is closer to beer in how it is made, which is probably why the US government now categorizes it as a beer. According to the 1984 National Minimum Drinking Age Act, "beer includes, but is not limited to, ale, lager, porter, stout, sake, and other similar fermented beverages brewed or produced from malt, wholly or in part from any substitute therefor." (Confusingly, while the US government might tax sake like malted beer, as of writing, it requires sake to be labeled like wine under the Federal Alcohol Administration Act.) But there are key differences. Both are brewed, but unlike beer, sake isn't made from malt. That

This special beer is made with German hops, imported malted barley and local, top-grade Yamada Nishiki rice.

heated in hot water, breaking down the enzymes into a sugary liquid called wort. Next, yeast is added, after which fermentation occurs, and beer is brewed.

Completely different steps, however, must be taken to make sake (see pages 41–67). Rice is starchy, but it needs the help of mold—and humans—in order to be converted into alcohol. Sweet mold-covered rice called *koji* is made with rice and *koji-kin*, the *Aspergillus oryzae* fungus. While koji is often translated as "malt" or "malted rice," this is not accurate. Malt, as defined by *Merriam-Webster*, is "grain (such as barley) softened by steeping in water, allowed to germinate, and used especially in brewing and distilling." Koji is rice that's covered with microorganisms (see page 95). It is slightly sweet; with the addition of yeast, those sugars are converted into alcohol. Unlike beer brewing, which is a series of separate steps, much of sake making happens all at once. In the fermentation process unique to sake, which is called "multiple parallel fermentation," production of sugars and alcohol occurs in tandem. The resulting brew is utterly unlike beer: sake isn't malty, bitter or frothy.

Even though the comparisons have existed for centuries and continue today, sake is not rice wine (nor is it related to any distilled drink like whisky). It's not rice beer, either. Sake is sake. There is nothing else like it.

hasn't stopped comparisons to beer over the centuries. In the 17th-century travelogue *The Travels of Monsieur de Thévenot*, by French traveler Jean de Thévenot, sake was compared to beer. In the 18th century, the *Encyclopedia Britannica* defined *sakki* as "rice beer," but added that it was "clear as wine and of an agreeable taste." Beer is made from barley grain that is malted, a process in which the grains are encouraged to germinate so that the starches create enzymes. The malted barley is milled then

## The Scientist Who Made Barley Sake

The German bacteriologist Oskar Korschelt thought he could use his beer-brewing expertise to improve upon the centuries-old sake-making process. He arrived in Japan in 1876 and took up a teaching post at Tokyo University Medical School. But he did other work, from soil analysis to pottery making.

Korschelt felt the sake-making process took too long and should take place year-round. His answer was to ditch the rice. In 1878, he began expressing his desire to make sake from barley. In Japan there exists a small tradition of making a fermented barley drink with koji. According to the 1898 book *Seisanfushi* (A record of the western Sanuki realm), drinks were made from barley in modern-day Kagawa Prefecture on the island of Shikoku.

Korschelt believed using barley would be cheaper and faster than rice, reasoning that it would produce the necessary starch to make sake while omitting the complex koji-making process and the need for multiple-step brewing. In 1879, he did two trials: one batch with rice and barley and another batch with barley only. Both reportedly had tasty results, though the barley-only brew sounds like, well, beer. In his report, Korschelt declared that the experiment

was "a total success," adding that he now had proof he could make sake from barley. "The smell of the liquor is refreshing and surpasses rice sake," he added.

Although barley sake never took off, Korschelt did leave a lasting mark on the sake industry. To combat the persistent problem of batches going to rot, he suggested that brewers add salicylic acid (a compound that is now used to fight pimples and dandruff, but back then was a beer preservative) to their sake. His advice sparked the increased use of additives in sake that were thought to be cutting-edge chemistry. But sake laced with salicylic acid was mildly poisonous, and by 1969, all brewers banned it. (Gekkeikan, the Kyoto sake-making giant, had already stopped using salicylic acid by the mid-1910s.)

In 1878, Oskar Korschelt learned that sake brewers had been using pasteurization techniques centuries before Louis Pasteur was even born.

ABOVE This is a *honnidaru*-style cask, traditionally covered in a straw matting emblazoned with the sake brand. Here, it reads Taketsuru (see next page).

# SAKE TO WHISKY: THE TAKETSURU NAME

**"This is difficult to talk about, but it's something I should say," says Toshio Taketsuru, taking a sip of green tea. "Initially, I didn't want to take over this brewery."**

Toshio Taketsuru is the 14th president of Taketsuru Shuzo in Hiroshima, a brewery known for its full-bodied sake. The family name is also known because Masataka Taketsuru was the father of Japanese whisky and the founder of the Nikka Whisky Distilling Company. Toshio speaks in a deep, clear voice, and shares the same strong jawline of his whisky-making ancestor.

Outside the brewery are posters of the famed whisky maker. A statue of Masataka and his Scotland-born wife, Rita, stands up the street. "Masataka didn't grow up in this house," explains Toshio. "His family home was about five minutes away, and his father Keijiro came here to brew sake when we needed help. That's probably how Masataka got interested in making alcohol." That, in turn, got him interested in whisky.

Toshio wasn't as keen to make liquor. The pressure of taking over the family brewery was daunting.

"My son is two now," he says. "He might want to be a policeman, a carpenter or a pro baseball player. But . . . he's a Taketsuru. Everyone in this town knows that. I started to gradually hate that expectation. I didn't want to be involved in the brewery at all."

After high school, Taketsuru won admission to prestigious Osaka University, where his father, Hisao, and Masataka before him had studied booze making. "I told my dad I got into Osaka University," says Toshio. "I didn't tell him it was to study physics. He found out during enrollment, and was a bit shocked." It seemed the brewery would not continue, which was especially sad considering the lengths his ancestors had taken to keep it going.

"My grandfather, Kyousuke Taketsuru, was killed in the atomic bombing of Hiroshima," Toshio says. "He had a bad leg, so he hadn't been able to join the military. Plus,

he was running a sake brewery, and the troops needed sake to drink, so that was part of the war effort." With the entire country weary and war-torn, Kyousuke felt he had to do something more; he couldn't just watch from the sidelines. "He went to Hiroshima to help put out fires," Toshio says of the grandfather he never met. He pauses, taking another sip of tea. "My grandfather didn't have to be in Hiroshima city, because he was handicapped and he was making sake," says Toshio. "But he went anyway." Kyousuke's wife was left with a four-year-old son, Hisao, and a sake brewery. The Taketsuru family did their best to make it through those difficult postwar years until Hisao was old enough to take the reins. There was no question whether or not he would run the brewery.

14

In the postwar era, multinational Japanese companies dominated the globe. Working in a brewery seemed old fashioned. "My father was resigned to the brewery not continuing." But as graduation approached, the younger Taketsuru started mulling over his career. "I really started thinking about the family business," he says. "I didn't have a burning passion for physics. I was just running away from expectations. I thought, was it worth casually ending a sake brewery that had existed for 260 years?" Toshio Taketsuru made up his mind. He was coming home.

"These breweries are passed down through the generations, but the youth are asked to make life-defining decisions before they've even drunk sake," Taketsuru says. "When you're 20, you still don't have a developed palate, and you're asked to devote your life to something you don't quite understand."

Taketsuru's young son scampers into the room. He's wearing a *Star Wars* T-shirt. I tell him that my youngest son loves *Star Wars* too. The boy smiles and darts out of the room. "Kids have their own lives and things they want to do," Taketsuru says. "And I guess we can always have more children."

ABOVE Toshio Taketsuru at his family's brewery. LEFT Taketsuru Shuzo uses both wooden tubs and metal tanks for brewing. CENTER Statues of Masataka Taketsuru and his wife Rita stand down the street from the Taketsuru brewery. BELOW Taketsuru Shuzo is closed to the public, but it's not uncommon for sake and whisky fans to make a pilgrimage just to take a snapshot of the brewery's exterior.

In 1987, the Shinkame Brewery was the first in Japan to switch all of its sakes to *junmai-shu*. Since then, the brewery has spearheaded the junmai-only movement among sake breweries. See page 243 for tasting note.

# TYPES OF SAKE

Sake comes in several major and niche types. The various categories are distinguished by the way they are made or their ingredients, and not by the rice variety used or the region.

## Pure Rice-Only Sake

**Junmai-shu** 純米酒**:** Literally "pure-rice sake," *junmai* is made from rice, *koji*, yeast and water. It doesn't have added alcohol or a minimum polishing ratio. The minimum polishing ratio of 70 percent (meaning 30 percent of the grain was milled or polished away) was abolished in 2003. Junmai-shu is often noted for being full bodied and having robust, even earthy flavors. Originally all sake was junmai-shu.

## "Alcohol-Added" Sake

In Japanese, alcohol-added sake is called *aruten*, which is short for *arukooru tenka*, literally meaning "alcohol added." The majority of Japanese sake made is aruten, and typically falls into one of the two following categories:

**Futsu-shu** 普通酒: Literally "regular sake," this everyday drink is about 60 percent of Japan's sake market. *Futsu-shu* is made from table rice, with added organic acids, amino acids, sugar and generous amounts of brewer's alcohol. What futsu-shu lacks in depth, it makes up for with easy, no-nonsense drinkability. There are exceptions: Japan's National Tax Agency can designate a junmai-shu as futsu-shu if it's made from low-grade rice, even if it doesn't have added alcohol. Moreover, if the sake is made with less than 15 percent koji, it will be categorized as futsu-shu.

**Honjozo-shu** 本醸造酒: Literally meaning "true brewed sake," *honjozo* is made from rice, koji, yeast, water and a limited percentage of high-proof alcohol which is added at the tail end of the fermentation process. The rice used in honjozo-shu must have a polishing ratio of at least 70 percent, meaning that 30 percent of the grain is milled or polished away. The added alcohol helps retain aromas, as scents easily glom onto ethanol, and it also results in a brew that is lighter, milder and easier to drink. The added alcohol also helps fortify and preserve the sake during storage.

## Well-Polished Sake

During the 20th century, better milling machines meant lower polishing ratios, which made super-premium sake possible.

**Ginjo-shu** 吟醸酒: At least 40 percent of the rice must be polished, leaving 60 percent of the grain. *Ginjo* sake is made from rice, koji, yeast, water and brewer's alcohol unless it's junmai ginjo-shu, which doesn't have added booze. Ginjo sake is famous for its fruity or floral fragrances. For more on ginjo-shu, see pages 18–19.

**Daiginjo-shu** 大吟醸酒: *Dai* means "great" or "big," and *Daiginjo* is the apex of ginjo. At least 50 percent of each grain is polished, generally resulting in brews that are even more aromatic (and expensive!) than regular ginjo-shu. Daiginjo-shu is made from rice, koji, yeast, water and added brewer's alcohol, unless it's a junmai daiginjo-shu, in which case the alcohol content is purely from rice.

Note that daiginjo and ginjo are typically brewed at lower temperatures of around 54°F (12°C). This slows the fermentation to up to five weeks, resulting in a sake with low acidity and

BELOW LEFT If you have any doubt about how much respect *honjozo* deserves, the country's most famous *toji* Naohiko Noguchi is famed for his excellent honjozo brews. For the tasting note, see page 221. BELOW Made with Kumamoto yeast, Kouro Ginjo is a classic *ginjo* sake. Check out the tasting note on page 219.

fruity aromas. Unless specified as junmai, ginjo and daiginjo sakes have added alcohol.

## Not-So-Well-Polished Sake

Before the 1930s, when vertical rice polishing machines were invented, sake rice didn't have the low polishing ratios achieved today. Milling removes fats and proteins that add flavor to rice. Through the 20th century until now, brewers have pushed polishing ratios lower and lower to isolate the starchy core of the grain known as the *shinpaku* (lit. "white heart"), which makes for easy koji production. The outer layers of the grain produce more body, but their compounds can be responsible for unwanted off-flavors. On the other hand, they also retain the taste of the rice, making for sake that is rich, heavy and acidic.

The tricky part of making sake with less-polished rice is pulling off the necessary balancing act. Typically, depending on the rice variety, breweries may decide they need to polish the rice more so that the koji spores can work their way into the grain. With softer rice, that might not be necessary, as spores can penetrate even if the grains have been barely polished. Then, the

fermentation times and yeast varieties will further affect the final flavors. Just because a sake has a high polishing ratio doesn't mean it's low quality or inexpensive; likewise, a low polishing ratio doesn't always ensure great sake. The barely polished brews are some of the most difficult sakes to make.

Tomita Shuzo, a 460-year-old brewery in Shiga famous for its Shichinoyari brand, has been conducting an interesting experiment. Its award-winning Junmai Wataribune 77% is made with local Wataribune rice, a relative of which was crossbred to make Yamada Nishiki, the top sake rice. Wataribune has been grown in Shiga for over 100 years, but by the 1960s, when Japan's population was growing rapidly, low-yielding rice like Wataribune was replaced by new easier-to-grow high-yielding varieties, like Koshihikari, Japan's favorite table rice. "Shiga-grown Wataribune has a large, starchy core, but it's not clearly defined like Yamada Nishiki," says Yasunobu Tomita, the brewery's 15th-generation owner. "Because of that, it's easy to impart the distinctive character of the rice to the sake."

Tomita Shuzo, which uses a handful of rice varieties, began brewing with Wataribune in 2008. It's very soft and not an easy rice to use, apt

Located in Shiga Prefecture, Tomita Shuzo's famous brand is Shichihonyari or "Seven Spearsmen," after the seven heroic leaders in the Battle of Shizugatake, fought nearby in 1583. The brewery, however, is older than that legendary battle. It is located on the Hokkoku Kaido road, an important route frequented by merchants and samurai.

# THE BIRTH OF PREMIUM GINJO AND DAIGINJO SAKE

Say "premium sake," and immediately *ginjo* leaps to mind. The kanji for *gin* (吟) in "ginjo" is the same as that in *ginjiru*, meaning "to chant" or "to recite" as in a poem. However, the "gin" in "ginjo" is actually derived from the word *ginmi* (吟味), meaning "scrutinize." For example, ginjo pioneer Kokuryu Sake Brewery in Fukui has long had the motto *ginmi shite kamosu* or "scrutinize and brew." The character *jo* (醸) in "ginjo" is from *jozo* (醸造), or "brew."

The word "ginjo" emerged in the late 1800s. Researcher Goro Kishi, who laid the foundation for the quick fermentation starter known as *sokujo-moto*, first mentioned the term "ginjo" in print with his 1894 book *Shuzou no tamoshibi* (The lamp of sake brewing). By the end of the century, several dozen breweries were using the "ginjo" designation to denote special competition brews that weren't for public consumption, iron-branding ginjo on casks to indicate sake "brewed with care." There were other terms, however, to convey excellence. According to antique expert Alan Scott Pate's book *Kanban: Traditional Shop Signs of Japan*, words like *gokinjo* (superior quality) and *daigokinjo* (best quality) were also used in Meiji-period advertising to denote excellent sake.

However, that early ginjo sake was quite different from today's ginjo, which is determined by a polishing ratio of at least 60 percent, which was first codified in 1975 within the sake industry. Later, the Japanese government legally standardized the ginjos in 1990 (along with official definitions for junmai and honjozo). This polishing ratio only became possible after the early

1930s, when high-tech vertical rice-milling machines were developed that could burnish away half the grain. World War II and the ensuing rice shortages, however, slammed the brakes on any further ginjo development. The war, fueled by booze taxes, led to the development and expansion of sake made with additives other than rice. Ginjo was all but forgotten.

During this time, when the emphasis was on quantity over quality, an important discovery was made that was paramount for future ginjo sake. In 1953, the yeast that later became known as association yeast No. 9 was isolated at the Kumamoto Prefecture Sake Research Center; the Brewing Society of Japan began selling the yeast in 1968. No. 9 made modern ginjo possible: its fermentation is robust at low temperatures, which results in a balanced brew with low acidity and signature fruity ginjo aromas of apples and bananas. No wonder the yeast and its derivatives are still widely used for ginjo.

According to a 2002 *Japan Times* article by sake writer John Gauntner, a small Chiba brewery released a ginjo-marketed sake in 1947 under the Fusa Masamune

Kokuryu Ginjo Icchorai is made from Gohyakumangoku rice that's been polished to 55 percent. It's a pleasant, easy-drinking ginjo with nice astringency, good complexity and subtle floral nuances. The name Kokuryu has become synonymous with ginjo.

brand. The brewery, Ishino Shoten, isn't currently operational and phone calls for confirmation went unanswered. "We don't really know who released the first ginjo to the general public," says author Jiro Shinoda, Japan's leading expert on ginjo-shu. In 1958, Hiroshima brewery Kamotsuru released Tokusei [special quality] Gold Kamotsuru labeled with the word *daiginzo* (大吟造), which means "*daigin* made," as the term *daiginjo* wasn't yet part of standardized parlance. According to Shinoda, Oita brewery Nishinoseki also released a ginjo *koshu* aged sake in 1961, but it seems it was sold as a niche product at airports. Ginjo brews weren't widely sold because the general public had no idea what the word meant. It was an industry term, reserved for sake entered into competitions. "The word 'ginjo-shu' wasn't commonly known until the 1980s," says Shinoda. Examples of "ginjo" appear in Japanese dictionaries as early as 1935, when the most complete dictionary of the day, *Daijiten*, defined it as "carefully brewed using selected ingredients." In the decades that followed, some dictionaries mentioned it, while *Kojien*, the Japanese dictionary held in highest esteem, did not define the word before1980. *Dai Kan-wa Jiten*, the most comprehensive postwar kanji dictionary, did not include it in the 1984 edition. In 1975, the year sake production reached its postwar peak, the Japan Sake Makers' Association released its "Standards for Description of Ingredients and Production Methods." These labeling and production standards, which were voluntary, defined ginjo-shu, including its polishing ratio. That same year, the Kokuryu Sake Brewery in Fukui released one of the first modern

daiginjos, Kokuryu Ginjo Icchorai (*icchorai* being a local expression for clothing, similar to "one's Sunday best" in English). It also released Kokuryu Daiginjo Ryu, which was one of the first daiginjo sakes. *Ryu* is Japanese for "dragon" (the brewery's name means "black dragon") and "dai-ginjo" was proudly written on the label. This sake had a polishing ratio of 50 percent (today's Kokuryu Daiginjo Ryu is polished even further, having a ratio of 40 percent) and was made from the highest grade of Yamada Nishiki rice. Kokuryu had sold its daiginjo locally prior to this release. But in 1975, Kokuryu launched this premium sake nationally, selling it

LEFT The Kokuryu brewery in Fukui uses soft water sourced from the evocative sounding Kuzuryugawa or "River of the Nine-Headed Dragon." BELOW For a rice to be *daiginjo*, it must be polished to 50 percent or less. Pictured are grains of Yamada Nishiki polished to 40 percent.

at 32 Takashimaya department stores across Japan. Daiginjo Ryu was one of the most expensive sakes of the day. One 1.8-liter (4-pint) bottle was 5,000 yen. The painstakingly made brew was a forerunner of future super-premium sakes made by brewers with relentless dedication to perfection. However, it would be another five years until the first mass-market ginjo was launched and Japanese sake drinkers went gaga for ginjo.

"Prior to that, ginjo-shu was made for the national brewing contest," says Shotaro Nakano, who, with his wife Akari, is the future of Dewazakura Sake Brewery in Yamagata Prefecture. "Even our brewery made ginjo-shu before 1980." The reasonably priced Dewazakura Oka went on sale in 1980, marketing ginjo-shu to a public that still didn't quite know what it was. The "ginjo boom" happened in the mid-1980s. According to Nakano, "Dewazakura Ouka ignited that fire."

Shinoda theorizes that the reason why the floral ginjo brews suddenly became popular was due to Japanese people's diet. "Before 1970, Japanese people

山田錦（40%）

were eating on average 18 grams (½ ounce) of salt a day," claims Shinoda. Foods like *yakitori* grilled chicken, *tsukemono* pickled vegetables and *umeboshi* pickled plums all have a high salt content. According to Shinoda, salty food makes people want to drink sweeter-tasting alcohol, which is why the heavier, richer sakes of Nada were so popular. "But that much salt isn't good for you, and mothers started complaining to elementary schools,

ABOVE Some breweries have their workers directly touch their rice with their bare hands, while others worry how that will impact flavor and require their brewers to wear gloves.
LEFT One of the most important aspects not only in ginjo sake making but in all sake making is cleanliness, which helps avoid unwanted flavors.
BELOW Two brewers at the Dewazakura Sake Brewery take a breather as they remove hot rice from the steamer.

and school lunches became less salty," says Shinoda. "This changed the Japanese diet." In adulthood, these children continued to eat less salty food, and therefore preferred the floral, drier sakes of the 1980s to the sweeter brews popular in the past. "Sake is always connected to food," says Shinoda. "This is why in the last 10 years, with more people eating salty takeout food, sweeter sakes have seen somewhat of a resurgence."

But ginjo sake was a game changer. "Compared to previous sake, the scent of ginjo—what's called the *ginjoka*—was quite different," says Nakano. The sake world was never the same.

to pick up more *nuka* (rice bran) during polishing compared to other rice varieties. Tomita must take extra care while washing to make sure all the clingy bran is gone, to make sure that no off-flavors will emerge during fermentation.

"Wataribune is a resurrected rice, so perhaps it might be better to use more of the grain," says Tomita. "But we wanted to offer a contrast and allow people to compare sake made at the same brewery with the same water, the same yeast and the same rice, but with different polishing ratios."

Tomita Shuzo's results are fascinating. The 77-percent polishing-ratio bottling has fatter flavors, but the richness of the rice comes through in the more-polished daiginjo version. Yet the brewery's less-polished version doesn't feel top-heavy, and it has a nice, clean finish.

"The more rice is polished, the more essential the brewing technique is for the final characteristics," says Tomita. "The less the rice is polished, the more important the flavors of the rice become."

## Cloudy and Undiluted Sake

These types of sake are closer to the uncut tipples either freshly pressed at breweries or made at home before do-it-yourself brewing became illegal in the late 19th century.

**Nigorizake** にごり酒: "Nigori" does not mean "unfiltered," as it's sometimes incorrectly translated; rather, it means "cloudy." Since *nigorizake* is *seishu* (refined sake), it is filtered—though not to the same degree. Created in the 1960s by Kyoto's Masuda Tokubee Shoten, it's a modern version of *doburoku*, or unfiltered sake (see page 154).

**Genshu** 原酒: Simply put, this is undiluted sake. Typically, sake is cut with water, bringing the alcohol by volume (ABV) down to 15 to 16 percent from its original 18 to 22 percent. No brewed drink has a higher natural alcohol

TOP Yasunobu Tomita holds a bottle of his brewery's excellent *junmai* Wataribune brew. ABOVE Unpolished Wataribune (on the right, in the plastic bag) is contrasted with Wataribune grains polished to 77 percent (on the left, in the round case).

percentage than sake. There are *genshu* brews that do have ABV levels as low as 15 percent, and a sake can still be considered a genshu if it has added water. However, the water cannot lower the alcohol content by 1 percent or more.

LEFT Just-pressed sake has a fresh, fizzy quality that vanishes during pasteurization and storage. That's not the case with this sparkling, cloudy sake. (For more, see page 223.) BELOW Bottles of sparkling Dassai.

## Styles of Starter

Brewing sake involves making a highly concentrated yeast starter called either a *shubo* (literally the "mother of sake") or a *moto* (the "base" of sake). Not only can the starter dictate how fermentation progresses, but the flavors in the starter can carry over to the final sake. This brewing stage is so paramount that sakes can be categorized by their starters.

## Sparkling Sake

Invented in America in 1939, sparkling sake made a comeback in Japan in 1998, when Ichinokura launched Ichinokura Sparkling Sake Suzune. There are several types of sparkling sake. One style takes already fermenting unpasteurized sake and does a second fermentation in the bottle, à la champagne. The other style bottles still-fermenting nigorizake for a fizzy, tart brew. Generally, since both styles are still fermenting, they should be refrigerated. These styles are called *kassei-shu* (the cloudy version is dubbed *kassei nigorizake*). Another style adds carbon dioxide to already-fermented sake, making for a sake that is stable, but perhaps lacking personality.

In November 2016, the Japan Awasake (*awa* means "foam") Association was established. The group has a handful of rules, such as: sparkling sake can only be made from rice, koji and water; the carbon dioxide must be naturally occurring (i.e., the fizz cannot be added); bubbles must be clearly evident when poured; and it must have a minimum of 10 percent alcohol by volume.

**Kimoto 生酛 and yamahai 山廃:** These terms describe two sake yeast starters, as well as distinct flavor profiles. They are genres unto themselves, amounting to just 10 percent of all sake produced—*yamahai* accounts for 9 percent and *kimoto* only 1 percent. Both starters require about three to four weeks.

Dating from the late 17th century and appearing to originate in Kobe's Nada brewing district, kimoto is a style of yeast starter in which the brewers mash rice and koji in small tubs of water into a creamy puree with oars and poles. The technique, called *yama-oroshi*, arose when it

LEFT Brewers at Kiku Masamune make *kimoto* starter. BELOW Clumps of rice are mixed with a paddle to help speed along saccharification.

wasn't possible to polish the rice to today's superfine ratios, and brewers thought mashing the rice and koji together was necessary to make the starter. Finely polished rice has eased this labor somewhat; however, it's still physically demanding work. Kimoto-style sake can have deeper and more complex flavors, due to the thoroughgoing way it is made. It can also be smooth, dry and acidic.

The yamahai method omits the yama-oroshi mashing step. Kinichiro Kagi, a researcher at the National Research Institute of Brewing, pointed out in 1909 that mashing the rice and koji together was superfluous, since the koji enzymes naturally dissolve the rice. He was correct, but as rice saccharification isn't helped by mashing, the rice might not dissolve as uniformly as in the kimoto style, affecting the final flavor. Yamahai-style sake has a flavor profile similar to kimoto, but often with gamy nuances. The name yamahai came from the Japanese love of making long words shorter: thus *yama-oroshi haishi* (*haishi* means "ceasing,") became "yamahai."

**Sokujo-moto** 速醸酛**:** The vast majority of sake is made with *sokujo-moto*, or "quick fermentation starter," which was codified in 1909 by brewing researcher Kamajiro Eda. This technique, used in making 90 percent of all Japanese sake, adds lactic acid to the mixture of steamed rice and koji instead of propagating it naturally, as the kimoto and yamahai methods do. Sokujo takes around two weeks; while the yeast microbes it produces are not as robust and active as those produced with the kimoto and yamahai methods, they can create crisp sakes with low acidity.

**Bodaimoto** 菩提酛 **(aka mizumoto** 水酛**):** *Bodaimoto* yeast starter produces some of the most acidic sakes available, which among wine drinkers might even elicit comparisons to German Riesling. *Mizumoto*, which literally means "water starter," refers to the method of leaving rice to soak uncovered in containers of water that become highly populated with

ambient lactic acid. The rice is removed and then steamed, after which the lactic acid–rich water, known as *soyashimizu*, is then mixed with the cooked rice, protecting it from harmful bacteria. Like sokujo, the bodaimoto (mizumoto) technique creates a starter with natural lactic acid, though it isn't nearly as stable.

This is one of the oldest styles of starters, dating from the Muromachi period (1333–1573). It is believed to have originated at the Buddhist temple Shoryakuji, located on Bodaisen mountain in Nara, home of the Bodaisen Shingon sect. Sake making was big business for Buddhist temples, which were cradles of learning and innovation in those days, akin to modern universities or research centers. Since bodaimoto was originally a summer brewing process, the practice fell out of use after the Tokugawa government restricted brewing to the winter months in the late 17th century. Although bodaimoto didn't die out completely—Shinto shrines continued to use the technique to make their sacred unrefined sake called *dakushu*—it declined even further with the wide acceptance of sokujo in the 20th century. However, on March 3, 1984, Okayama's *Sanyo Shimbun* newspaper reported that local brewery Tsuji Honten was reviving bodaimoto to make a nigorizake.

"Mizumoto" and "bodaimoto" refer to the same process, but because bodaimoto has the kanji characters 菩提 (*bodai*, meaning "enlightenment"), the term carries strong Buddhist associations. There is (as yet) no bodaimoto association comparable to the International Trappist Association, which has certain

Every year, breweries gather at Shoryakuji Temple, famous for *bodaimoto*, to make a modern version of this traditional yeast starter. The breweries use that starter to create a variety of bodaimoto brews, such as this one, reviewed on page 218.

# ADDING BREWER'S ALCOHOL

**Brewer's alcohol can be made from cereal grains or sugarcane molasses. However, the law forbids the use of chemically produced synthetic alcohol. Some breweries do insist on using brewer's alcohol made from rice, which is more expensive. The raw sugarcane is distilled into a crude spirit—often done in Brazil—and then imported to Japan, where one of the major distillers runs it through their high-tech multistory-tall column stills repeatedly until they produce a pure, clean alcoholic spirit. Even though the brewer's alcohol might technically hail from another country, it would not be in any condition to put into *honjozo-shu* or *futsu-shu* without the expertise of Japanese distillers.**

There is also a tradition of adding distilled spirit to sake to fortify the drink, just as there is a long history of adding alcohol to fortified wines like port and sherry. According to *Domo shuzoki* (loosely "Brewing for dummies), a brewing guide from 1685, adding the distilled spirit *shochu* will help bring out flavors and fend off bacteria that could cause spoilage. Another brewing text, dating from 1771, states that adding shochu does improve the sake, but also makes it drier. Contemporary breweries like Abekan Shuzoten in Miyagi Prefecture and Konotomo Shuzo in Hyogo Prefecture add their in-house distilled shochu to make a sake style known

as *hashira jikomi*. What makes this practice even more remarkable is that only a handful of breweries have the necessary equipment to distill their own spirit, and shochu fetches good money on its own. Tamanohikari, a pioneer of the *junmai-shu* revival, has its own still with a worm-tub condenser that could produce excellent spirits, but since it doesn't add alcohol to any of its sake, the brewery doesn't make the hashira style. Cost and ability aside, most brewers now prefer to use the light, high-proof brewer's alcohol because it doesn't have a strong character like shochu does and it won't affect flavor. Brewer's alcohol is added for its

effect on the sake, not because of its inherent flavor or properties.

During the 20th century, inexpensive brewer's alcohol was added to sake for different reasons. During the late 1930s, rice shortages poised a threat to sake production, which in turn hurt alcohol taxes. To retain a high level of production, cheap brewer's alcohol was pumped into sake. In the 1940s breweries were required to add alcohol, so *junmai-shu* vanished until the 1960s. The practice of "tripling" the sake with added alcohol continued even after shortages ended, ensuring high profit margins. This gave the practice a bad reputation.

Today, the vast majority of all sake made in Japan contains added brewer's alcohol, the vast majority of which is inexpensive, flavorless distillate. Even the brews that win at the country's National Sake Competition typically have added brewer's alcohol, though, so if you dismiss the practice, you might miss out on some excellent sakes.

Maru from Hakutsuru and Tsuki from Gekkeikan are two popular futsu-shu brands. Table sake is often sold in cartons. The first paper-packed sake in Japan was Hakosake Ichidai, which launched in 1967 from Hiroshima's Chugoku Jozo brewery.

stipulations for Trappist beer, such as that the beer must be brewed by monks in a monastery (or at least under their supervision). However, there is an annual bodaimoto brewing event every January at Shoryakuji, the Buddhist temple where the technique was perfected.

### Raw and Unprocessed Sakes

*Nama* sake varieties constitute a category unto themselves. The word can mean "pure," "raw," "undiluted," "unprocessed" and even "genuine." In sake, there are several different kinds of nama brews, which give folks the closest opportunity to taste freshly pressed sake, which is always a real treat. Typically sake is pasteurized, matured, filtrated, cut with water and pasteurized again before it is bottled and shipped. (The second pasteurization sometimes happens after the sake has already been bottled.) The different nama brews eliminate one or more of these steps. Nama-zake should be refrigerated and enjoyed in a timely manner.

**Nama-zume-shu** 生詰め酒: Literally "live bottled sake," this brew follows the same post-pressing steps as regular sake, but skips the final pasteurization.

**Nama-chozo-shu** 生貯蔵酒: Literally "live stored sake," this brew also follows the same post-pressing steps as typical sake, but it forgoes the first pasteurization.

**Nama-zake** 生酒: In this case "nama" means "raw" or "unprocessed." This sake is diluted, but is not pasteurized. Unless the label reads *muroka* (無濾過), meaning "unfiltered," it has been filtered to balance the flavors. The increased use of chilled shipping containers and the proliferation of refrigeration in sake storage has meant more *nama-zake* has become available not just in Japan but around the world.

**Nama-genshu** 生原酒: This is the "raw" or "unprocessed" version of *genshu*. It skips both pasteurizations and goes straight from pressing to bottling with filtering, unless it's muroka ("unfiltered").

# PREMIUM SAKE RISING

### The Return of Junmai

"My father was the first person to bring back the sake made from 100 percent rice that today we'd call *junmai-shu*," says Hiroshi Ujita, owner of Tamanohikari in Fushimi, Kyoto. It was 1964, the year of the Tokyo Olympics, and for the first time since World War II ended, pure sake was back. "Before the war, all sake was junmai-shu," says Ujita. Moments ago, he had been working on a laptop in a conference room, but leaped up after hearing me ask about his brewery's history. His eyes are lively, and his voice is booming. This is important history, and his father, Fukutoki, had a major part in it.

"Up until 1940, Japanese law said that sake was made from rice, *koji* and water," Ujita says. During the war and in the years after, rice shortages meant that brewers had to make sake

Yucho Shuzo brewery goes to great lengths to bottle the freshest *nama-zake* possible. Their Kaze no Mori sake, pictured here, is reviewed on page 235.

with little or even no rice. As in the past, the government needed an alcohol tax to raise funds. "So, sake started being made with added brewer's alcohol, glucose and amino acids." The additives were cheaper than making sake from just rice. But it was the customers who ended up paying a different price. "You drink that stuff and the next day, you're going to end up with a pounding headache," says Ujita. "My father didn't want to sell sake that gave people nasty hangovers. The answer was to make sake as it had been before the war."

The sake business, however, was rolling in money, thanks to added-alcohol brews. The profit margins were enormous, and other brewers, as well as the Japanese tax office, probably weren't thrilled with the idea of cutting into those margins by ditching brewer's alcohol and other additives. But by 1961, rice shortages had ended and surpluses actually became a problem. Without that extra rice, it would have been difficult to make the shift back to additive-free sake.

At that time, the term "junmai-shu" did not exist. Tamanohikari used the word *mutenka-shu*, or "additive-free sake." (These days, the term is used to refer to sake made with ambient, not added, yeast.) It might seem innocuous now, but at that time, the descriptor was confrontational. It strongly implied that other sake makers were adding things. "It was like dad was picking a fight," says daughter Chiyoko Higashi, who sits on the brewery's board of directors.

Tamanohikari's mutenka-shu went on sale in 1964. It was a revolutionary moment in post–World War II sake history, but this was initially lost on the country's sake drinkers. Higashi explains, "After my father had made up his mind,

the resulting sake was expensive, and customers at that time didn't understand why." From 1940 to 1993, the Japanese government categorized sake into different grades and taxed them accordingly. Tamanohikari didn't submit its expensive pure-rice sake to the tax office, reasoning that it would be taxed less to help keep its already high price down, even though the country would classify it at a lower grade. "It was grade-two sake," says Ujita—the cheaper stuff—even though Tamanohikari's sake was a premium sake at a premium price.

"It was comical, because, at department stores, the staff would say, 'This is Tamanohikari and it's made from 100 percent rice,' " says Ujita. "The customer would ask what grade it was, be told it was grade two, and then say they couldn't buy lower-grade sake as a gift. The customers wouldn't even listen." (Japan's gift-giving culture, incidentally, helped ensure steady sake sales during the postwar era; companies would send

The sign reads *Kanzen mutenka seishu tamanohikari* or "Completely additive-free refined sake Tamanohikari."

LEFT A Tamanohikari worker sorts bottles as they come down the bottling line.
BELOW Tamanohikari Black Label is a *junmai daiginjo* made with Omachi rice polished to 35 percent, which is quite a feat considering how difficult polishing Omachi can be. The tassels are all tied by hand. For more on Omachi, see pages 80–81.

bottles of sake for summer and winter gifts.) Fukutoki Ujita knew that pure-rice sake might not catch on if people didn't understand what it was. "He had to change perceptions, and he needed regular folks to understand," says the younger Ujita. "Which is why he opened a restaurant, our first, in Tokyo Station." That was in July 1969.

While the general public might not have yet embraced the pure-rice sake, other sake makers were starting to. In Hiroshima, Kamoizumi Shuzo began making its own mutenka-shu in 1965, and after some trial and error made what would be considered a junmai ginjo today. "We didn't aim to turn junmai-shu into a luxury product," says Kamoizumi's Kazuhiro Maegaki. "In 1965, when the limits on the rice supply were lifted, it became possible to brew sake without adding brewer's alcohol." The brewery did a series of tests, attempting to manage the higher cost of raw materials as well as adjusting the different flavors and clarity of those early junmai revivals. Finally, in 1972, Kamoizumi released its all-rice brew. "When it went on sale," says Maegaki, "it wasn't labeled as junmai-shu, but rather, mutenka seishu" (that is, additive-free refined sake). During that same period, Hiroshi Uehara, a sake consultant and researcher,

worked with brewers in Tottori to bring back junmai-shu in 1967, while in Kyoto, Masuda Tokubee Shoten was already seeing how its junmai brew would age. Chiyonosono Shuzo, a brewery in Kumamoto, launched its own junmai-shu in 1968.

The next decade put the pure-rice sake revival into high gear. In 1970, there was a rice surplus, which led to the repeal of a law that allotted only a certain amount for sake production. Suddenly, brewers were able to get their hands on as much rice as they needed. The Junsui Nihonshu Kyoukai (Pure Japanese Sake Association) was founded in 1972; its members included Tamanohikari and Kamoizumi. In the years that followed, breweries began labeling their sakes as "junmai-shu" ("pure-rice sake") instead of "mutenka-shu." In 1987, the Shinkame Brewery in Saitama because the first brewery in the postwar era to switch all of its production to junmai-shu only, something that is now standard in many craft breweries.

"As of 2017, junmai-shu comprises 25.9 percent of the sake made in Japan," says Ujita. "Meaning that nearly three-quarters of it still has added alcohol." It also means that junmai-shu still has room to grow.

## Niche Sakes

These niche offerings may be hard to find, but that doesn't mean they are less important or less delicious than more common brews.

**Kijoshu dessert sake 貴醸酒:** This sake was born in 1973 after the National Research Institute of Brewing decided there should be a luxurious *nihonshu* to serve at diplomatic functions instead of wine or champagne. A researcher named Makoto Satoh devised a sweet brew that used sake in the later brewing stage instead of water. When sake is adding during the final stage, fermentation stops. The yeast is overwhelmed by all the sugar, and producing

acidic compounds. All the sugars that should have been converted into alcohol are left behind, resulting in a delightfully sweet, yet highly acidic brew. According to an imperial manuscript dating from 927, there was a similar historical precedent for this sake, but *kijoshu* is very much a modern invention. For more on kijoshu, see pages 150–151.

**Koshu aged sake 古酒:** Literally "old sake," *koshu* has no legal definition. Within the sake industry, any sake that has been matured within the brewing year is technically koshu, and the term *jukusei koshu* (matured koshu) is used for brews with older vintages of three years or more. However, consumers tend to refer to any sake that's aged for an extended period of time as koshu, with the longer maturation period resulting in rich flavors that will appeal to whisky, sherry and brandy drinkers.

In 1966, the Kyoto brewery Masuda Tokubee Shoten, a favorite of renowned film director Akira Kurosawa, revived koshu. The brewery's president at the time discovered a description of

Shiga Prefecture brewery Emishiki is known for its *kijoshu* dessert sakes. Here is a collection of releases at the brewery.

koshu in *Honcho shokkan* (A mirror of our country's food), a compendium of Japanese food published in 1697. "*Shinshu* is newly brewed 100 percent rice sake, and koshu is 100 percent rice sake that is over a year old," reads the text, which also notes that koshu's aroma does not become pleasant and its flavor doesn't deepen until the three-year mark. The maturation process, with sake aging in jugs, was also described. Masuda Tokubee Shoten brewed what would become its first koshu in 1966 from Yamada Nishiki rice with a polishing ratio of 35 percent and released it a decade later as Kohaku Hikari (Amber Light). It was a domestic-only premium product, then priced at 5,000 yen for the smaller 720 ml (1½-pint) bottle and 10,000 yen for the larger 1.8-liter (4-pint) bottle. Masuda Tokubee Shoten still makes its 10-year Kohaku Hikari, which it now ships around the globe.

Now, in the brewery's attic, more than 1,200 20-liter (5-gallon) ceramic jugs are stacked up like casks to age. The stopper of each jug is made

from paulownia wood and sealed with *washi* (Japanese paper). There are glazed and unglazed ceramic jugs; the unglazed ones are highly susceptible to evaporation in Kyoto's notoriously humid summers. Like whisky and wine in casks, a portion of the koshu in jugs evaporates into the air. In English, this is called the "angel's share," which is literally translated into Japanese as *tenshi no wakemae*. But what percentage of koshu evaporates each year? Masuda Tokubee Shoten brewer Guillaume Ozanne reckons it's difficult to give an exact number, because while the ceramic jugs look largely uniform, each one is handcrafted and therefore has its own unique properties. How much koshu evaporates can ultimately depend on the jug, and the brewers won't find that out until afterward. Sometimes, they can lose 20 percent, while other times, they actually lose 100 percent. "We were the first to bring back koshu, and we're still the only ones to age it like this," says the Normandy-born Ozanne.

After Masuda Tokubee Shoten revived the brewing of koshu, a small number of breweries, such as Sawanotsuru, followed suit (see pages 131–33). To avoid evaporation during maturation, other breweries either cold-store their koshu or age it at low temperatures.

**Taruzake** 樽酒: Meaning "cask sake," *taruzake* comprised pretty much all sake sold until the advent of bottles in the 20th century. In those days sake was shipped and sold in cedar casks, which had the side effect of imparting woody notes onto the sake. These days, taruzake is hardly standard fare, but Kiku Masamune in Kobe's Nada brewing district has continued to make it, even employing coopers to craft the casks. Typically, sake is stored in the casks only for a couple days, so this is more of a flavoring

In the foreground is a bottle of Sawanotsuru's *honjozo* aged sake that was brewed in 1973.

LEFT The maturation cellar at Masuda Tokubee Shoten, filled with ceramic jugs.
BELOW Masuda Tokubee Shoten brewer Guillaume Ozanne hails from Normandy in France and worked at French yogurt-maker Dannon, before moving to Japan.

than prolonged aging. (To read more about cask aging, see page 34.)

## The Return of Koshu

During the Edo period (1603–1868), records state that koshu was fetching two to three times more than other sake. It was a premium product. Samurai sake aficionados no doubt liked koshu's savory and sweet flavors and were aware that to make koshu, you needed precious time. According to one Edo shopping guide from 1824, nine-year-old koshu (yes, there were age statements!) was more than double the cheapest koshu and three times the price of the least expensive new brew. But during the Meiji period (1868–1912) and the years that followed, old sake became a relic of the past.

"Now when we make sake, we are taxed on the sake we ship from the brewery," says Hiroyuki Konno, the assistant brewing manager at Sawanotsuru. "But during the Meiji period, breweries were taxed on the sake they made."

That meant storing sake was a tax liability, and breweries began selling sake as soon as possible to recoup costs. In both the Russo-Japanese War and World War II, the Japanese government wanted sake breweries to make and sell as much sake as possible to pay for its military machine. During World War II, especially, when there were rice shortages forcing breweries to make imitation sake, aging sake was inconceivable. "In 1954, the law changed," says Konno. "Breweries were taxed on what they shipped, but by that time everyone had forgotten about koshu."

"This koshu dates from 1973," says Konno. On a table in this meeting room are 11 bottles of koshu dating from 1973 to 2014. The sake comes in shades that you don't typically see in sake—cream, amber, honey and marmalade. "Do you see these different hues?" Konno asks, holding

31

up a glass of koshu from 1991. I take a sip. The flavors are more pronounced than in typical sake, and the aromas remind me of brandy or even whisky, though more reserved, and without the oak notes. I nose a 2010 junmai ginjo koshu: there are flowers and old books. The 2008 junmai daiginjo koshu is creamy vanilla. But in the background and the finish, there's umami, and depending on the koshu, the savoriness can range from that of a light broth to a much deeper one reminiscent of soy sauce. At the end of the table are the older vintages. Light streams through a lace curtain, softly illuminating the koshu. I nose a 1973 junmai koshu. It's like a delicious Sunday breakfast, with maple and pancakes. "We haven't released that one just yet," Konno says. "I think it needs more time." I think it's fantastic.

Today, koshu comprises just a tiny percentage of all sake. There are less than 30 breweries nationwide in Japan's Association for Long Term Aged Sake, of which the Nada brewery Sawano-tsuru is a member. The group defines jukusei koshu (matured koshu) as sake that has been aged for three years, because at that point the savory flavors and aromas are apparent. During

its second year of maturation, the differences become noticeable, but this period is koshu's awkward adolescent phase, and the changes are not necessarily for the better. By the third year, the savory flavors and aromas associated with koshu start to appear. Incidentally, this is also how long Scotch spirit must age in oak to be called whisky.

Stepping out of an elevator, Konno walks down a dark hallway to one of Sawanotsuru's koshu cellars. Inside, it's a cool 55°F (13°C) and the room is packed with 22 two-ton green enamel tanks. Koshu was originally aged in clay pots known as *kame*, so the enamel tanks might not be historically correct, but they do create an environment in which the sake can mature without its flavor being influenced. Rocks and cinder blocks sit on top of the tanks' lids to keep them closed. At Sawanotsuru, junmai and futsu-shu are left to mature at room temperature. However, junmai ginjo sakes are in maturation

**Different styles of sake age differently. From left to right: a *kimoto junmai* from 2014, a *junmai-shu* from 1991, a *junmai-shu* from 1973, and a *honjozo* from 1973.**

rooms set to 59°F (15°C), while the delicate junmai daiginjo age at a lower temp of 41–50°F (5–10°C). The reason for this difference between room and low temperature maturation is the intent: Sawanotsuru wants to see how much junmai and futsu-shu change during aging, while the brewery wants to slowly age its premium ginjo and daiginjo for rounder flavors. Once it reaches the optimum flavor profile, like the 1973 vintage, it is stored in a maturation room at 41°F (5°C) to keep it from aging further.

If there is no interaction with wood, where does Sawanotsuru's koshu get its amber and brown hues? "A big difference between sake and distilled spirits is that if you leave, say, whisky alone, it won't change color. Sake will." The reason, says Konno, is that distilled spirits do not have components that will change color. "Sake changes its hue by simply leaving as is, because it has amino acids, organic acids and sugars.

"But after that, the sake starts to mature nicely, becoming richer and changing color as sake sediment collects at the bottom of the tank," says Konno. "All that intensity reaches a peak, and then the sake settles down and becomes smooth and crisp to drink." These changes happen over decades, and the brewers don't just leave the sake to age in a temperature-controlled room. They check the flavors annually. Furthermore, every decade, depending on how the sake is maturing, they remove some—but not all—of the sediment, which consists of rice and yeast particles and other material, in a process known as *oribiki*, or "sediment removal." The koshu is then placed in a new tank. The whole process is complicated and time-consuming. Yet, that effort isn't always reflected in the price tag.

"Compared to vintage wine and old whiskies, koshu isn't expensive at all," says Konno. "That's because people in Japan don't yet fully appreciate its value." Drink up while you can, because one day, that might change.

TOP The Nada-gogo brewing district in Kobe is famous for its hard water (for more, see pages 90–91). However, its success was also due to local rivers like the Toga River (pictured) that helped power the waterwheels that made previously unseen rice-polishing rates possible for delicious sakes. ABOVE Hiroyuki Konno fills a glass with Sawanotsuru's vintage sake.

# THE MASTER CASK MAKER

"I've been making casks for over 30 years," says master cooper Takeshi Tamura. Using a blade, he splits a long strip of bamboo down the middle. His movements are practiced and precise. He then takes the strip and whips it round like Indiana Jones. In seconds, he's made a perfect hoop called a *taga*. Apprentices spend months mastering these motions before they begin making the actual cask. "You start with the taga," Tamura says. "If you can't learn that, then you can't move to the next step." Today, Tamura is making about 10 casks for Kiku Masamune brewery's *taruzake* (cask sake).

Since its founding in 1659, Kiku Masamune has been making taruzake. Before the 20th century, taruzake was commonplace. If you were drinking sake, it was most likely transported and stored in wood. Today, most sake breweries don't make taruzake, and the ones that do typically don't make their own *taru*, or casks. Before glass bottles appeared in the late 1800s, sake was carried in taru casks from Nada in western Japan to modern-day Tokyo via ships known as *taru-kaisen*, which literally means "cask cargo vessels." It would take around 12 days to transport the casks from western to eastern Japan. Once the sake arrived in Tokyo, liquor shops would keep it in the casks it was shipped in. Storing the brew in cedar casks added extra flavors.

During the 20th century, when other breweries moved away from cask maturation, Kiku Masamune continued making taruzake, even during the Second World War, when the confusion and chaos pushed aside time-consuming and expensive traditional methods. In 1966, the brewery launched a bottled version of taruzake that is still sold today—in 2017, it produced 1,180 kiloliters (311,723 gallons) of the stuff. For Kiku Masamune, one of the biggest breweries in Nada, cask-aged sake is a signature part of its lineup. For the sake industry as a whole, though, it's still a niche product, because most breweries are unable to employ master coopers. Kiku Masamune, however, makes all its casks in-house, thanks to the increasingly rare skill set possessed by Tamura and his fellow coopers. "Taruzake is a lot of work," he says, "but it's worth it."

Tamura begins fitting 16 staves, called *kure*, in place. Japanese casks are much smaller than their Western counterparts, holding 72 liters. The small size allows greater interaction between the brew and the wood. Kiku Masamune stores its sake in casks for a brief time, but does not ship it in casks; its aim is to flavor the brew with *sugi*, or Japanese cedar.

"We always make our casks from Yoshino sugi," Tamura says, holding up a stave. "I've only ever made casks from that sugi." Yoshino, a small Nara town with less than 10,000 residents, is famous for two things: cherry blossoms that have inspired centuries of Japanese art and poetry, and high-quality sugi cedar with a long grain and no knots. Only Japanese sugi that are over 100 years old are large enough to be turned into cask lumber.

The wood has a fresh, green aroma. "That's the scent of the organic compound terpene," says Toshinari Takahashi, the production manager at Kiku Masamune. This brings out the refreshing dryness of Kiku Masamune's sake. It also has a sharp taste, so the sake only gets a quick finish in the casks for two or three days; any longer might make the brew overwhelming for modern tastes.

Tamura turns over one of the staves, showing the side that must line up perfectly with the stave next to it. "This side is called the *shojiki* surface," pointing to the side. "Shojiki" means "honest," "upright" or "frank." The word perfectly describes the approach to Japanese cooperage. Before the staves are fitted in place, their sides are shaved with a special plane called a *shojiki-dai*, so that they fit together, which also releases the flavors in the wood. Glue and nails aren't used, so everything needs to line up perfectly.

With a couple of thwacks, Tamura hammers two taga hoops into place, flips the cask on its side and begins shaving the inside to make it smooth and uniform. The staves are various heights, with some jutting up slightly higher. Flipping the cask over again, Tamura takes a two-handled drawknife called a *sen*, lays it against the edge and pulls it toward his body, making the top edge even and sending little wood chips flying. He takes a cask head, or lid, bending it slightly, and then pushes it flat into place at the top, sealing the cask, before hammering on four more taga, shaving the bottom staves so they align perfectly, and then putting in one last taga.

When the cask is finished, it's ready to be taken into the filling room, where it's filled with sake for a quick two-week maturation, enough to give the sake elegant forest notes without overpowering the brew. Since only fresh casks are used, once the maturation is finished, casks are resold to shops that make *tsukemono* pickled vegetables.

Tamura stops, wipes his brow. This is the first cask of the day; only 10 or so more to go.

FACING PAGE, LEFT Takeshi Tamura fits the staves together. FACING PAGE, RIGHT With taga hoops holding the staves in place, Tamura shaves the cask's inside. THIS PAGE, LEFT Tamura works with a two-handled drawknife called a *sen*. THIS PAGE, RIGHT The cooper pounds the cask's lid, which is known as a *kagami*.

# THE SEASONS OF SAKE

Sake has long reflected seasonality. The brewing season starts in fall and ends in early spring, although many producers these days brew year-round. Traditionally, brewers worked in fishing or agriculture, whose low seasons coincided neatly with the sake-making season. Even further in the past, however, sake was made throughout the year. Different seasons meant different styles of sake as well as varied production methods. For example, the *bodaimoto* (aka *mizumoto*) yeast starter was developed at a Buddhist temple by the 1300s, so monks could brew sake during the summer with fewer batches going to rot. But *kanshu*, sake brewed during the winter, was the most expensive.

In 1673 the Tokugawa shogunate restricted brewing to the winter to ensure a stable rice supply and create seasonal brewing labor. The seasonal brewers became a staple of sake making until the late 20th and early 21st centuries, when production dropped significantly and more rural young people either migrated to cities or lost interest in the low-paying, backbreaking work of sake brewing, which required them to be away from home for months at a time.

But sake brewing is suited to cold weather. Steaming, *koji* making and fermentation give off natural heat, which is easier to manage in the winter. Temperature control is one of the most important elements in sake production. Before refrigerators and air-conditioners, winter brewing made this easier. If brewers needed to adjust the temperature of the yeast starter, they could add a *dakidaru* (a water- or ice-filled container). Analog temperature control wasn't only important in the winter. The outside walls of breweries were painted white to reflect light, keeping things cool.

With the advent of refrigeration during the 20th century, sake breweries were able to stay in production throughout the year. Year-round breweries were built in Hawaii and Taiwan at the turn of the 20th century, as the warmth of the local climates made batches of sake susceptible to rot-inducing bacteria. In 1961, Gekkeikan in Kyoto and Reimei Shuzo in Nagasaki each built Japan's first year-round breweries to meet the demand of the nation's skyrocketing population.

**A line-up of fall-release sakes. To learn about the different subgenres reflecting the micro-seasons of Japan's autumn, see facing page.**

## The Brewing Year

Although the winter brewing season starts in the fall and ends in the spring, the 12-month brewing year starts on July 1 and ends on June 30. The brewing year, denoted by a "BY" on the bottle's back label, corresponds to the imperial era, which needs to be converted to the common era for Westerners to know the vintage. For example, Reiwa 2 (the second year of Emperor Naruhito's reign) is 2020. Thus, sake brewed between July 1, 2020, and June 30, 2021, would actually have the brewing year of R2, or 2020. The staggered brewing calendar and the imperial conversions can make the brewing year seem rather opaque. Some breweries have switched over to common-era yearly markings to make their vintages easier for non-Japanese customers to understand.

Is there a best time to buy sake? Nope! However, there are certain seasonal releases to keep in mind. Currently, there are no legal definitions of the seasonal brews listed on the following pages.

Limited-release summer sakes. The tags recommend serving these brews chilled. The bottles are blue to underscore that point.

### Spring

**Nama-zake** 生酒: *Nama* means "raw," and here refers to unpasteurized sake from the just-ended brewing season. While it's available year round, early spring is when the freshest nama-zake is available. Fresh, lively and even sharp and brash, nama-zake is the perfect spring brew.

### Summer

**Natsu-zake** 夏酒: This designation is often given to nama-zake specially packaged and bottled for summer (*natsu* in Japanese). There are also unpasteurized and unfiltered versions that pack an extra punch. Usually, *natsu-zake* is light and fresh, but some are zesty and deep. Often they are best ice cold or chilled. However, there are some exceptions, like Kinoshita Shuzo's summertime-only Ice Breaker release, which, even though it's a summer exclusive, is fantastic hot. Stock up on a few bottles for fall and winter.

ABOVE My co-author Takashi Eguchi trims a *sugidama*. Even this small one can take over six hours. No glue is used at all. RIGHT A browned sugidama outside Imanishi Shuzo brewery in Sakurai, Nara, where the sugidama was born.

## Autumn

**Aki-agari** 秋上がり: This is sake sold in fall (*aki* in Japanese). It is brewed during the coldest months of the previous season and aged through the summer, resulting in a milder flavor profile with rounder tastes. *Aki-agari* sake is pasteurized before its six-month storage and gets a second pasteurization before shipping. Aki-agari sake is good hot, eaten with Japanese fall foods like *matsutake* mushrooms, salted fish and hot pot.

**Hiya-oroshi** ひやおろし: Like aki-agari, *hiya-oroshi* is matured through the summer and pasteurized before storage. However, as it is not pasteurized a second time, it keeps some of the freshness and desired sharpness of nama-zake. Chilled storage is necessary and stated in the name "hiya-oroshi"—*hiya* means "cold" and *oroshi* means "wholesale," or "being taken down" (as if off a shelf). Some hiya-oroshi taste best chilled, while others shine at room temperature or hotter.

Within hiya-oroshi, there are three subgenres, which each reflecting different micro-seasons:

**Nagoshi-zake** 夏越し酒: Literally "over the summer sake," this hiya-oroshi is released in September, when the weather is still warm. It's often best drunk chilled or at room temperature.

Note that modern *nagoshi-zake* differs from the traditional *nagoshi-no-sake*, which is used in a purification ceremony at a midsummer Shinto festival called Nagoshi-no-Harai.

**Akidashi ichibanzake** 秋出し一番酒: Released in October, this hiya-oroshi brew is typically well balanced. *Akidashi* means "release in fall," and *ichibanzake* means "number-one sake."

**Banshu-umazake** 夜秋旨酒: Aged the longest of the hiya-oroshi releases, *banshu-umazake* (literally "late fall good sake") is mellow, round and ripe, typically with more umami than the other releases. Released in November, this sake is worth the wait. Usually, it's best heated.

## Winter

**Shiboritate** 搾り立て: "Just pressed." One of life's great pleasures is tasting sake right after pressing. Shiboritate is often fresh, full bodied and young, but can be spunky and sharp. As it's unpasteurized, more of the rice flavors are apparent. It's not strictly a winter release, but is often at its best late November through February. However, it is available through March.

**Shinshu** 新酒: Though there is no legal definition, *shinshu* (new sake) is typically assumed to be made from rice harvested during the current brewing year. Sake shipped by the end of June is technically shinshu. Sake that is then aged over the summer is either aki-agari or hiya-oroshi, depending on the pasteurization.

In years past, when the shinshu was ready, breweries would hang a *sugidama* (literally "Japanese cedar ball"), also known as a *sakabayashi* ("sake thicket") out front. Many breweries now keep a sakabayashi out year-round as a sake-brewing symbol. The Japanese cedar branches are fanned out and painstakingly trimmed to form a perfect sphere. Initially, the needles are green, indicating fresh new sake.

Fittingly, the sakabayashi turns brown as the sake ages and mellows over the summer.

The sakabayashi is said to have originated at Ohmiwa Shrine, one of Japan's oldest, as an offering for the deity. Mount Miwa, home of the shrine, is covered in cedar trees, which traditionally were used to make brewing equipment. It is unclear what the round shape symbolizes.

Sakabayashi are hung wherever sake is made, be it a brewery or the National Research Institute of Brewing in Hiroshima, which makes sake for research purposes. Even bars, restaurants and liquor shops hang a sakabayashi out front as a decoration.

ABOVE The precincts of Ohmiwa Shrine in Nara. The Japanese cedar in the foreground is sacred, which is denoted by the *shimenawa* rope tied around it. The shrine sits at the foot of Mt. Miwa, which is also worshipped as a sacred deity. LEFT Shrine maidens carry *omiki*, which is sake offered to the gods, during the annual Ohmiwa Shrine sake ceremony in November.

Brewers at Nishida Sake Brewery in Aomori Prefecture break up clumps of steamed rice.

# THE TEN THOUSAND METHODS: HOW GREAT SAKE IS MADE

## SAKE-MAKING STEPS

The steps of sake making appear simple: wash and soak the rice, steam it, inoculate it with the *koji-kin* fungus, mash the *koji* with rice and water in multiple stages, press the resulting brew and bottle. But the chemistry is so complex and the skill required is so high that it's a wonder good sake is made at all. Yet, walk into any liquor store in Japan, pull a bottle of sake off the shelf, and most likely you'll end up with something that tastes good. How do brewers do it?

The saying *sake zukuri banryuu* means "ten thousand methods of making sake." Throughout Japan, sake makers put their own spin on the process. Even within the same region, there are differences that come down to rice polishing ratios, yeasts, or fermentation times—all resulting in varied sakes. Heck, significant variations can be found between breweries on the same street! But the basic brewing framework is largely the same everywhere.

The process of making sake is a seemingly endless series of choices, with many of the steps occurring simultaneously and influencing each other. Some of the decisions are already made for the brewery, such as the climate and water supply. However, with climate-controlled rooms and complex water filtering, even those have become increasingly negligible. The brewery needs to decide what kind of sake it wants to make and then make choices during the production process that move toward that goal.

### Polishing the Rice

First, the rice is polished to the desired percentage. Many breweries outsource the polishing process, as rice-polishing machines, which are several stories high, are expensive to buy, run and maintain. The machines also must be housed separately from the brewery so the powder from polished bran doesn't accidentally mix with the fermenting sake. The outer layers of a rice grain are packed with vitamins, minerals,

# THE RICE-POLISHING REVOLUTION

**"Early brewers were driven by a desire to make better sake, and realized that improving the rice polishing ratio was essential,"** says Isao Aramaki, vice president and general manager at Kamotsuru Sake Brewing in Saijo, Hiroshima. Aramaki sits in a leather chair, the tea before him untouched. He's too busy talking rice polishing.

Images of rice being pounded are among the earliest in Japanese art. Bronze bells from the Yayoi period (300 BC – AD 250) depict stick figures pounding rice to remove the husk and the bran. For the next 2,000 years, Japanese people would gradually develop better technology to polish those grains, taking unpolished brown rice to highly polished white rice, from stone mortar to wood, from foot-powered milling to water-powered milling, which polished the grains like never before.

It was in Hiroshima that rice polishing was revolutionized forever. In the Edo period (1603–1868), the region's sake simply wasn't as good as the booze flowing from Kobe's Nada brewing district, where rice polishing contraptions powered by waterwheels helped produce truly

delicious sake. But the Hiroshima town now known as Saijo would become one of Japan's most famous brewing districts in the 20th century thanks to the advent of high-tech rice polishing machines. While Saijo's good medium-soft water makes excellent ginjo sake possible, it doesn't have anything to do with the town's technological feats. "There is no direct connection between soft water and the development of the rice polishing technique," says Aramaki. The main reason was the way locals embraced the new machine-driven tech. In Saijo, Riichi Satake started it all.

The son of farmers, Satake was born in the Saijo area in 1863. He excelled at school and was hailed as a child prodigy. In his teens, he began thinking there had to be a better way to polish table rice than

Riichi Satake, inventor of Japan's first modern, mechanical rice polisher.

the exhausting foot-pedal-powered method originally imported from China. During his 20s and early 30s, Satake oversaw public works projects, including the construction of train lines. He met Wahei Kimura, the founder of Kamotsuru Sake Brewery, by chance. The two struck up a friendship, and Kimura became a surrogate father to the younger engineer and inventor, who had lost his dad at a young age. In 1895, Satake began working on what would become Japan's first power-driven rice-polishing machine. A year later, Satake had developed the "quadruple-mortar machine," with

This Hokusai woodblock print is taken from the series *Thirty-Six Views of Mount Fuji*. For sake making, brewers would harness waterwheels like this to achieve previously impossible polishing ratios.

custom parts he made himself. His first customer was Wahei Kimura.

Japan's first power-driven rice polisher didn't come out of nowhere. Hiroshima was rapidly industrializing by the late 19th century. In 1877, for example, a massive state-of-the-art textile factory opened in Hiroshima, outfitted with thousands of the latest English-made mechanical looms. By the late 1880s, Hiroshima was home to a large military base, so there were plenty of thirsty troops ready to drink locally brewed sake. In 1894, when war broke out with China, Hiroshima was connected by rail to Tokyo, providing a flow of troops into the city and, as Hiroshima's sake improved, a way for Hiroshima brewers to reach larger markets; furthermore, the city's harbor was bustling with boats. That fall, as the military conflict with China continued, Emperor Meiji and the imperial court temporarily relocated to Hiroshima until the following spring so the court could keep a closer eye on the war. Hiroshima was more important than ever.

The power-driven rice polisher was not invented in Japan, but in the United Kingdom, in the early 1860s. The country was not a major producer or consumer of rice, but untapped Asian markets offered lucrative opportunities. In 1888, the Engelberg Huller Company of Syracuse, New York also launched a smaller machine for grain hulling and rice polishing. With new technology flowing into Hiroshima, and inventive minds eager to embrace it and develop and adapt their own, it was not surprising that Hiroshima came up with Japan's first power-driven polisher.

"Satake's power-driven machine paved the way for the development of the vertical rice polishing machine," says Aramaki. As Hiroshima grew and modernized, Satake continued improving his rice polishers, developing a new abrasive roller in 1922. Everything changed eight years later in 1930 with the Vertical Abrasive Power-Driven Milling Machine Type C. Unlike horizontal polishing machines, which are used for table rice, the vertical design used gravity to drop the rice through the center chamber, which was outfitted with a center grindstone coated with carborundum. Horizontal polishing machines have the rice grains rub each other, but the Type C polished the grain with the abrasive center roller to achieve a 40

**Riichi Satake handmade all the parts for his first rice polisher. At that time, the resulting machine was twenty times more effective than other manpowered rice-polishing contraptions.**

percent polishing ratio, removing 50 percent of the rice grain. In comparison, the water wheels of the previous generation, which helped make Nada's sake the best in Japan, could only achieve an 80 to 70 percent polishing ratio, buffing away 20 to 30 percent of the rice. The Type C revolutionized everything and became the standard, resulting in more uniform, finely polished grains that didn't chip or crack. The sake industry can be divided into pre– and post–Type C. Without it, ginjo-shu and daiginjo-shu as they're now defined would not be possible. The Satake Machinery Factory, now the Satake Corporation, has become a global giant with a 50 percent share of the Japanese market.

All of which shows that Aramaki is right when he states, "We can say that the history of sake is the history of rice polishing."

**Satake continues to innovate, making advanced, high-tech rice polishers. The company is now a multinational corporation with branches and offices worldwide.**

LEFT Kenbishi in Nada can do its own rice-polishing in-house. Many breweries cannot. ABOVE Polished rice at the Daishichi Brewery. RIGHT Rice used to be hand washed, but now compact machines like this at the Kamotsuru Shuzo Brewery in Saijo, Hiroshima make the job easier.

proteins and fats. While these might make rice taste good, they can adversely affect sake's flavor. That said, some brewers might want the flavors produced by those outer layers. Outer layers are removed for *ginjo* and *daiginjo*, whereas breweries aiming for rich, full-bodied flavors keep the polishing to a minimum.

Not all rice polishing is the same, either. Typical milling results in little beads of rice for brewing. However, the starchy white cores in, for example, the Yamada Nishiki rice variety are not round, but flat spheres. If you cut open a grain of Hyogo-grown Yamada Nishiki, the starchy core looks like the filling in an ice-cream sandwich or a moon pie. If Yamada Nishiki is polished to 40 percent with a typical mill, the tips of each grain will be removed, but the midsection, with all its unwanted proteins and oils, remains. The flat rice-polishing method, devised by Tomio Saito of the Tokyo Regional Taxation Bureau in the late 1980s, aims to reduce that by polishing away the middle. The Daishichi Brewery in Nihonmatsu furthered that technique with its in-house method known as "super-flat rice polishing." The average width of a Yamada Nishiki grain is 2.1 mm, and according to brewery

president Hideharu Ohta, conventional rice polishing only brings that down to 1.9 mm. "So for Yamada Nishiki, with a 35 percent polishing ratio, lengthwise it's actually polished to 20 percent, but the middle is only polished to 90 percent," says Ohta. "It's like you're blending rice with two different polishing ratios." Instead, the super-flat method can bring the width of a 2.1mm grain of Yamada Nishiki down to 1.5mm.

## Washing, Then Soaking

The rice is washed to remove any fine powder (called *nuka* in Japanese) that may have been left on the grain during polishing, which would negatively affect fermentation, because the point of polishing is to remove the outer layers. Rice can be machine washed or washed as it's piped through the brewery. The delicate grains of polished rice can be washed by hand or by hi-tech rice-washing contraptions.

After washing, the rice is soaked. Soaking slightly polished rice takes a bit of time, while finely polished ginjo grain soaks up water in minutes; the process is monitored by stopwatch. Brewers must make sure the grains absorb the

FAR LEFT Rice steams at Tamano-hikari in Fushimi. LEFT A brewer scoops out steamed rice at the Miyoshino brewery in Nara. ABOVE A peek inside an enclosed brewing tank.

desired amount. If the rice soaks too long, it becomes sticky once steamed, making it hard to work with during the koji making. Soaking is one of the most important steps in making sake.

## Steaming

The soaked rice is steamed in a large tub or tank called a *koshiki* for around an hour. Water is not added, because the rice has already soaked in water and contains the necessary moisture. Ideally, the resulting steamed rice has a hard exterior and a soft inner core. The steam breaks down the crystalline molecular structure of the rice starch, setting the stage for the enzyme reactions that follow. *Koji-mai* is the steamed rice destined for koji making, while steamed rice that's cooled and added to the main-mash is called *kake-mai*. Out of each steamed batch of rice, the breakdown between koji-mai and kake-mai is around 25:75, but a percent is also set aside for the yeast starter rice.

## Koji Making

Steamed rice is high in starch, but doesn't have enough sugars for yeast to eat and produce alcohol. Enter *koji*. In English, the word "koji" is used interchangeably to refer to the mold and the inoculated rice. In Japanese, koji-kin means the koji mold spores; in sake making, koji refers to rice inoculated with the mold. The term *kome koji* (rice koji) is also used, typically shortened to simply "koji."

Around 20 percent of the steamed rice is cooled to 86–95°F (30–35°C) and transferred to a sauna-like room paneled with cedar or stainless-steel called the *koji muro*, where the temperature is 82–86°F (28–30°C) and the humidity is 80 to 90 percent. It is placed on a large table and covered with a cloth for a few hours so the temperature and moisture can equalize.

The steamed rice is unwrapped and spread out. Koji mold spores are then sprinkled over the rice; the mycelium will work its way inside the grain, seeking moisture in the starchy core. The rice is kneaded into a mound and covered with a cloth to prevent loss of heat and moisture. Another method is for breweries to sprinkle koji-kin on the rice as it comes down the conveyor belt on a cooling machine.

For mass-produced sake, rice is inoculated mechanically with koji-kin spores as it passes through tubes.

Over the next 20 hours, the rice is unwrapped and kneaded twice more. When white mold dots the grains, the rice is moved into wooden trays or boxes. During the next eight hours, the rice is moved around in the trays, which are stacked and restacked in the koji muro to ensure uniform heat and moisture. Some breweries use cedarwood trays; others use trays made from plastic or metal.

The chemical process continues to give off heat until the temperature surpasses 100°F (38°C). The koji muro becomes a sauna, fogging up your glasses and drenching your shirt, explaining why some brewers work shirtless and barefoot. Once koji-kin covers most of the grain and koji's telltale chestnut aroma hangs in the air, the koji is removed from the room, spread out on cloths and raked. Some breweries make patterns in the koji to indicate that it's finished, or to indicate which batch of sake the koji is slated for. Sometimes, however, the designs are just that—designs.

This is the traditional koji-making process. But there's more than one way to make koji. Another is to place hand-inoculated rice in temperature-controlled chambers that look like ovens. Koji for mass-produced sake can also be made in automated temperature-controlled koji chambers with large combines that turn the koji. These giant rotators stir massive amounts of rice and produce huge koji batches. Ultimately, what matters most is the quality of koji produced.

## Yeast Starter

As previously mentioned, the Japanese word for yeast starter is *moto* (which means the "base" of sake), or *shubo* (which means "the mother of sake"). Good shubo means good sake, so brewers aim to make excellent (and healthy) yeast starter for brewing. This is why starter is used to create a small, pure yeast culture of lactic acid that protects the starter from undesirable bacteria. Lactic acid either propagates naturally or is

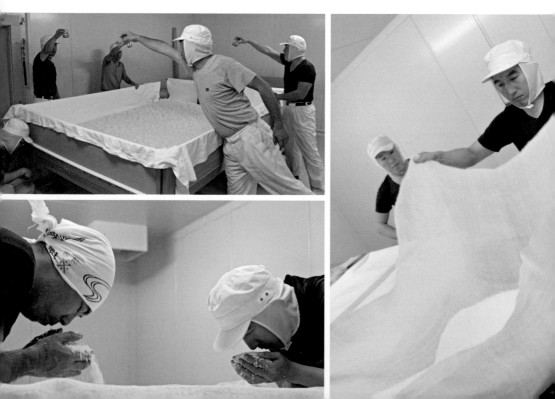

added. The main starter styles are *kimoto*, its offshoot *yamahai*, and *sokujo-moto*.

## Kimoto

Kimoto (literally "pure yeast starter") is one of the oldest styles of moto still used, dating from the 1600s. There is no official definition of how to make kimoto, nor are there any regulations that define the style. Generally, it's characterized by mashing the rice and koji together with the oar-like poles in a technique known as *moto-suri* (often translated as "grinding the yeast starter") or the more evocative sounding *yama-oroshi* ("grinding down the mountain"), referring to the mounds of rice in the mixing tubs.

To start the kimoto process, steamed rice is wrapped in cloth and cooled for 10 hours. (This step is essential; if skipped, sticky, glue-like rice will result, leading to subpar starter.) Once cooled, the rice is mixed with koji and water in small tubs called *han-giri oke*. When the rice has absorbed the water, brewers begin the work of mixing by hand or with small paddles.

Depending on the brewery, the next day can start with *moto-fumi* (or "stepping on the moto") when brewers cover their boots in plastic and stomp on the rice to help break up the clumps. Since modern sake rice is polished more (and thus is softer), many breweries skip this step in making kimoto. Next, the process of pounding the rice mixture with oar-like poles, which must be done every three to four hours, begins.

In the past, brewers sang songs to stay awake during late-night moto-suri; the rhythm and tempo of the song helped make sure everyone was moving in unison. Moto-suri is carried out until the mixture reaches a puree-like state. The puree is then put into a single starter tank, during which nitric acid is converted into nitrous acid; this, along with sugars from the koji and the low temperatures, inhibits the growth of undesirable wild yeasts. Microorganisms living in the brewery, as well as in the wooden tubs, also contribute to the kimoto sake's flavor.

Temperature control is paramount. It is accomplished by placing small sealed containers

FAR LEFT, CENTER and LEFT *Koji* making involves inoculating the rice with *koji-kin*, checking the aroma of the rice, and placing the koji-innoculated rice into wooden trays. ABOVE *Toji* Yuji Nakamura of Eigashima Shuzo inoculates just-steamed rice with koji-kin as it's transported down the cooling machine. Nakamura is the only toji who is also a master whisky distiller. When not brewing sake, he's making Eigashima Shuzo's White Oak–branded whisky.

# THE ELEGANCE OF TRADITIONAL SAKE

**The Daishichi sake brewery is unlike any other in Japan, with vaulted ceilings, wood paneling and marble floors. Landscape paintings cover the walls, and beautiful sculptures adorn nooks and crannies.**

Daishichi's specialty is the *kimoto* method. It uses this starter for its full lineup of sakes, which all feature good acidity and excellent umami. They're sturdy, well-put-together brews that, if stored properly, improve with age. "Sometimes we get calls from customers who turn up old bottles of Daishichi, wondering if they're still drinkable," says brewery president Hideharu Ohta. "Our reply is, 'If we still had that sake here, we'd sell it at a premium price.'"

Located on a quaint main street in Nihonmatsu in Fukushima Prefecture, a town that is famous for furniture making, the current brewery was built during the 2000s. Over the course of several years, production was moved into this new structure from the old brewery so the microorganisms clinging to brewers and employees gradually made the move too. "With kimoto, it's not just the yeast, but the lactic acid, in addition to the numerous micro-organisms, that make a sturdy sake."

The first-generation owner, Saburoemon Ohta, founded the original brewery in 1752, making Ohyama- branded sake. The third-generation owner, Shichiemon, focused the family's business exclusively on sake, using the kimoto method. The brewery's eighth-generation president, Ohta's grandfather, made the fateful decision to continue that tradition.

"My great-grandfather passed away young and my grandfather took over the brewery when he was only 16 years old," says Ohta. "Around that time, *sokujo-moto* was invented. According to the government, sokujo was easier than kimoto and harder to mess up." Countless breweries went under due to bad batches

TOP Brewery president Hideharu Ohta. ABOVE and RIGHT The sake-making process at Daishichi includes hoisting steamed rice into a cooling machine, innoculating the rice with *koji*, mixing it and wrapping it. Daishichi brews some of its most special sake in *kioke* wooden tubs. The oldest of these is about 90 years old and made from Fukushima cedar.

produced by the kimoto method, which requires superb technique and impeccable hygiene. "The government directed breweries to use the sokujo method, and my grandfather thought it might be the future." The brewery became the first in the region to begin test-brewing the new quick starter. "My grandfather found that no matter how hard he tried, he couldn't make the flavors he wanted with sokujo, so he decided not to give up kimoto," says Ohta. "Daishichi was quick to try sokujo and quick to say it was no good."

During World War II, the brewery had to temporarily abandon the kimoto method because the brewers were enlisted to the army and there wasn't sufficient manpower. After the war, Ohta's father was keen to return to kimoto, but there still weren't enough brewers, so he decided to try *yamahai*. "Yamahai sake, like sake made with kimoto, has personality, but it's heavier and the acidity stands out noticeably,"

says Ohta. With the yamahai method, the rice is left to dissolve, but according to Ohta, the starch might not completely saccharify, leaving a starter with a high percent of dextrin, which results in in a heavier sake. It wasn't the Daishichi style, and the brewery soon returned to kimoto.

Later, I watch *toji* Takanobu Sato work a pole into a small stainless-steel tub of starter. His movements are controlled, but he's not crushing the grains into a paste; rather, he's moving them around into a puree. The Japanese word Ohta uses to describe the mixture is "*sara-sara*," which is used to describe silky hair or smooth grains of sand. Looking closely, I see that the individual rice grains are intact as Sato carefully wipes the end of the pole and sides of the tub.

Around four weeks later, this finished starter will be taken to the main brewing room at Daishichi, where it is added to uncovered

tanks. The in-house yeast is a foaming yeast, allowing the brewers to check on the fermentation progress. When the brew is ready to be pressed, the brewery has different options, including modern Yabuta automatic presses and traditional wooden presses.

"At first, when I was still in my 20s, I thought using sokujo would be better because it can easily make prize-winning sake," says Ohta over a plate of sushi at lunch. "But by the time I was 30, I realized even though no one then respected kimoto, one day they would, and kimoto would again become the pinnacle of sake brewing." Ohta knew Daishichi had to be ready. "I wasn't sure if I'd be alive when that day came," Ohta says. He pauses, takes a sip of warm sake. "I didn't found this brewery. I'm following in the footsteps of those who went before. My father left this brewery for me, and I am going to leave something for the generation that follows."

# NIIZAWA BREWERY'S SUPER-PREMIUM, SUPER-POLISHED SAKE

**It's unseasonably warm for February. Patches of snow dot the soggy earth. Nestled against a lush green mountain, Niizawa Brewery's metallic silo glimmers in the morning light as a monkey scampers across the clearing. Here in the remote reaches of Miyagi Prefecture in the north of Japan, some of the world's most expensive sake is being brewed—costing upward of $1,000 a bottle—as well as award-winning budget sakes such as Atagonomatsu.**

Iwao Niizawa, the burly fifth-generation head of the brewery, strides through the building as workers raise a net filled with freshly steamed rice. All the brewers are young—in their twenties and thirties. "Sake breweries are unfair," he says bluntly. "They ask people to work for low wages so they can make a profit." Niizawa is different. Brewers are paid a living wage and given the opportunity to manage the brewery's subsidiary companies, such as its rice-polishing business. Promotions aren't based on age or gender, but skill. The *toji* (head brewer), a 22-year-old woman named Nanami Watanabe, is speaking to other brewers through a headset to ensure they're all in constant contact.

Niizawa, who took over the family's brewery at the tender age of 25 in 2000, knows that greater age doesn't necessarily make one a great toji—talent does. Niizawa was the youngest master brewer in Miyagi Prefecture, and the first not to belong to a toji guild. At that time, 90 percent of the family's sake was inexpensive *futsu-shu*. But the younger Niizawa wanted to make delicious sake that would enhance meals. Once he started

realizing his vision, sake lovers took notice. By 2005, Japan Airlines was serving the brewery's Hakurakusei-branded *junmai* in Executive Class. Five years later, Hakurakusei was the official sake of the FIFA World Cup and being served to the world's most famous musicians at the Grammies. Then, disaster hit.

On March 11, 2011, a massive earthquake rocked the northeast of Japan, unleashing tsunami waves that left death and destruction in their wake. Fortunately, no one was killed. But the brewery was destroyed, as was its inventory. Niizawa moved to its current remote Miyagi location because of the prime, unspoiled soft groundwater.

Excellent water isn't the only secret to Niizawa's premium sake. The brewery has been blazing trails in rice polishing. In 2009, Niizawa released Zankyo Super 9, made from Kura-no-hana rice with a 9 percent polishing ratio, milling away 91 percent of the grain. Zankyo means "reverberation"; true to this name, its impact was felt throughout the sake industry.

Niizawa wanted to make a sake a transcendent experience. He used

the brewery's in-house rice mill to see just how low the polishing ratio could go. At that time, the number was 9 percent. In 2014, the brewery had reached Super 8. A year later, Niizawa hit a *seimaibuai* (polishing ratio) of 7 percent. Polishing the rice alone took 350 hours. The super-premium sake won fans, but drew denunciation for the amount of rice that went unused. "People criticize the 7 percent polishing ratio because they haven't drunk it," Niizawa says. "It's like explaining what a Ferrari is to someone who's never driven one." The battle lines were drawn. A polishing war was underway. And Niizawa felt as though rival breweries were ripping him off.

Things had turned into the sake industry equivalent of the arms race. Tatenokawa, the first junmai-only brewery in Yamagata Prefecture, released its own 7 percent super-premium sake called Shichiseiki (the name refers to a seven-starred samurai battle flag) in 2017. That same year, Tatenokawa also released a sake with a 1 percent polishing ratio called Komyo, or literally "great achievement." This was the first time a brewery had made sake from rice with 99 percent of the grain milled away.

Polishing rice down to these teeny percentages is costly. The brewers discard more than 90 percent of the grains, and thus have to use more rice to brew. Rice can also crack during the polishing process.

RIGHT Niizawa brewery's shop and main office are located in Osaki, Miyagi Prefecture. Originally the brewery was located there too, but after the 2011 Tohoku earthquake and tsunami, it was destroyed. A new brewery was opened about an hour away. BELOW Niizawa's Hakurakusei Junmai Ginjo is reviewed on page 230.

Once the polishing ratio enters single digits, it becomes harder, though certainly not impossible, to use traditional sake rice.

Niizawa wasn't content to give up the rice-polishing crown. "We've made a sake with rice that's been polished even more—to zero percent," he says. "It's a limited release, with 500 ml (1 pint) going for 350,000 yen." But how can the brewery release sake with a zero polishing ratio?

Released in November 2018, the sake was Reikyo Absolute 0 Junmai Daiginjo. "Reikyo" literally means "zero reverberation." The reaction within the sake industry has been far from zero. But the name underscores the definitive and absolute quality the sake has.

Until July 1, 2019, Japanese tax regulations stated that decimal points for seimaibuai were always rounded down. So, for example, a polishing ratio of 6.9 would be 6 percent. Under the old regulation, when Niizawa reached 0.85, the

sake's label should legally read zero. "When we went to get the label approved, we were criticized for possibly leading customers astray," says Niizawa.

It wasn't Niizawa that was the problem, however, but the liquor regulations. "I wasn't trying to mislead customers," says Niizawa. "I was trying to be a rice-polishing pioneer." His Absolute 0 sake showed that the old regulations needed updating, which they

ultimately were. "Until then, I could sell my zero sake." The rice polishing alone took over seven months, costing $200,000. Niizawa had too much invested to give up now. Since it takes so long to polish rice to this percentage, and since the window during which zero percentage sake could legally be labeled was so short, Niizawa knew he'd have the final word in the rice-polishing race. That he did.

called *dakidaru* into the tank. They are filled with ice or hot water depending on the condition and needs of the starter. Dakidaru canisters containing hot water are used to raise the temperature. (Heating plates, can be used but they don't ensure the same even distribution of heat.) The mixture starts at 46°F (8°C) and is slowly raised to propagate healthy lactic acid bacilli, which create the lactic acid that prevents the propagation of undesirable bacteria, producing an optimal environment for the yeast. But the mixture is so acidic that it first inhibits the nitrate-reducing bacteria and then the lactic acid bacteria.

The koji enzymes turn starch into glucose; yeast, whether introduced or ambient, will withstand the acidity and gobble up the glucose to make alcohol. These days, yeast is typically added to the starter mixture about 14 days after the process begins, but during the Edo period (1603–1868), ambient yeasts in the brewery naturally worked their way into the starter. Meanwhile, increasing amounts of lactic acid in the kimoto mix kill off unwanted bacteria and microorganisms, making a highly concentrated yeast culture. The increased acidity and alcohol

levels make the lactic acid bacilli die off, leaving only the sake yeast. The whole process can take four weeks. The result is a robust starter ready to make durable and versatile sake.

## The history of kimoto starter

Although kimoto dates from the 1600s, the word does not appear in that period's brewing manual *Domo shuzoki* (loosely, "Brewing for dummies"), as the term had not been yet coined. Originally, it was called *kanmoto* (midwinter yeast starter). At that time, sake was made year-round, with different starters for different seasons. For example, *bodaimoto* (see page 24) was made in summer, because it thrived in hot weather. The kanmoto style, however, was tailored to saccharify the rice at low temperatures (41–42°F, or 5–6°C). But in 1673, the Tokugawa shogunate banned year-round brewing in a crackdown on sake making. In 1657, it had introduced a brewing licensing system known as *sakekabu*, essentially a "sake certificate" which was required for a brewery to make sake. But once the system was instituted, the government would not grant new certificates, allowing it to control the sake business and its rice consumption. Those who hoped to get into sake making had to either buy or lease a sakekabu from a mothballed brewery, although unlicensed sake continued to be made. The government also put a 50 percent levy on sake, causing a drop in production and a spike in prices, resulting in less sake to tax. In 1709 the tax was abolished.

Brewers at Kiku Masamune in Nada mix mounds of rice to prep for kimoto's *moto-suri* step. Making kimoto is physically demanding.

However, the seasonal restrictions on brewing would shape sake making for the next several hundred years. It led to rise of the kimoto starter, which by the late 1800s was so dominant that it was known as *futsu-moto* or "standard yeast starter." It also gave rise to the *toji* system, in which a toji (master brewer) and his workers would travel to a brewery, where they would live during the winter and make sake. Since the toji and his team were typically farmers, sake brewing gave them work after the harvest and often ensured that the folks who were making the sake had intimate knowledge of rice. This system worked well until the second half of the 20th century when sake sales dropped and brewery salaries fell with them. Young people left rural areas to live in cities like Tokyo and Osaka, and backbreaking work in cold, damp breweries lost its appeal in an increasingly wealthy country.

The earliest style of kimoto was developed in the Itami area, near Osaka, but was originally mixed by hand, not with oar-like poles. The late 17th-century brewing text *Kanmoto tsukuri-yo gokuiden* (The essentials of kanmoto brewing), which introduced Itami sake-making techniques, details how brewers mixed the starter using small hand-held paddles in small tubs in a technique called *temoto*, "hand yeast starter." Even now rice and water are first mixed together by hand before being mashed with oars in the later stages. However, the pole-mixing technique, which turns the rice into a puree, is not mentioned in this text from the 1600s. That process seems to have been perfected in neighboring Nada during the next century, and it no doubt improved the quality of Nada's sake.

## Yamahai

Around 9 percent of all sake is made with *yamahai*-style starter. Developed in 1909, this technique omits kimoto's laborious pole-ramming mashing process. "Yamahai" is short for

This *shubo* yeast starter at the Kasumi Tsuru Brewery is made with the low-foaming version of association yeast No. 7. As is evident from this photograph, low-foam does not mean no foam.

*yama-oroshi-haishi-moto*, or "yeast starter that omits yama-oroshi." Before the 1980s, yamahai wasn't widely known; it started as an offshoot of the previous decade's *jizake* (local sake) boom, which placed importance on older methods.

Process-wise, the difference between yamahai and kimoto happens in the first few days. For kimoto, the starter is mixed in multiple smaller tubs, while yamahai happens in one tank. Yamahai omits the mashing stage, but during the first few days brewers can mix the yamahai batch, using baseball bat–like poles to break up the rice so it can saccharify evenly. These initial mashing steps are how the kimoto and yamahai starter processes differ.

Note that there is also a spin on the yamahai method called *kaisoku yamahai* (high-speed yamahai) in which lactic acid is added to the

yamahai fermentation tank. This isn't a new process—it dates back over half a century—but it cuts the yamahai starter brewing time in half, saving time and money. Since yamahai doesn't have a legally defined process, kaisoku yamahai enables brewers to feature the yamahai name, even as they sacrifice flavor nuances. Even with this shortcut though, flavors have more depth than typical *sokujo-moto* quick yeast starter, making kaisoku yamahai an interesting addition to the brewer's arsenal.

### Are kimoto and yamahai different?

Yamahai is said to produce much gamier or wilder flavors than kimoto because it doesn't use kimoto's pole-ramming method, which affects

A selection of *kimoto* sakes. LEFT This Sakura Masamune kimoto sake is made with association yeast No. 1. See tasting note on page 232. CENTER Maruto is a well-made kimoto from Nagano. See page 239. RIGHT Under current brewery head Yusuke Sato, Aramasa shifted to all its sake to kimoto. See page 215.

saccharification, so more funky compounds end up in the starter. But according to Kazuhiro Fukumoto of the Kasumi Tsuru brewery—one of the few in Japan to brew exclusively with kimoto and yamahai starters—the difference between yamahai and kimoto is more nuanced.

"If you are making kimoto and yamahai, they end up resembling each other," says Fukumoto. "That is if your brewery is like ours, and is trying

Tools called *kaburagai* are used to make kimoto. The ones pictured here are used by the Kasumi Tsuru brewery in Hyogo Prefecture.

A selection of *yamahai* sakes. LEFT Yuki no Bosha from the Saiya Brewery in Akita. See page 231 for tasting note. CENTER This Tenon brew is a rich, well-balanced yamahai. See page 227. RIGHT The Furosen brand is synonymous with yamahai. Read the tasting note on page 247.

to offer kimoto and yamahai at their best." What he means is that at Kasumi Tsuru, there is a difference between kimoto and yamahai sake, but the difference is clearly understood. "Yamahai is easier to drink when freshly pressed, which is why we sell it that way," says Fukumoto. "Newly pressed kimoto has a hard mouthfeel and a mineral taste, especially if the rice isn't polished to less than 60 percent." Kasumi Tsuru feels its yamahai is better young, while its kimoto can be put down for a year,. "But if the yamahai and kimoto are highly-polished *ginjo* or *daiginjo* sakes, there really isn't this difference." This discrepancy might be due to the way the fats and proteins in less-polished rice break down.

This certainly doesn't mean yamahai doesn't age well. On the contrary, Philip Harper at the Kinoshita brewery (see page 127) is making excellent aged kimoto and yamahai sakes.

### Sokujo-moto

*Sokujo-moto* starter is by far the most dominant yeast starter, used in 90 percent of Japanese sake. A lactic acid solution is added, so that the time needed to brew the starter is only two weeks. This is far less than the kimoto and yamahai methods; hence the name, which means "fast brewed." The result is a clean, crisp sake.

Niigata brewer and researcher Goro Kishi conceived what would later become sokujo-moto. In 1894, Kishi published a technical manual on sake production that used science to explain brewing principles and to improve sake. At that time, the approach to making sake was shifting from the intuition of the *toji* to one based on empirical methods. Besides an in-depth look at soft-water brewing, which was invaluable to Niigata brewers, Kishi was the first to mention the addition of lactic acid to the yeast starter. Later, this idea was refined, and the National Institute of Brewing codified the sokujo-style starter in 1909.

### Multi-step Brewing

The yeast starter makes up only around 6 percent of the total brew. So, much like concentrated juice or powdered milk, it must be evened out to create a full batch. This is accomplished through a four-day process called *sandan jikomi*, or "three-step addition."

On the first day, steamed rice, *koji* and water are added to the starter. On the second day, known as *odori* (literally "dance"), the mixture is

left as is so the yeast can grow. The next day, steamed rice, koji and water are added again. The fourth day sees another addition of steamed rice, koji and water. The sake mash, or *moromi*, is then left to ferment for up to four weeks.

Sometimes a "four-step addition" is used. Depending on the brewers' aim, the fourth addition could be shubo, sake *kasu* (lees), *amazake* (sweet non-alcoholic sake), water or sticky rice. Ozeki, one of the country's largest sake makers, even has a premium sake produced with a 10-step addition process.

### Kai-ire: mixing up the brewing mash

One of the most common sights in a sake brewery is brewers jamming poles called *kai* into tanks and tubs of sake. This is called *kai-ire*, or "putting in the kai," an essential part of the process that helps even out the mash, keeps a constant temperature and releases trapped carbon dioxide. Brewers have their own techniques for handling the kai and mixing up the mash. However, Shoichi Washizu, the legendary toji at Niigata's oldest brewery, Yoshinogawa, figured out that by using massive tanks, the kai-ire process wouldn't be necessary: so much gas would be created during fermentation that the mash would agitate itself during brewing. Others in the industry thought his plan would never work, but it did—and beautifully— allowing Yoshinogawa to keep prices low and production high. These fermentation tanks are as tall as three-story buildings. Each batch produces 5,000 *isshobin* (1.8-liter or 4 pint-bottles) of sake. "If you drank one isshobin

LEFT It's easy to see why the *fukuro-tsuri* (hanging bag) style of pressing is also called *kubi-tsuri*, meaning "hung by the neck." For more, see page 60. BELOW CENTER Fresh sake passes through metal mesh. BOTTOM Some *daiginjo*, typically pressed in hanging bags, is then added directly to 18-liter (5-gallon) glass jugs known as *tobin*.

everyday, it would take over 13 years to drink all the sake in one tank," explains Yoshinogawa spokesperson Masayuki Yokomoto. While Yoshinogawa's award-winning sake is very good, drinking an entire isshobin of it every day isn't recommended, for obvious health reasons!

## Adding Alcohol

For certain types of sake, brewer's alcohol is added right before pressing. Of course, it is not added to pure rice junmai sake. For more on brewer's alcohol, see page 25.

## Pressing

There are three basic ways to press alcohol once the fermentation is complete. One is by using an old-fashioned press called a *sakabune* ("sake boat"). Cloth bags are filled with sake, folded and stacked on each other in the rectangular sakabune box. Since only careful folding keeps the sake from spilling, even these initial steps take tremendous skill. Typically made from hard woods like cherry or gingko, these all-wood presses can impart a scent to the sake, which might impair certain brews. For this reason, some sakabune are lined with easy-to-clean material like stainless steel.

It can take up to three days to press the sake in the sakabune, after which all the bags must be cleaned. Most large sake breweries in Japan no longer use this method—though the Kariho Brewery in Akita has a whopping six sakabune in use! It's not uncommon for smaller breweries to still use sakabune for various reasons. Some use them to achieve a certain nuance; for others,

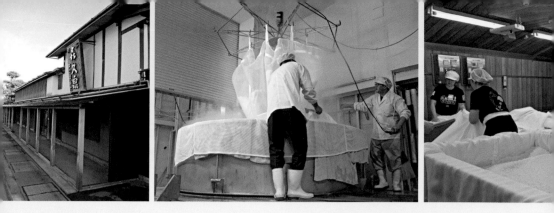

# DENSHU SAKE: THE RELENTLESS PURSUIT OF PERFECTION

**A sprightly 59 years old, Tsukasa Nishida bounds through the Nishida Shuzoten Brewery in khaki pants and a pair of Adidas Stan Smiths. It's not unusual to see a brewery president pulling double duty as *toji*, especially in a small boutique outfit like this. But Nishida isn't the master brewer. His second gig is brewery worker, so he ties up canvas bags of steamed rice, pushes carts and cleans up. Don't be fooled, though: he's the one making the final call.**

Tsukasa Nishida is all smiles after a long day of working in the brewery.

"The other brewers here don't see me as the president," Nishida says, taking a quick break after the morning brewing. When he's working in the brewery, he's just another hand. "But I have to be out here on the floor. That's the only way I can know what's really going on and make the necessary changes to improve what we do and what we make." Nishida Shuzoten's most famous sake is Denshu. Launched in 1974, the name literally means "rice-field sake." The idea was that this was a brew made directly from rice. It was promoted and labeled as a *junmai-shu*, marking a return to the days when sake was made without any added alcohol.

Nishida Shuzoten uses interesting rice varieties, including Kojo Nishiki, a variety named in 1968 that was bred from the second-most- commonly used sake rice, Gohyakuman-

goku, and Benkei, a sake rice variety dating from 1924 that fell out of favor once Yamada Nishiki, the king of sake rice, arrived in 1936. What makes Denshu so good is that it is exceedingly balanced, with equal emphasis on in the rice, *koji* and yeast. There is umami and depth, but nothing overpowers or distracts. "The kind of sake that is popular these days is good for that first impact, but loses its luster the more you drink," says Nishida. "Our sake is something that you can keep drinking, and it doesn't get in the way of food, so you can finish the sake and your meal too."

But Denshu wasn't always this good. "When I came to this brewery in 1992, the stuff they were making was awful," says Nishida. Denshu was cruising along on its brand name, not its flavor. "I knew things had to change." Nishida,

whose wife's family owned the brewery, had been working at Toshiba in nuclear energy. "I never thought I was going to work here," he says. "I wasn't born into this brewing family." He asked his father-in-law for a part-time gig. For the first three years, he was working in the brewery from the crack of dawn to 10 or 11 pm, staying overnight when necessary.

"My dad was a fireman," Nishida says. Coming from a world outside the brewery he saw everything with fresh eyes. But he had to work

The sake-making process from behind the picturesque facade of the Nishida Shuzoten Brewery, including hoisting rice out of the steamer to place in the cooling machine, making koji in the koji room, and bottling.

harder than everyone else to catch up. While he didn't have experience making sake, he did have loads of experience drinking it, and he knew that, at that time, Denshu was no longer up to snuff.

In November of 2004, Nishida took over the family business. "The toji in those days was getting old, and because what we made was still well received, he didn't want to change anything," says Nishida. "He was complacent, and I wasn't." Nishida asked him to step down, hiring a younger toji. "I'm never satisfied, and I always want to improve."

Every year Nishida contemplates how they can make better sake. "If we make sake that's only as good as the last, I think we can't satisfy customers. We need to push forward every year." But now that the brewery is making top-level sake, isn't it

getting hard to improve? "There's always something you can fix," he says. For example, he bought a new pressing machine because sometimes the batches would be ready to press at the same time, and one batch would have to be selected over the other. Investing in another Yabuta filtration press means that the brewery can now press every batch at the right time, ensuring they're bottling the best sake possible. Over the years, continual changes—and investments—like this have improved the brews. "I didn't get another press to increase the quantity, just the quality," says Nishida. "I only spend money on improving quality. Customers want more sake, but if we increased production, then the quality might drop. If the quality were to drop, I wouldn't want to make the sake."

The model here isn't what the brewery has done before, nor is it another famous sake brewery. Heck, Nishida isn't even thinking of Denshu and the brewery's other brand, Kikuizumi, as mere drinks. He looks to France for inspiration—and not to the country's wine industry. "France is famous for its bag makers with long histories," he says. "What I'm aiming at is Hermès, not Louis Vuitton. The difference is that Hermès increases quality, while Vuitton increases production. Vuitton is no good, right? Me, I'm for Hermès."

A collection of colorful Denshu bottlings. Denshu, however, isn't the brewery's only brand. On the far left is a bottle of Utou-branded sake.

it is simply the equipment the brewery has (automatic presses are expensive!). These days, sakabune often sit forlorn and unused in the brewery, covered in plastic or moved to a permanent exhibit in the brewery museum.

The most common press is the rectangle-shaped accordion-style automatic press, which uses air compression to press the sake, leaving behind easy-to-clean sheets of sake lees between the mesh dividers. It's faster, easier, doesn't result in sake oxidation, and is the preferred method.

The Yabuta automatic press, invented in 1963 by Noboru Yabuta of Daiwa Sake Brewing, dominates the sake industry. It is also used to press soy sauce, rice vinegar and red bean paste.

In the *fukuro-tsuri* ("hanging bag") style of pressing, bags filled with sake are hung so that the contents slowly drip out over the course of eight hours or so, with deeply elegant results. It's also known as *fukuro shibori* ("bag pressing") or *shizuku-shibori* ("drip pressing") as well as the grim-sounding *kubi-tsuri* ("hung by the neck"). The modern version was codified in 1965 at the Kumamoto Prefecture Sake Research Center. However, it's believed the style could be a modern take on a centuries-old method that

made *sumisake* (refined sake). Bureaucratic records written on wooden tablets in the 8th century, unearthed in the imperial Heijo Palace ruins in Nara, mention sumisake. The assumption is that unfiltered sake, now called *doburoku*, was somehow run through a cloth. Since this gentle method isn't ideal for large volumes, it's often reserved for special *daiginjo-shu*.

A modern spin (literally) on the gravity-powered hanging-bag style of pressing is centrifugal separation, which speeds up the slow-drip method. Here, the sake is put into a stainless-steel centrifuge machine and spun around to press the sake. This produces a brew that is similar in character to drip sake. The process, was patented in 2005 and only around ten sake breweries own the pricey machine. Asahi Shuzo, maker of the brand Dassai, was the first in Japan to press its sake in this way.

BELOW LEFT A brewer at Miyako Bijin on Awaji Island wears a rain jacket while filling bags to press sake. To-be-pressed sake drips out of the spout as he folds the bags and stacks them one by one. BELOW The old-fashioned tenbin shibori process at Miyako Bijin is helped along with a modern forklift.

The *tenbin-shibori*, or "balance press," was common in the Edo period, but is now a rare way to press sake. Tenbin-shibori uses a sakabune-style press—bags of sake are filled, folded and stacked in a rectangular box. Unlike in modern sakabune, where the pressure is applied mechanically, the tenbin-shibori method uses rocks balanced from a beam to press the sake.

Miyako Bijin on Awaji Island is one of the few breweries in Japan that still uses this time-consuming method. "We had a sakabune and wanted to do something with it," says brewery president Hirotsugu Hisada. The beam is *kashinoki*, a type of Japanese oak, brought all the way from Kyushu. During the late 19th century, when Japan modernized rapidly, much of the prime lumber, which takes over 100 years to reach suitable size, was chopped down for domestic needs and export. Finding strong, hard lumber of this size today is not easy.

Then, there's the amount of time it takes to press the sake with the tenbin-shibori method. At Miyako Bijin, brewers spend an hour just filling all the bags with 1,000 liters (260 gallons) of unpressed sake. It takes 46 to 48 hours to squeeze it all out. During this period, brewers must move the weight and the position of the rocks on the beam to the correct balance so that the sake is uniformly pressed. "We have to do this slowly," explains Miyako Bijin's toji Kunihiro Yamauchi, "so that the bags don't explode." The whole process takes three days. In comparison, an automatic hydraulic press can squeeze 3,000 liters (800 gallons) of sake in just 12 hours. Tenbin-shibori is taxing, which is why Miyako Bijin only does it about seven times a year, using an automatic press for most of its sake. The effort is worth it. "Tenbin-shibori is more gentle than a modern sakabune," says Yamauchi. "With

TOP This isn't sake, but rather, bottles of Miyako Bijin's brewing water. Sake makers are proud of their water and will often offer visitors a taste, or even bottle and sell it. ABOVE Miyako Bijin's *toji*, Kunihiro Yamauchi, holds a cup of sake just pressed by *tenbin-shibori*.

tenbin-shibori, the sake is pressed slowly and delicately, so you end up with a very soft sake."

## The parts of a sake-pressing run

The initial sake that leaks through without any additional pressure is called *arabashiri* (meaning "rough run"). This happens before the pressing starts in a sakabune, as the sake-filled bags are laid on top of each other, or at the very start of the bag-hanging method. It's called "rough" for good reason, but it's certainly drinkable, and sake makers proudly bottle it.

The most desirable part of the pressing run is the middle phase, known as the *naka-dare*

TOP At the Taiyo Sake Brewery in Niigata, sake kasu (lees) are chopped into squares, weighed and bagged for sale. ABOVE When it comes to cleaning, hot water is used to clean tools instead of soap, which leaves a residue and impacts flavor. Pictured is the Kamotsuru Shuzo Brewery in Saijo.

*shizuku-zake* or *shizuku-shu*, is known for being both aromatic and subtle. Since the sake can slowly drip, drawn solely by gravity, flavors and compounds emerge, giving shizuku-shu complexity. All the time and effort that goes into the process comes across in the flavor, aromas—and the price tag. This ain't cheap.

## Sake lees: the stuff left behind

The sake-pressing process leaves behind lees known as *sake kasu*. This by-product can be used to make a delicious winter soup called *kasujiru*, or to pickle vegetables, or as a marinade for fish or even to bake sake-kasu cake! The lees can also be used to make *amazake*, a sweet, low-or-non-alcohol drink. Typically, sake breweries have more sake kasu than they know what to do with. The modern automatic compression filter creates sheets of sake kasu that can easily be cut into pieces, bagged and sold.

## Cleaning

If you visit a brewery, you'll see someone is always cleaning something. This is to ensure unwanted bacteria don't run amok and ruin the sake. In a country with a long-standing bathing culture and a native religion (Shintoism) centered on cleanliness, the incessant washing doesn't seem out of place. During production, hot water is preferred, as it disinfects without adversely affecting flavor.

## Filtering

All sake is filtered (except *doburoku*, see page 154) even *nigori* (cloudy) sake. Pressing sake filters it. Sake is typically filtered a second time to remove sediment and tweak the flavor. The filtering process may also remove the natural yellowish hue to give a crystal-clear sake. Filtering techniques can even out a sake, but may inadvertently reduce its character. This is why some drinkers prefer their sake *muroka*, or "unfiltered."

(middle drops), *naka-gumi* (the middle draw) or *naka-tori* (taken from the middle). It's the heart of the press. When making premium *ginjo-shu* sake with the bag-hanging method, the middle cut is slowly collected drip by drip in glass bottles known as *tobin*, which means a "one-*to* bottle" (a "to" is an old measurement of volume corresponding the roughly 18 liters). The bottle has a small mouth, protecting the prized middle run from contamination and reducing air contact before sealing. The resulting sake, called

## Pasteurization and Bottling

Thanks to modern conveniences, such as refrigerated shipping, and technology like microfiltering that can rid raw sake of unwanted microorganisms, it's easier than ever to enjoy unpasteurized *nama-zake*—at least in Japan, where sake makers have a close relationship with retailers and can ensure that a shop's stock is properly stored and old bottles are switched out for fresh ones. But some brewers want fresh, nama-like aromas and flavors without the worry of dealing with unpasteurized sake, which will go bad if not properly cared for once it leaves the brewery.

In Japanese, pasteurization is called *hi-ire*. Bringing the brew's temperature to the neighborhood of 150°F (65°C), will rid the sake of potential nasty bacteria as well as inactivating enzymes, changing the sake's character. Pasteurization can be done prior to storage, right before bottling or once bottled. Originally a Chinese technique, pasteuriza-

Bottles of sake are pasteurized in hot water under a watchful eye at Hayakawa Shuzo in Mie Prefecture. As the temperature rises, so does the sake in the bottles. To cool them, a sprinkler sprays them with water, bringing down the temperature. Hayakawa Shuzo is known for its Tabika brand.

tion was utilized at least three centuries before Louis Pasteur. The *Tamon-in nikki* (Tamon-in diary), an account of Buddhist priests in Nara in the 1560s, mentions sake being boiled. Buddhist priests who traveled to China for religious studies often brought back the latest learning; it's very likely they brought back this practice, too.

There are several different methods of pasteurization. One is to run sake through a pipe immersed in hot water. Another is to move the sake through a series of metal heating plates, bringing the brew up to 158°F (70°C) in a second or so. Another is to put bottled sake into a pasteurizing machine. The bottles move through on a conveyor belt, getting heated and

# A VISIT TO HAKUTSURU: JAPAN'S BIGGEST-SELLING SAKE BREWERY

**"The temperature in here is the same as the average for November,"**
**says Mitsuhiro Ban, *toji* for all three of Hakutsuru's Nada breweries.**
**I think it must be colder, though—I can see my breath. The third**
**floor of the brewery is all shiny metal and grated walkways and**
**looks like something out of a sci-fi film. Greenish tubes pipe in the**
***koji* and white tubes shoot steamed rice into the metal vats.**

"Forty percent of all our sake is made in this brewery," says Ban, who's friendly and upbeat, speaking in the local dialect. The brewery has the rather ho-hum name of *3-go kojo* (Number Three Brewery), but what goes on here is nothing short of remarkable. "The Number Three Brewery makes around 5 percent of all sake produced in Japan." Fully 5 percent—right here. Over a hundred million gallons. That's staggering. The brewery's most famous sake is its Maru brand table sake. Moments earlier, we toured the floor above, where Yamagata-grown table rice polished to 78 percent is washed and soaked in big metal vats—3.5

tons of rice in one go—before being steamed on conveyor belts. Every day, this brewery steams 25 tons of rice.

The rap on mass-produced sake is that an operator sitting at a control panel simply presses a button and, bam, sake is made. In fact, there is a big panel with lighted buttons, but the operator—or rather, the brewer—walks over to the steamed rice, picks up a handful and rubs it on a wooden board to test the elasticity. "We might need to change the steaming time a little," says Ban, stretching the rice in his hand. "Here, let me show you how the koji is made."

I stick my face up against a small enclosed metal compartment with a glass top. Inside, a mechanical rotary flicks up koji spores that are sent down a tube into another tube carrying steamed rice, inoculating the grains in the process. The rice is transported to massive automatic, temperature-controlled koji machines with large combines that mix it as necessary. The koji is then moved and mixed with the steamed rice and the yeast starter in the third-floor tanks. And there is the hand of another brewer, who mixes each one with a long metal pole. This is mass-produced sake, but not devoid of the human touch. The process shows how a brewery can churn out huge quantities of sake.

In an small alcove, a handful of brewers are making the *shubo* yeast starter, using Yamada Nishiki polished to 38 percent. This brewing is all being done by hand on a small scale. "These brewers are making *daiginjo* to enter in the Annual Japan Sake Awards," says Ban. "Earlier this year, this brewery's daiginjo came in first place out of 850 entries at those awards." He's beaming, inviting me over to smell the shubo. The scent of juicy pears and elegant Fuji apples tickles my nose. It is going to make a spectacular daiginjo brew.

Hakutsuru is one of Japan's most famous sake brands. Its brewery building looms large over the Nada district.

Just before I leave the brewery, Ban brings out two bottles. One contains a daiginjo that won the 2018 Annual Japan Sake Award, and which was sold in very limited quantities. The other contains Hakutsuru's budget-priced daiginjo. "This is sold at convenience stores. It was created for people who might want to try daiginjo," he explains. He pours me a cup of the budget sake to taste first. It's exceedingly light and balanced. No fireworks, but that's not the point.

"Here, try this," Ban says handing me a cup of the award-winning daiginjo. When I smell it, that lush elegance is still there, but the aromas are more poised, well-defined and confident. I could nose this daiginjo all day. I take a sip. The whole brew just falls into place, exquisitely. Childhood memories of

pulling out honeysuckle stems and tasting that sweet nectar come flooding back. It's incredible. "That first impact is the secret for the daiginjo we enter into contests," Ban says.

"The brewers who made this are the same ones you saw upstairs making a batch for this year's entry," Ban says. "They are also the

same ones who make Maru, our table sake," says Ban. This isn't a special elite team, either. They're the brewery workers who make the best daiginjo in the country while they're also making widely available, mass-produced table sake. For Hakutsuru, this isn't an either-or choice, but a decision to strive for excellence in both.

TOP Toji Mitsuhiro Ban poses in front of brewing tanks. In the background, a brewer mixes up the brewing mash. CENTER, LEFT to RIGHT Toji Mitsuhiro Ban takes steamed rice and kneads it on a wooden board to check water absorption. Many breweries have omitted this step but Hakutsuru still believes it's important. RIGHT Hakutsuru uses massive disk-rotating koji-making machines. This contraption can make nearly 3,600 kg (8,000 pounds) of koji in a single batch. It was first installed at Hakutsuru in the 1960s.

then sprayed with water to bring down the temperature. This machine helps make sure all the bottles are evenly pasteurized, but it isn't cheap, costing around $70,000.

The trickiest, most time-consuming way is to manually heat the bottles in hot water, a process known as *bin hi-ire*, meaning "bottle pasteurization." Heating the sake in the bottle keeps flavors intact. "I want to retain the aromas of fresh sake, but I wanted to avoid the issues that can arise with shipping *nama-zake*," says Toshihito Hayakawa, toji at Hayakawa Shuzo in Mie Prefecture. "I thought bin hi-ire was the best way to preserve that and still have the longer shelf life of pasteurized sake." At Hayakawa Shuzo, all sake gets a single bin hi-ire pasteurization before it is sent out for sale.

Bin hi-ire isn't just a matter of heating up the bottles; it's an involved process. Brewers need to decide how much of the bottle to submerge in

the hot water. Some say putting the bottles in deeper water ensures a more even heat distribution, while others say it causes more bottles to explode. As in much of sake making, temperature control is key. There are different schools of thought as to whether the sake should be heated slowly or quickly. "Between 86° and 122°F [30–50°C], it's easy for bin hi-ire to get unwanted stale odors," says Hayakawa. "So we feel it's necessary to raise the temperature as quickly as possible during this stage."

It takes 20 minutes or so for Hayakawa Shuzo to raise the temperature inside the bottle to the desired 145.4°F (63°C). Then, the brewery turns on its do-it-yourself mist machine for another 20 minutes to drop the temperature of the sake in the bottle to 122°F (50°C), so that the brew can stabilize. If this step is not properly done, a musty smell can result. "I found out that there's a company in Hiroshima selling a high-tech misting machine with sensors for around $100,000," says Shunsuke Hayakawa, the brewery's president, who, with his son Toshihito, is only one of three people making sake at Hayakawa Shuzo. "We made our mist machine a while back for under $500," he says with a proud grin. After misting, the bottles are removed and put under a cool shower, where their temperature quickly drops to 73.4°F (23°C). Then the bottles are moved into refrigerated storage, where over the next hour, the temperature drops to zero.

## Maturation

After pressing, sake is typically stored for six months to a year. After storage, it's usually cut with water and blended to achieve consistent flavors. The sake is then bottled and shipped.

The maturation cellar at Kasumi Tsuru brewery in Hyogo Prefecture is filled with long-aged *koshu*. Each bottle is numbered and labeled with its brewing year and yeast starter type.

RIGHT Toji Shigeru Mukuda of the Kamotsuru Shuzo Brewery in Saijo noses one of his sakes. BELOW Niizawa Jozoten is one of Japan's more diverse breweries.

# MEET THE SAKE MAKERS

To brew sake, a group of people must come together to make the drink. Traditionally, the teams of brewers were large, but due to increased automation and costs, they are becoming smaller. Places like Kenbishi in Nada, which brings in 80 seasonal brewers every October to brew until spring, are a rarity.

## Kurabito

The word *kurabito* literally means "brewery person" and is used to refer to the brewers. In olden times, kurabito were part of the team assembled by the *toji* (chief brewer or master brewer) who traveled to the brewery. Kurabito traditionally worked in agriculture or fishing, often giving them intimate knowledge of rice.

## Toji

The term *toji* is not limited to brewing; there have also traditionally been rice-polishing toji, a key position in the milling process. The term is also used for soy sauce and vinegar brewers.

Traditionally, the toji knew the brewing secrets that the *kuramoto* (brewery owner) did not. They were hired for seasonal work, assembling a team to use their skills, experience and intuition to brew up some delicious sake. A number of

# BREWING SAKE FOR 7 DECADES: NAOHIKO NOGUCHI

**It's a glorious summer afternoon in Ishikawa, on the Sea of Japan coast. Rocky mountains, green rice paddies and blue skies provide a spectacular backdrop. I had arrived 10 minutes early so as not to keep Naohiko Noguchi waiting. With 27 gold prizes at the Annual Japan Sake Awards and recognition from the Japanese government as a master craftsman, he is one of Japan's most respected and accomplished sake masters.**

Noguchi, a sake icon, has been brewing sake for over seven decades. He's waiting patiently for me inside the brewery that bears his name, the Noguchi Naohiko Sake Institute, sipping green tea. The brewery, established only two years prior, is a way for the legendary *toji* to pass what he knows to the next generation.

He springs up as soon as I enter, hand outstretched, flashing a pearly smile. Later, he tells me he had to have all his teeth replaced in his forties when they rotted after eating *koji* each night to check its quality. Without good koji, you cannot make good sake. For Noguchi, if ensuring the koji's quality means extensive dental work, so be it.

"This morning, I was doing tastings," Noguchi tells me, in his thick, local dialect. He doesn't really drink though, he says. "If I drink even a little, my face turns red. I'm one of the 30 percent of Japanese who can't break down alcohol." But tastings are part of the job. "My face got all red this morning," he says with a chuckle. "I got a little tipsy." Even though Noguchi doesn't drink sake for pleasure, he knows exactly how it should taste.

"I can imagine how a sake is going to taste before I brew it. I know what the yeast and the koji will produce with each variety of rice. If the result is different, then I know something went wrong." I ask how long it took him to learn that. "Oh, 20 years of brewing." That was still early in his career.

"I entered the sake business when I was 16 years old," says the 86-year-old. "By the time I was 27, I was a toji in charge of brewing *daiginjo*." At that time it was almost unheard of to become a toji so young. Noguchi came of age during World War II. During that time, he was at high school, but not in class. The schoolyard had been converted into a farm, and young Noguchi spent his days growing vegetables. Adult men were either off fighting or working in factories making weapons. His father and grandfather both worked as toji, and in 1949 the teenage Noguchi found himself working at a brewery called Yamanaka Masayoshi Shoten. "During the war, I lost the chance to study at school but others lost their lives. So compared to that, it wasn't a major loss."

It was fall 1961 when Noguchi became toji at Kikuhime in Ishikawa.

He would go on to make his name at that brewery, but his first year was a bust. Before joining Kikuhime, Noguchi had cut his teeth in Mie Prefecture, where, at the time, a lighter style of sake was preferred. "For the mountain folk here in Ishikawa, a thinly-flavored, lighter sake was not satisfying." Lumberjacks toiled all day up in the mountains, and when they came down to the town, they didn't want a watery-sake. Noguchi took note and learned a lesson that still guides him more than half a century later. "It's no good for you, the toji, to dictate the style of sake. You must meet the needs of the people," he says. "I learned that I need to make sake that will bring enjoyment to the people drinking it," he says. "Since I don't drink sake, I'm always listening closely to what customers want. What's the point of making sake that nobody drinks?"

After his first season as toji, Noguchi began to look to other styles of sake that would allow him to create more depth and flavor. He hit on *yamahai*, a style that wasn't widely used or known at the time. He traveled to the now-shuttered Miyako Shuzo in Kyoto to learn from a yamahai master. The style is now closely associated with Noguchi, and his flavorful yamahai sakes are reminiscent of intricate woodwork sculptures: finely grained, nuanced and expertly done. The traditional way to make yamahai is to mush up the yeast starter with bat-like poles called *bougai*. It is exhausting physical work. "About ten years after I started making yamahai, I heard about brewers at Kodama Shuzo in Akita using electric mixers," Noguchi says. "I immediately tried it for myself." With a mixer, it takes 30 to 40 minutes to mash up the rice. "Sake-making techniques have constantly evolved since the olden days," he says. "Just because something is labor-intensive, that doesn't mean it's better." Noguchi points out that whether brewers use old-fashioned poles or electric mixers, the goal is the same: to break up the rice. "If less-taxing methods can get you the same results, you should use them."

In the 70 years he has been brewing, trends have come and gone. sweet sake, light sake, the *ginjo* craze, acidic sake and more. Noguchi has always been flexible enough to change with the times so that he's making sake that's of its day. "I can't decide the flavor of sake," he says. "That's dictated by the times—not by me." In the past, people in Japan ate meals at home. *Kan-zake* (warmed sake), he says, allowed them to take their time. Now, fewer people are cooking or eating at home. If they are, they might just be heating something up from the fridge. More people are eating alone. Buildings are air-conditioned, and most people work indoors. "This is why a softer style of sake has become popular," Noguchi says. "For each generation, sake changes. It is up to the toji to meet the needs of the day."

Noguchi asks if I'd like to see the brewery. We walk down a long hallway. Huge glass windows over-

look the brewing floor where the sake making will start in the fall. A timeline of his career and photos covers the walls, marking milestones along the way. Noguchi's career has kept going and going, with multiple retirements and comebacks. He first retired when he was 65. "It was company policy at Kikuhime," he says. "But after I retired, another brewery, the Kano Brewery, asked me to brew for them." He stayed there for another 14 years, raking in more awards, including one of the highest, the Ribbon Medal of Honor. Then, in 2012, he retired again, but returned to brewing at age 80 before retiring yet again in 2015. Offered a chance to set up his own brewery, Noguchi came out of retirement in 2017 at the age of 84. Making sake is not merely a job. He has given his life to brewing. "I didn't go to school, and I didn't study, so I had fewer options as a kid," he says. "The only choice for me was to become a *shokunin*—a craftsman. So I gave it my all."

"When I was young, I was really quite vigorous," he says, walking downstairs. At 86, he still is. Making sake is demanding—physically and mentally. Noguchi still lives at the brewery during the winter season, waking up at 4 am, making sake with brewers a third his age. "I sometimes hear them complaining that their backs hurt or they're tired." Noguchi opens the door to

Naohiko Noguchi stands in front of the noren curtain at his new brewery in Ishikawa Prefecture. Noguchi has influenced an entire generation of brewers and delighted generations of drinkers with his sake.

his office. It's spartan: on the desk are just some neatly stacked papers, pens, a calculator, and a telephone. There are no knickknacks or other distractions to take his focus off the task at hand: making delicious sake.

"This is the only profession where I can make others happy. I will brew sake as long as I can, and as long as there are customers I can please. For them, I am grateful." Later, American-born brewer Gordon Heady tells me about a time he was working at Noguchi's brewery, shoveling snow for an hour outside the toji's office on a crisp blue day. "I don't think he looked up once from his desk to acknowledge the view or me," Heady said. "He was completely absorbed in his notebooks, where he keeps all his sake data." Like his sake, this is a testament to his focus.

breweries today do not use the term "toji." They prefer titles like "production manager," "leader" or "person in charge of brewing."

## The meaning of "toji"

It's unclear where the term "toji" originated. One theory is it comes from the old word meaning "matron" to refer to the head of the household, in the days when simple sake was made at home by women. During the Heian period (794–1185), the jug used for brewing sake for religious offerings was also referred to as a "toji." *Wakun no shiori*, a dictionary from the Edo period (1603–1868), confirms the religious connection and states that women handled the sake making at Shinto shrines. But by the Muromachi period (1336–1573), male brewers were referred to as toji. Another theory is the word evolved from the word *shashi*, "Shinto priest." Another is that "toji" refers to Du Kang, who made first alcohol

LEFT Shoichi Washizu was a legendary, award-winning *toji* at Yoshinogawa in Niigata Prefecture. The Japanese government awarded him a yellow ribbon Medal of Honor in 1983. ABOVE Maho Otsuka, female toji at Shoutoku Shuzo in Kyoto's Fushimi is part of a trend away from male domination of the sake industry.

from sorghum in China's Xia Dynasty (2100–1600 BC). In Japanese, Du Kang is pronounced "Tokou"; supposedly, "toji" is derived from this legendary Chinese liquor maker.

## The rise of the female toji

For centuries, men have dominated the sake industry. Sake making was traditionally a seasonal occupation: brewers left their homes to go live at the brewery and make sake. In eras when women were expected to keep house, it simply wasn't possible for them to leave to make sake. But in the past few decades, as sake breweries began to use fewer seasonal workers and a generational shift happened in the industry, women started working in breweries.

In 1980, Kazuko Shiiya, a brewer at Ichishima Shuzo in Niigata, caused a national sensation when she scored level 1, the highest rank, on the National Trade Skills Test for brewing. "I have often thought that if I had been a man, I could have become a toji one day," Shiiya told the *Japan Times* in 2002. "But ask me if I envy housewives stuck in the kitchen, and I'd have to say, 'Absolutely not.'"

There are no official numbers, but in 2016, out of the Japan Sake Brewing Toji Union's 694 members, 16 were women. There could be other female toji in Japan who aren't in the union.

"These days there are more female toji, and many of them are the daughters of brewery owners," says Shikou Kimura, president of Shoutoku Shuzo, a Kyoto brewery in Fushimi dating from 1645. "But our female toji, Maho Otsuka, is different: she started out as an employee here and rose through the ranks."

After getting a master's in agriculture, Otsuka felt like the world of the *shokunin* (artisan) would be a better fit than a white-collar job. "It wasn't easy looking for a sake brewery job in 2000," she recalls. "Sake consumption was declining and breweries weren't hiring. Also, women brewers were exceedingly rare." During her first year at Shoutoku Shuzo, she pulled double duty, working in the office like the most women in the sake industry and, when she could, in the brewery. "I would come in at 3 am when the other brewers arrived so I could learn from them and show I was serious."

By her second year, Otsuka was working in the brewery full-time, learning everything she could from the toji, who was about to retire. Today, it's common for apprentices to be told what to do, but the old style was tight-lipped. "The toji just wanted me to do what he did, and watch him

closely." Today, she also likes to lead by example. "But I often have to remind myself that the younger generation needs to be told explicitly."

At some point, after the toji retired, Otsuka started being introduced as the sake-brewing leader. "Then I noticed my business cards had 'toji' written on them." That was in 2005. It was official—Otsuka was her brewery's toji.

While the way Otsuka learned the trade was old-school, she wasn't willing to the life of a sake brewer, with its notorious early mornings and late nights, as a given. In 2010, Shoutoku Shuzo went to a 9-to-5 work schedule for breweries. Otsuka worked as a toji during her two pregnancies. But even after working hours, she comes back to the *kura* when necessary. "I'll bring my kids sometimes. They're so encouraging. They also love eating the rice." Brewers have families; they always have, but times are changing. They have lives outside of making sake. "If revamping the schedule affected the sake we produced, we wouldn't do it, but it hasn't," she says. "I want other breweries to know that they can have their kurabito keep more normal hours and still make delicious sake."

## Kuramoto

Literally meaning "origin of the brewery," *kuramoto* denotes the brewery owner. Traditionally, sake brewing is a family-owned business, and the breweries are passed down from one generation to the next. In the past, the kuramoto was not connected to the actual brewing process; instead, he hired a toji who assembled a team to brew sake. Only a few decades ago, the idea of a *kuramoto-toji* who both owned the brewery and led the brewing was inconceivable. Now, however, among smaller breweries, it's become increasingly commonplace.

Plump grains of premium
Yamada Nishiki rice in Hyogo
Prefecture are still weeks
away from harvest.

# THE ESSENTIAL INGREDIENTS: RICE, WATER, KOJI, YEAST AND SOIL

## RICE

Wherever you look in Japan, there is rice. The countryside has spectacular mountainside rice terraces. Cities squeeze in tiny rice fields in open lots. The Japanese word for cooked rice is *gohan*, which also means "meal." The inference is that rice is the main event and the other dishes, including the meat or fish, are mere sides.

Wet-rice cultivation in paddy fields was introduced to Japan as early as 2,800 years ago, but dry-field rice farming existed before that. Wet-rice cultivation slowly spread through the country. The earliest archaeological sites date from around 1000 BC and are located in far western Japan in Kyushu, whose geographical location is close to China and the Korean peninsula. Remains of prehistoric paddies are found throughout Japan.

Rice is essentially a tropical or subtropical crop. For a September harvest, it needs day and night temperatures during the summer months that don't dip below 68°F (20°C). Japan's climate is not uniform, so some areas of Japan, especially those in the north, harvest rice later. Moreover, in centuries past, those cooler areas have been more susceptible to famine. Thanks to improved fertilizers and stronger, high-yielding rice strains, they have become better able to not only feed themselves, but the entire country.

These days, the traditional diet is changing, and Japanese people eat more bread than rice. According to a 2011 Japanese government survey, nonagricultural families of two or more spent the equivalent of nearly 100 dollars more on bread than rice. This was a first since the government began the survey in 1946. Still, rice, especially white rice, remains synonymous with Japan. This wasn't always true.

### The Valuable Grain

Japan's oldest book, the *Kojiki* (Record of Ancient Matters), from AD 712, lists rice as

merely one of the "five grains" (*gokoku*). The concept of five main grains originated in China, though some of Japan's five grains were different. According to the *Kojiki*, they were adzuki beans, barley or wheat, foxtail millet, soybeans and rice. Legend had it that these grains were born from the corpse of a slain goddess, with rice sprouting out of her eyes and the other grains emerging from other orifices. The *Nihon Shoki*, Japan's second-oldest text, dating from 720, lists the five grains as barnyard millet, barley or wheat, beans, foxtail millet and rice.

For centuries, a mix of grains—not just rice—helped provide the Japanese diet with the necessary caloric intake. Members of the upper class, including the royal family and high-level samurai, ate rice year-round, but other grains still found their way into imperial bellies. Lower classes ate less rice and more of the other grains. However, out of all those grains, rice became the one with the greatest spiritual and cultural importance. It also became the most economically valuable.

As early as 1500 BC, rice was one of several commodities that was used for barter. During the centuries that followed, Japanese minted coins as well as importing coins from China. Yet rice remained a precious commodity, as it kept well and the crop had a high yield-to-seed ratio. The Taika Reforms of AD 645 leveled a 3 percent tax on rice fields—paid in rice—further cementing

Planting by hand simply isn't efficient. Small and large farmers alike save time and energy with modern equipment. Many large breweries get their rice from farmers, with whom they have close relationships and long-time contracts. However, in summer 2016, Yoshinogawa in Niigata began growing its own rice, starting with Gohyakumangoku (pictured, center).

FAR LEFT Sake makers often hold planting events. Sometimes fans participate, while here, brewers from Sawanotsuru in Nada roll up their pants to plant rice by hand.
CENTER Large breweries need large amounts of rice. Pictured is a greenhouse in Niigata.
LEFT Gohyakumangoku is the second-most-used sake rice. It can impart different flavors from Yamada Nishiki and suits the typical Niigata brewing style. These seedlings are waiting to be planted.

its economic value. After rapid inflation during the mid-10th century, coins were no longer minted in Japan; by the 11th century, rice was again a commodity currency, along with silk (used to make kimono) and hemp (for sacred ropes at Shinto shrines, clothes, fishing nets, paper and bowls). Japan's commodity currency system was based on credit, as samurai elites couldn't carry around granaries in their purses.

After the mid-12th century, coins came back into use. Rice was still used as currency, though this faded as more coins flowed through the economy. According to Nobuo Harada, author of *Kome wo eranda nihon no rekishi* (A history of Japan choosing rice), loans were based in the grain right up into the 1800s. Rice wasn't just food; it was money—hence its association with Inari, the Shinto god of business. It also became increasingly connected with purity, thanks to the development of polishing technology that could turn brown rice white. Because it could be made into sake, it was also basically yen you could drink, and thus a perfect crop.

Prior to the 1500s, it's best to think of rice as an imperial tribute. But with a burgeoning merchant class with greater wealth than the higher-status samurai, more and more people started eating rice and drinking sake. Consumerism was taking hold of Japan. By the late 1600s, polishing techniques made white rice

# ORGANIC RICE

**The overwhelming majority of rice eaten and brewed in Japan is not organic. Farmers use chemical pesticides, fertilizers and treatments to ensure a stable crop year after year. Kotaro Oku of the Akishika Brewery in far north Osaka says, "I'm not against non-organic food—I eat it all the time. I just don't want to grow it."**

Ever since Akishika's founding in 1886, the family has grown rice for brewing. "Many *kuramoto* [owners] don't want to get in their hands muddy in rice paddies," says Hiroaki Oku, kuramoto and *toji* of Akishika. "I grew up in rice paddies and so did my son Kotaro." As of this writing, 20 percent of the rice used in brewing here is organically grown; the rest is purchased from other local farmers.

"The number might seem low, but that's because the crop yield isn't as high as it would be if we used agricultural chemicals. We're not

going for quantity, but quality." According to the elder Oku, organic rice makes excellent *koji* and produces sake that's worth all the extra effort. By using organic rice, Akishika can ensure that unwanted flavors and nuances aren't lurking in their brews. The brewery doesn't even use manure to fertilize its rice, as it can't be 100 percent sure the animals were not given hormones in their feed. Instead, it makes compost from rice husks for its Yamada Nishiki and Omachi crops. Akishika's rice fields look wild and overgrown, with weeds peeking through and

rice stalks growing at different heights. "Other rice farmers have these neat, uniform fields made possible by agricultural chemicals," says Kotaro. "So they're gob-smacked when they see this. But this is how rice fields used to look."

While other breweries might charge nearly double for organic rice sake, Akishika charges the same as it does for its non-organic brews. If organic production increases, however, that might not remain possible. The goal is to grow 70 percent of the rice it uses, keeping 30 percent contracted from local farmers just in case.

"I don't know if we'll reach that number," says Kotaro, "but we want to try."

ABOVE When people hear Osaka, they think of a packed urban city. However, Osaka Prefecture has lovely rural spots like Nose (pronounced "no-say," not the thing on your face), where Akishika is located.

LEFT The younger Oku stands in front of a field of organically-grown Omachi. Akishika's goal is *ikkan-zukuri*, which means from seedling to sake.

possible, and fashionable foodies and wealthy urbanites wanted to eat it. (As a side note, all that polishing removed nutrients like vitamin B, and white-rice connoisseurs started developing beriberi, a vitamin-deficiency disease that affects the nervous and cardiovascular system.)

What would later become the Dojima Rice Exchange in Osaka began operating in 1697. It would become the world's first commodity futures exchange, booking and recording trades in rice. The entire Japanese economy was based in the grain, with samurai elites paid in the rice and not gold coins, similar to how Roman soldiers were paid in salt. Eating rice, especially white rice, wasn't only filling, but an act of extravagance; drinking it, even more so. One of the most significant economic changes of the Meiji era (1868–1912) was the revision of the tax code stating that taxes must be paid in cash, not rice. The grain was left for eating—or better yet, brewing.

## Sake Rice and Table Rice

There are two types of rice for Japanese sake. One is regular table rice, which is used to make around 80 percent of all sake. The rest is made with sake rice, specialty breeds that are not generally eaten, but make delicious brews.

While the official Japanese name for sake rice is *shuzo koteki mai*, literally "rice suited for sake brewing," most simply refer to it as *sakamai* or "sake rice." Less then 5 percent of all rice grown in Japan is sake rice; the vast majority of *futsu-shu* is made from table rice. But these specialty grains are the result of science, patience and luck. Sake-rice grains have been bred to be larger than table rice and they have a big starchy white center, which, for many brewers, is the desired part of the grain. It's also less glutinous than sticky table rice, making it easier to work with once steamed. (Non-sticky varieties of table rice are also used for sake making.)

In addition to having larger and heavier grains, sake rice grows taller than table rice and can be more susceptible to falling over during late-summer typhoons when the grain is ripening. This causes the stalks to bend, cutting

ABOVE RIGHT Sake rice tends to grow longer than table rice. On the left in the top photo is Yamada Nishiki, the most famous sake rice. On the right, with the last white placard, is Koshihikari, Japan's favorite table rice. The long stalks make sake rice more vulnerable to typhoons and other severe weather, which can wreck havoc on fields. RIGHT Table rice harvested in late September in the Osaka region.

# REVIVAL RICES

**During the years following World War II, when the population of Japan was increasing rapidly, low-yielding rice varieties fell out of favor. Old strains like Omachi were overtaken by crossbred varieties that were easier to grow, stronger and had higher yields. In the early 1990s, one of the oldest varieties, Ise Nishiki, was resurrected.**

"After learning about rice varieties native to Mie Prefecture that reflect the region, we began cultivating Ise Nishiki for brewing," says Shimpei Gensaka, managing director at the Gensaka brewery in Mie. The brewery received seeds from the local agricultural research center and worked with local farmers to bring the rice back.

In the late 1840s, rice was selectively bred in Mie Prefecture with seeds from a variety known as Yamato. In 1849, the new rice was christened Ise Nishiki. According to the essay "History of Rice in Japan" by Chukichi Kaneda of Kobe University, when regular folk went on pilgrimages to shrines and temples during the Edo period (1603–1868), travelers would bring back rice varieties as souvenirs. The rice varieties, explained Kaneda, were given names such as Ise Nishiki or Zenkoji after sacred spots like Ise Grand Shrine in Mie or Zenkoji Temple in Nagano. Sake brewers noted the size of the Ise Nishiki grains and the large, clearly defined *shinpaku* at the center.

But during the 20th century, Ise Nishiki seemed to disappear. "The big reason was that this ancient rice was not suited to modern farming methods," says Gensaka. The stalks grow as high as 160 cm (5 feet), making them prone to toppling in late-summer and early-fall typhoons. "Back then, rice was grown naturally—there weren't chemical fertilizers and pesticides like today. But starting during the Meiji era [1868–1912], the country pushed to modernize farming, and crossbreeding replaced selective breeding. New varieties designed to be used with chemical fertilizers appeared, and old strains like Ise Nishiki had too many drawbacks, especially with the rice shortages during World War II and the post-war years. So it vanished."

Bringing it back was no easy task. The Gensaka brewery, which grows its rice on-site, leaves space between plants to allow offshoots to fan out, strengthening the stalk to lower the risk during typhoon season. Older varieties can lose quality over time, especially if

there isn't strict supervision over which seeds are distributed. It's like making photocopies of photocopies; the end result simply isn't as good as the original. Some older rice varieties have been mixed and matched with other varieties to improve yields. According to Gensaka, however, Ise Nishiki is still a pure breed, and it doesn't appear to have changed much from its original incarnation.

"With Ise Nishiki, what kind of sake you can make really depends on the personality of the brewery, so I cannot say it produces a specific type of brew," says Gensaka. At his brewery, though, you can say without a doubt that Ise Nishiki makes excellent sake.

**BELOW LEFT** Harvesting Ise Nishiki in Mie Prefecture for Gensaka sake. **BOTTOM RIGHT** Grain falls into the hopper. **BELOW** Resurrected Ise Nishiki awaiting harvest.

off necessary nutrients. New hybrids like Hyogo 85, which took three decades to develop, have stronger stems. The biggest threat, however, isn't storms but climate change, which is why more growers are planting late in the summer and harvesting later. Sake rice isn't cheap: on average, it costs 20 percent more than table rice.

If you eat sake rice and table rice side by side, the intrinsic differences between the two become clear. The rap on sake rice is that it tastes bad but brews well—the truth, however, is a bit more nuanced. The sake rice that is used by breweries is typically highly polished, with the minerals, fats and proteins in the outer layers removed. Then, the rice is soaked, steamed and dried, resulting in a flavorless packet of starch, which is not appealing. Sake rice that hasn't been polished to standard white rice levels (at least 90 percent) before being cooked tastes all right, if you don't mind the chewier texture.

However, there are intrinsic differences between the two. A cross-section look at Yamada Nishiki shows a clearly defined oval-shaped *shinpaku* core that looks like the marshmallow filling in a moon pie (or a Choco Pie in Japan). The grain is able to withstand intense milling because it isn't too hard, and its outer layers are easy to polish without chipping. It also dissolves evenly during brewing. The combination of all these factors is ideal for making *ginjo* sake.

In comparison, table rice, such as Japan's most popular breed, Koshihikari, typically doesn't have a clearly defined shinpaku, which means certain types of sake are challenging. A cross section shows proteins and minerals dotted throughout, which makes for delicious table rice, but is not ideal for ginjo sakes. Table rice can't endure intense milling, and often chips. For these reasons, it's typically reserved for futsu-shu—though there are delicious exceptions.

For the vast majority of sake's history, it has not been made from specialty rice. Sake rice didn't appear until the second half of the 19th

Yoshiaki Yano shows off one of his fields of Yamada Nishiki in midsummer.

century. Before that, brewers might have only known that a certain farmer or a particular paddy yielded grain that was excellent for sake making, but there was no clear division between rice for eating and rice for brewing as there is today. Modern sake rice isn't sold for mealtime consumption, and even if it were, it wouldn't compare favorably to sticky and flavorful table rice. As of writing, there are over 120 varieties of sakamai, most of which have debuted in the past few decades. The modern emphasis on variety and provenance overlooks the fact that historically, brewers didn't always know where their rice originated. The grains were mixed and stored in large granaries. Sake rice, along with notions of regionalism and traceability, are modern concerns that brewers and consumers have the luxury of considering.

These days when sake fans hear "table rice," many immediately think of inexpensive brews mass-produced by automation. That's not always the case. "If you polish the rice to appropriate levels and use a good *koji-kin*, sake rice isn't necessary," says Chobei Yamamoto, president of the small Yucho brewery in Nara. Yucho uses both sake rice like Yamada Nishiki and table rice like Kinuhikari, among other grains. But you've got to know what you're doing, and a taste of Yucho's Kaze no Mori sake (see page 235) proves that, at this brewery, they do.

## The Discovery of Sake Rice

During the late Edo period (1603–1868), sake makers started noticing they preferred certain rice from certain farmers. They might have not known the complex chemistry, but they did know good sake.

In 1859, a farmer named Jinzou Kishimoto was returning from a pilgrimage to modern-day Tottori Prefecture when he spotted the large-grained stalks of what is now considered the first pure-breed sake rice, Omachi. Kishimoto took two stalks to plant at his home in Omachi Village in Okayama. Kishimoto dubbed the rice "Nihon Kusa," which literally means "two stalks of grass" but is also a homonym for "Japanese grass." Locals ignored his clever names and simply called it "Omachi," a name that stuck as the large-grained rice gained fame in neighboring towns. Originally a table rice, this pure strain became the go-to grain for local sake breweries. What is now known as the first sake rice led the way for numerous varieties to follow.

However, prior to the discovery of Omachi, brewers were already aware that certain types of table rice made good sake—and also that certain farmers grew good rice for brewing. Today, the skill of the farmer remains vital to good sake rice. "My family moved to Hyogo Prefecture from the island of Shikoku in the 1840s," says Yoshiaki Yano, a sixth-generation rice farmer. Now he grows Yamada Nishiki, the king of sake rice, which wasn't developed until the 20th century. The town where he lives, Miki, in Hyogo Prefecture, is a famous area for Yamada Nishiki. It's not far from the big Kobe breweries and has long had a closer relationship with them.

Yano's family, like other rice farmers in the area, grew the Benkei variety as well as Yamadabo, the mother of Yamada Nishiki. "At

that time, rice wasn't divided into sake rice and table rice," says Yano. "It was all table rice, and brewers just happened to like certain farmers' rice better than others. My family grew Benkei to meet the needs of the brewers." Ever since then, his family has worked to ensure a stable supply of sake rice.

## Varieties are the Spice of Sake Rice

There are over 270 varieties of Japonica rice in Japan. Out of those, an increasing number are sakamai or "sake rice." The concept of sake rice is relatively new; the term "jozo yo genmai," which differentiated sakamai from table rice, wasn't official until 1951.

Yamada Nishiki is the most widely used sake rice. In 2016, 37.1 kilotons (41,552 tons) of Yamada Nishiki were produced in Japan, followed by 24.7 kilotons (27,664 tons) of Gohyakumangoku. In third place was Miyama Nishiki, originally from Nagano, at 7.51 kilotons (8,411 tons). The Akita brewing rice Akitashu Komachi follows at 2.67 kilotons (2,990 tons) and Omachi at 2.48 kilotons (2,777 tons). After that, the remaining varieties get increasingly niche. Yamada Nishiki and Gohyakumangoku dominate because they're easy to use.

Just because one region uses a particular type of sake rice doesn't mean the variety is suitable for all areas. For example, Hyogo Prefecture, the birthplace of Japan's most famous sake rice, Yamada Nishiki, also grows Gohyakumangoku, a famous Niigata sake rice, in the colder northern part of the prefecture. It is a better fit for those winters on the Sea of Japan than the local creation Yamada Nishiki, which thrives during hot days and cool nights.

Niigata, where Gohyakumangoku was born, is famous for its *tanrei karakuchi*, a light, crisp and dry style. People often mistake those flavors for being associated with the intrinsic qualities of the rice instead of a series of choices made by the brewer. In the 1960s, for example, Niigata was

With its big plump grains, it's easy to see why Hyogo-grown Yamada Nishiki is so desirable among sake makers. Hyogo Yamada Nishiki has a large, clearly defined starchy white core known as the *shinpaku*.

making sweeter, heavier sakes that were reminiscent of those produced in Kobe's Nada district. During the 1970s, Niigata toji from the Echigo guild were becoming masters at using activated charcoal filtering to pair down their brews. Using innate qualities in the local rice, they created drier-tasting sakes. Not all brewcries followed in their footsteps, but many did, creating a new regional style that contrasted with the full bodied, sweet sakes of the day. Thus, just because a brewer uses Gohyakumangoku rice, it doesn't automatically yield the region's signature dry sake.

Each sakamai variety has a range of possible flavors, depending on the polishing ratio, the type of koji made, the yeast and the skills of the brewers. For Yamada Nishiki, that range is wide, while for Gohyakumangoku it is more narrowly defined. The perceived notion is that Gohyaku-mangoku produces a light, refreshing and dry sake, but it isn't limited to that, and brewers can create a variety of sakes with that rice. For brewers, Yamada Nishiki is versatile and forgiving. Its large shinpaku makes for excellent koji. The inner layers contain no compounds that produce unwanted off-flavors, and the grain breaks down well during fermentation. Yamada Nishiki, brewers say, easily makes delicious sake.

When evaluating sake rice, it's important to consider how easy it is for brewers to work with. Will its grains resist chipping and breakage in the polishing machine? How high a polishing ratio can be attained? Does it absorb water well during soaking? Does it make good koji? Of course, the flavor of the rice contributes to the sake's overall profile, but much of the grain is polished away so it doesn't interrupt the flavors and aromas created by the yeast and the koji. For example, Omachi can chip in polishing machines. Its shinpaku is large, and while it's not as pronounced as Yamada Nishiki's white core, this means Omachi doesn't really need to be polished more than 50 percent. Because of this, Omachi is best for sake with lots of body. "Omachi has wide flavors, and because of that, I think it's the best rice to reveal the characteristic style of a brewery," says Toshihito Hayakawa, toji at the Hayakawa brewery in Mie Prefecture. It is a soft rice that saccharifies quickly, making it one

Teiji Fujikawa isn't called "The Father of Yamada Nishiki" (after all, he didn't originally cross-breed the grain), but rather, its foster father.

of the more difficult sakamai. Numerous breweries in Japan swear by it, however, and are up to any challenges Omachi presents.

## Yamada Nishiki: The King of Sake Rices

It all started in 1923, when a team of Hyogo Prefecture botanists led by researcher Shigeharu Nishiumi crossbred Tankan Wataribune rice, a shorter type of Wataribune grown in Shiga, with Yamadabo, a rice of uncertain origins. The resulting new breed, originally a table rice, was later dubbed "Systematic Number 161," with 161 referring to the sequences of crossbreeding.

In 1928, a team of sake rice researchers led by Teiji Fujikawa took over the project. Fujikawa realized the sake potential of Systematic Number 161. Today, growth rates are tracked via computer, but back then Fujikawa did laborious, detailed drawings by hand, measuring the grains as they grew bit by bit. In 1932, he and his team planted the rice in a test paddy. Every day, rain or shine, Fujiwara bicycled nearly 4 miles (about 6 kilometers) to check on the rice, which had been nicknamed "Ootsubu 50-7," literally meaning "Big Grain 50-7" (50-7 referred to the line and branch numbers), and "Yamato 50-7." In Japanese, Yamato 50-7 is written as 山渡 50-7; the character *yama* (山) derived from the cross-breed's mother Yamadabo, and the *to* character (渡) came from its father, Tankan Wataribune (短桿渡船). The new breed, however, would get another name—in fact, another two names.

While the exact date is not recorded, it was likely in late 1935 when researchers registered a name for this rice, calling it "Showa." The name, a reference to the Showa era, which began in 1926, sounded new and modern, fitting for a rice developed by serious science. However, the name Showa was already being used for a rice in Yamagata Prefecture, so the researchers had to find a new one. On January 31, 1936, a meeting began at 11 am at the Hyogo Prefectural Agricultural Experimental Station in Akashi. That afternoon, the 60 people in attendance chose a new name for the rice: Yamada Nishiki. "Yamada" referred to Yamadabo, the new crossbreed's mother, but as for "Nishiki" (which means "brocade" in Japanese), its inclusion is less clear. Even now, the Japan Agricultural Cooperatives, the country's agriculture collective, doesn't know why the word was added. One guess is that it refers to Ise Nishiki, an early sake rice. Since then, other sake rice varieties have been given the Nishiki appellation—most famously Takane Nishiki, developed in 1942, and Hattan Nishiki, developed in 1973.

After being officially registered in 1936, the variety has surpassed all other sake rices with its award-winning record and dominance. Yamada Nishiki is two or three times as expensive as other varieties, but its name has become a brand and a mark of quality. More than 540 breweries across Japan use Yamada Nishiki, typically reserving it for their most expensive ginjo brews. Its use for high-end brewing has become so prevalent that modern daiginjo brewing has developed around it. This is one reason why it's become so hard to replace.

Not all Yamada Nishiki is the same. Different, even lower-quality versions of the rice are harvested throughout the country, especially closer to Japan's colder northeastern regions. The most famous Yamada Nishiki is grown where the rice was born, in southeastern Hyogo Prefecture. Days are hot, and nights are cold, and the temperature variation results in a good crop. The soil is rich in minerals. Yamada Nishiki has long roots that are able to tap those minerals and moisture for a strong, and healthy crop, even helping the rice survive droughts.

Yamada Nishiki checks all the boxes for the ideal sakamai. The grain's structure is strong enough to withstand intense polishing without chipping or breaking. The grain size is large and heavy; 1,000 grains weigh around 28 grams (about 1 ounce) on average, compared to the table rice average of 22 grams (about ¾ ounce) per 1,000 grains. Yamada Nishiki has a large starchy center for easy koji-making, and the starch's short amylopectin chains give Yamada Nishiki optimum solubility. The result is fragrant and delicious sake.

"Yamada Nishiki is a forgiving rice," says Takuma Sugimoto, senior researcher at Hyogo Prefecture's Agriculture and Horticulture Department. Other varieties make excellent sake, but there is less room for error. "Yamada Nishiki is hard to screw up."

## How Sake Rice Is Created

Even today, crossbreeding is exhausting and exacting work. The basic technique hasn't changed in over 80 years. Manual crossbreeding is done in August and early September when rice flowers. "We have to pick which one is the father and which one is the mother," explains Takuma Sugimoto, senior researcher at Hyogo Prefecture's Agriculture and Horticulture Department, where Yamada Nishiki was created. "We pick the mother based on the quality of sake the rice makes," he continues. "It has to be good sake." The father is selected on different parameters, such as having a suitable height and strong immunity to diseases.

Early in the morning, Sugimoto goes into a

LEFT Researcher Takuma Sugimoto stands at the research station where Yamada Nishiki was originally developed. He holds sake made with a rice called Hyogo 85. ABOVE Hyogo Nishiki, bred from Yamada Nishiki, is a new variety with stronger stems.

# ANCIENT JAPANESE RICE GRAINS MAKE UNIQUE SAKE

**"You've never seen red or black rice?"** says Kuniko Mukai, *toji* at Mukai Shuzo in northern Kyoto, before she darts off and returns with a cupful. Even after nearly two decades in Japan, I confess that I have not. **"***Sekihan***, the red rice that's made for celebrations, is made with red adzuki beans these days,"** she says. **"But before that, it used to be made from** ***kodaimai.***" **In English, that word means "ancient rice."**

*Kuromai* (black rice), which includes the dark-purple varieties, as well as *akamai* (red rice), are kodaimai that, by the Edo period (1603–1868), were increasingly viewed as low class, as people passed them over for luxurious white rice, much as white bread supplanted whole-grain loaves in the West during the late 19th and early 20th centuries. Colored rice was cheaply valued and even banned from annual tributes.

Today, however, these ancient varieties are expensive health foods, boasting a variety of benefits that far surpass regular white rice. Kuromai like the dark purple Murasaki Komachi in Mukai's "Ine Mankai" sake (see page 241) contain antioxidants called anthocyanins as well as vitamin C. Since

Mukai Shuzo only polishes the dark grain to 91 percent—the polishing ratio for table rice—it remains rich in minerals. The dark rice is blended with the sake rice Gohyakuman-goku, which is polished to 83 percent for brewing. The resulting reddish sake has wonderful chewy rice notes, wrapped in a sweet tartness. The first variety the brewery used, the red rice Asa Murasaki from Kyushu, didn't suit the northern Kyoto climate and didn't properly color the sake. Mukai finally settled on Murasaki Komachi, a Niigata variety that's easier to grow, with strong stems, and that gives Ine Mankai the desired purplish-red luster.

Mukai's family brewery, which has been in business for over 250

**Mukai is the first woman brewer to join the Tajima Toji, one of Japan's most famous *toji* guilds.**

years, sits on the Sea of Japan coast. Little two-story wooden houses line the bay, with boats docked in watery first-floor garages. The brewery is surrounded by fishing huts. "As a kid, I didn't want to become a sake brewer," says Mukai. "This is a fishing town, and all my friends' fathers were fishermen, so on the way home from school, their dads would call out to them from the boats where they were working." Mukai's father was the only one not out in the bay. "I didn't like that," she says. "I didn't like that my family made sake; I wanted a job related to the sea." When it came time for Mukai to go to college, her father wanted her to attend Tokyo University of Agriculture to study brewing. "We had a massive fight," she says. She told her father that she wouldn't get in—but she did.

"At the Tokyo University of Agriculture, my professor, Masahisa Takeda, pointed out that this country's rice polishing techniques were exceedingly high, so everywhere you looked it was easy to find delicious sake," Mukai says. "He often said if we don't make interesting, individualistic sake that stands out, we wouldn't survive. If I hadn't met him, I probably wouldn't have become a brewer." In Takeda's lab, a testing ground for cutting-edge sake, Mukai got her first experience working with flower yeasts from cherry blossoms and yeasts from pine trees, as well as white *koji-kin*, decades

LEFT Boxing bottles of Mukai Shuzo's distinctive brew. For a tasting note, see page 241. ABOVE A road separates the brewery shop and the kura. BELOW At the brewery's shop, Mukai Shuzo sells the *kuromai* (black rice) it uses in sake making. It doesn't just make delicious sake: adding some to a pot of regular white rice makes for a tasty staple. When cooked, it turns a violet color.

before they drew the focus of today's avant-garde sake makers. "This was over 20 years ago, when the majority of brewers were simply aiming to make sake that tasted good," says Mukai. "The types that were far more unusual didn't get much notice." Yet.

When Mukai returned home from Tokyo she was 22, and her head was packed full of brewing knowledge. Her first year home was spent washing and cleaning the brewery. The second year, she became the toji. "All the other brewers, who had been so nice to me, suddenly went cold," recalls Mukai. She would tell them what to do, but nobody listened. "It wasn't because I'm a woman, but because I was young and inexperienced." So she started coming in before anyone else and doing everything by herself. The other brewers gradually came around. Her father, who had pushed her to study brewing, was completely hands off, leaving his daughter in charge of running the brewery. "I realized that the toji's job isn't just ordering people around," she says. "It's leading, it's teamwork and creating a positive atmosphere." A bad brewery atmosphere, she says, will produce bad sake.

In 1999, she debuted her most successful brew so far, the ruddy Ine Mankai. "Other friends of mine have worked in other breweries," she says. "I haven't, and I think if I had, I wouldn't have made something like that." Looking back, Mukai says she didn't know the rules—a good thing, because Ine Mankai broke them all. While opinion on the brew was divided sharply, customers snapped it up. The first run sold out as soon as it went on sale, making it clear that Mukai Shuzo had a hit on its hands. Since then, Mukai has continued to experiment with kodaimai rice varieties, aging sake, and even using a 100-year-old yeast strain.

"I've tried to make sake like others, and it wasn't fun," Mukai says. Together we look out the brewery window as sunlight reflects off the bay, and the morning mist starts to clear. "I think in the future, there is going to be more and more sake that stands out."

greenhouse, making sure all the doors and windows are firmly shut in order to cut off any possible breeze that could blow the pollen around. Temperatures reach well over 100°F (38°C). Just as breeders have done for nearly 100 years, he cuts the tips of the selected mother grains. He doesn't cut just one, but multiple grains on a stalk.

Then Sugimoto waits for the father to bud, which can take a few hours, and collects pollen from multiple flowering grains. The pollen is only good for 24 hours. Using tweezers, he then must manually pollinate the mother's stigma on each grain. Once they've been pollinated, he covers each ear of rice with a long, thin white paper bag to prevent unwanted pollen from hijacking the process. The resulting crossbreed can then be planted, and researchers will identify specific qualities in the results. As this process of trial and error is repeated hundreds of times, it's easy to see why producing a successful breed takes years. Sugimoto previously worked on a sake rice called Hyogo 85, which took over 30 years to create. His predecessors began working on the rice in 1985 when he was still in junior high school, long before he ever decided to become a horticulturist.

"The plan has been to make a sake rice that's better than Yamada Nishiki, but result after result has shown no improvement," says Sugimoto. "We haven't been able to surpass Yamada Nishiki." Sugimoto says it's not just the excellent intrinsic qualities of this variety, but also that much of the brewing industry has geared itself to it. So polishing ratios, fermentation times and even expected flavors are based on 80-plus years of Yamada Nishiki. A new rice, no matter how good, is at a disadvantage, because it won't match those parameters.

But researchers aren't giving up. They're also trying to create breeds that, while they might not surpass Yamada Nishiki, respond better to the increasingly changing climate, whether with stronger stems to withstand typhoons or better endurance for the summer heat. "With our crossbreed Hakutsuru Nishiki, we weren't simply trying to surpass Yamada Nishiki, but we wanted to create something that could exist alongside it," says Mitsuhiro Ban, toji at Hakutsuru in Nada. To make this crossbreed, Hakutsuru went to Yamada Nishiki's origin and did its own crossing of the famed sake rice's parents, Yamadado and Tankan Wataribune. Registered in 2007, Hakutsuru Nishiki is certainly a contender for one of the more successful recent rice varieties. It has since been embraced by other breweries,

The two bags on the right contain unpolished Yamada Nishiki and Yamada Nishiki polished to 38 percent. On the left are bags containing unpolished Hakutsuru Nishiki and Hakutsuru Nishiki polished to 38 percent. Hakutsuru has done an admirable job of creating a new brewing rice.

The Japanese characters on these bottles of sake read "Yamada Nishiki." The rice itself is now so famous that sake makers will slap its name on labels as a way to sell sake.

including Takagi Shuzo, maker of the Jyuyondai sake that in the 1990s inspired a generation of young kuramoto to take the reins of their breweries and make bold and fruity products.

"We might be able to make a super sake rice with genetic engineering," says Sugimoto. "We know how to make sake rice with strong stems and disease-resistant breeds, but we don't know how to make big, strong shinpaku." The center core of the grain isn't decided by a single piece of DNA, but a multitude of them. This means significant trial and error is required in cross-breeding to fix the perfect combination, turning the creation of optimal sake rice into a genetic engineering challenge.

## The Second-Most-Popular Sake Rice

Officially designated in 1957, the name Gohya-kumangoku literally means "5 million *koku*" (one koku of rice roughly corresponds to 330 pounds or 150 kilos). The name refers to Niigata establishing its dominance as a rice grower by breaking through five million koku. Out of all Japan's prefectures, Niigata has the largest number of sake breweries, with nearly 90 sake makers in the Niigata Sake Brewers' Association. Nationally, the prefecture's total production is third, behind Hyogo and Kyoto. It also grows the most rice in Japan on an annual basis. In 2017, for example, Niigata produced 611,700 tons of rice, edging out Hokkaido (581,800 tons) and Akita (498,800 tons).

"Gohyakumangoku is a very hard variety, so we can't polish it like Yamada Nishiki," explains Satoshi Murayama, president of Niigata's Taiyo Sake Brewery. "The shinpaku is quite large, and it breaks easily." This is because it's not as clearly defined as Yamada Nishiki. Also, because Gohyakumangoku is so hard, the grain can crack during intense, prolonged polishing. This is not a bad thing, but means that more of the proteins and fats in the outer layers carry over to the final brew. The resulting sakes don't have the same rich, honeyed sweetness of Yamada Nishiki. The hard grains dissolve slowly, requiring an extra week or two of brewing—but this suits the soft water of Niigata, which performs best under

extended low-temperature brewing. Hard rice, soft water and long fermentation are the secret of Niigata's crisp and dry *tanrei karakuchi* style that took the sake world by storm in the 1980s.

Since Gohyakumangoku isn't suitable for polishing to the daiginjo level, Niigata developed a new variety called Koshi Tanrei, which can be polished to high levels. Released in the early 21st century, this is crossbreed of Yamada Nishiki and Gohyakumangoku that makes richer flavor profiles possible. Climate change has also made it possible to grow Yamada Nishiki in Niigata, which was unthinkable in decades past. Despite these changes, it would be foolish to expect Gohyakumangoku to be cast aside anytime soon.

# WATER

"Can you make good sake without good water?" I once asked this question to Akira Tanaka, the director at Kinshi Masamune in Kyoto's Fushimi district. "Nope," he answered promptly. "It's impossible."

Japan is lucky to have been blessed with excellent water. A month-long rainy season battering down on a country that's 80 percent mountains helps keep the streams, rivers and lakes from getting stagnant. Europeans in the late 19th century marveled at Tokyo's water grid and its clean water. Without Japan's good water, its sake culture would not be what it is today.

## Soft and Hard Water

The majority of water in Japan is soft water, called *nansui* in Japanese. The softness depends on how many minerals the water picks up as it passes through soil and underground rock layers. Soft water contains low concentrations of calcium and magnesium. In regions where there is heavy snow, soft water can be the result of melted snow. For sake making, soft water requires a longer brewing period, because the lower mineral content leads to a less-vigorous fermentation.

Fushimi, Kyoto's most famous brewing district, is known for its soft water. Its sake is often called "feminine" as compared to Nada's macho brews. The city of Kyoto is located on a

basin, with rivers feeding into a large under-groundwater table, but Fushimi sits atop a granite slab. "Civilizations develop based on the water supply," says Kinshi Masamune's Tanaka. Kyoto is not an exception. Water flows underground down the surrounding mountains, passing through layer upon layer of sediment. "Fushimi is on an incline," Tanaka explains, "so the water goes through a natural and thorough filtration." Other areas of Japan are also famous for soft water, such as Niigata, where brewing water comes from snowmelt. This helps produce the clean, crisp sake the region for which the region is famous.

Much of Kyoto's water is soft, thanks to the underground sediment that filters the water naturally. This is why the city is famous for its tea: minerals like calcium and sodium can negatively impact the aroma and flavor of the tea. The soft water is also behind the excellent coffee served at the city's cafés. Water influences cuisine; this is why Kyoto's traditional food uses light and elegant dashi stock, and why its elaborate tofu cuisine developed. None of this would be possible with hard water. Hard water, however, pulls out the savory flavors of meat much better than soft water. Kobe beef actually

CENTER Snow begins to fall in front of Yucho Shuzo. ABOVE This Nara water is used to grow the same rice that Yucho Shuzo brews with. RIGHT As well as good water, Kinshi Masamune has a shrine dedicated to Inari, the Shinto god of rice and wealth.

tastes better when it's served with the area's hard drinking water.

In Japanese, hard water is known as *kousui*. Rocks and soil rich in lime and chalk lead to higher concentrations of calcium and magnesium, which produces much more active fermentation than soft water. This results in robust sake, and also makes for tasty drinking water. For example, Yucho Shuzo, located in the town of Gose, Nara Prefecture, uses hard water for its floral Kaze no Mori–branded sake (see page 235). Like many breweries, Yucho Shuzo lets locals fill bottles of its brewing water free of charge. "I can't use this for cooking Japanese cuisine because it has too many minerals," said one chef said as he filled a plastic bottle. "But it's perfect for drinking water."

The most famous water for sake in Japan, *miyamizu* (for more, see page 90), is also mineral-heavy, but even it falls short of famous

# THE DISCOVERY OF THE MOST LEGENDARY SAKE WATER

A gleaming tanker truck pulls into the grounds of the Sakura Masamune brewery in Nada's Uozaki area. It carries Japan's most famous sake-brewing water, *miyamizu*. Originally the water was called "Nishinomiya no mizu" (Nishinomiya water), but that was shortened to miyamizu. "In 1840, sake brewer Tazaemon Yamamura VI discovered miyamizu in the Nishinomiya area," says Norihide Harada, a *toji* at the famed Sakura Masamune. It would be the first time a brewer realized just how water could influence sake.

"Before that, sake brewers thought water was water," says Harada. "They didn't recognize the difference that water could make."

In the first part of the 19th century, Yamamura owned two breweries: one in nearby Nishinomiya and the other at Sakura Masamune's present location (though the current brewery is a modern building constructed in the mid-1990s). Yamamura wondered why the Nishinomiya brewery's sake was superior, so he swapped out the brewery workers. Yet the Nishinomiya sake was still better. He then used the exact same brewing process and the same rice at both breweries, but Nishinomiya was still making superior sake. It had to be the water. "So he brought the miyamizu here by oxcart," Harada says. "Apparently, the other Nada breweries were surprised by this and thought he was nuts." The resulting sake, made in Uozaki from miyamizu, tasted as good as the Nishinomiya sake. Yamamura had figured it out: the difference was indeed the water. Oxcarts began bringing miyamizu to Uozaki on a regular basis so that it could be used for sake making. "The water was also brought in by boats," Harada says pointing in the direction of the adjacent harbor.

Miyamizu is underground well water that flows from the Rokko mountains, the range that provides spectacular views of the Port of Kobe. Most water in Japan is soft, but miyamizu is hard water that's rich in magnesium, calcium, potassium and phosphorus, which makes fermentation fast and robust. This water also has only trace amounts of iron, if any. *Koji* produces compounds that bind with iron and turn the sake a reddish color, also imparting bad flavors and aromas. In miyamizu, iron is either undetectable or present in such minuscule amounts that treatment to bring it under the 0.02 ppm threshold isn't necessary. But unlike sake made with soft water, which tastes terrific just after it's pressed, sake made with miyamizu needs some time to settle in. Harada notes, "For sake that's made with hard water with lots of minerals, letting it mature over the summer makes it delicious by fall." The resulting brew is full-flavored and dry, with good acidity; it's traditionally been called *otoko-zake*, or "manly sake."

Miyamizu was brought to the brewery by ox and cart.

"If you were to compare Japanese sake regions to French wine regions, Nada is like Bordeaux, because we use miyamizu, which makes full-bodied sake," says Harada. "Sake from Kyoto, which uses mainly soft water, is known as *onna-zake* or 'feminine sake,' which would be closer to Burgundy or the lighter Pinot Noir."

In the Edo period (1603–1868), Tazaemon Yamamura VI started using miyamizu to make flavorful sake that fetched the highest prices in Edo (modern-day Tokyo). Other Edo breweries which had previously ridiculed carting in water, started using miyamizu as well. Uozaki was right next to the ocean, so sake could be shipped to Tokyo with ease. "This area now accounts for around 25 percent of all sake made in Japan," Harada says. "This success has been built on miyamizu."

Prior to the change in water, the sake from Yamamura's Uozaki brewery was called "Shinsui"—a name that, like many sake brands at that time, was that of a famous kabuki actor. For the new and improved brew, Yamamura chose the name "Sei-shuu" (正宗), a reference to the *Rinzai Sei-shuu*, a Buddhist text. It was also meant to be a pun on "seishu" (清酒), the Japanese word for refined or clear sake, but the joke flew over the heads of sake connoisseurs, who were losing their minds over the new Nada brew. The kanji characters for "Sei-shuu" were misread as "Masamune," and the name stuck. The brew was so popular that other sake makers started calling their product "Masamune," too. "In Japan, there are over 100 sake breweries that use the name Masa-

mune," Harada says. "Ours was the first." He points to an old Sakura Masamune sign in the company's marble entryway.

In an age before copyright law, there was not much Yamamura could do but continue to produce excellent sake. In the late 19th century, when a rapidly modernizing Japan finally got trademark laws, the sake maker attempted to register "Masamune" as a brand name, but was turned down. "It had become a generic name throughout Japan, so we couldn't trademark it," explains Harada. As a workaround, the brewery added "Sakura" (meaning "cherry blossoms") and registered the name "Sakura Masamune," which is still used. Harada pauses, looking up again at the sign. "We might not be such a famous brewery outside the industry, but so many things began right here."

This well at the Hakubotan brewery in Saijo has been used for over 300 years. The brewery itself dates from 1675, making it one of Hiroshima's oldest.

French mineral waters, like Evian and Vittel, which have about twice the calcium. It's not just hard water that makes robust sake, though. What the Yucho brewery's water and miyamizu have in common is a lack of iron, a mineral that is highly detrimental to sake making. The koji fungus produces a compound called deferrifer-richrysin, which can bond with iron and subsequently turn sake brownish red. This is why sake-brewing water must have less than 0.02 ppm of iron—far less than the 0.3 ppm of iron maximum set by Japanese law for tap water. Miyamizu is ideal for making robust brews because it's mineral-rich with very little iron.

"Classification as soft or hard is different from nation to nation, region to region," says Isao Aramaki, vice president and general manager at the Kamotsuru Shuzo Brewery in Hiroshima's Saijo district. Within the same region—the same city, even—water hardness can vary due to different flow paths. Another factor is how hard and soft water are measured. The World Health Organization defines water with 0–60mg/L of magnesium and calcium as soft, 61–120mg/L as medium, 121–180mg/L as hard and 181mg/L or

higher as extremely hard. "However, people generally say 0–100mg/L is soft, 101–300mg/L is medium, and more than 301mg/L is hard," says Aramaki. According to this definition, he continues, the water in both the Kyoto brewing district of Fushimi and the Hiroshima brewing district of Saijo have a medium hardness of 60–80mg. "But, of course, there are some exceptions," says Aramaki. "For example, the *gokosui* water of Fushimi, the water from Ishii well in Saijo, and the water of Akitsu in Hyogo, birthplace of the soft-water brewing method, are extremely soft, at under 50mg."

Even if a brewery's water doesn't suit its needs, it can be processed and changed, thanks to modern filtering technology. That's not true for rice. "We can't change rice's intrinsic components," explains Aramaki. "In this sense, the polishing technique is very important, and this is why in the past, the polishing master or *seimai toji* had the same authority as the brewing toji."

## How Does Water Affect Sake?

There are two obvious ways water affects sake. First, the water hardness influences the vigor of fermentation. Sake brewed with mineral-rich hard water will have a very active fermentation, leading to robust flavors. Since soft water has less magnesium and calcium, fermentation is less active. It's possible to brew dry sake with either hard or soft water. Sweet, rich, and fragrant sake can also be made regardless of water hardness.

Obviously, soft water has a different mouthfeel than hard water, and this is most noticeable in the water used to dilute the *genshu* (undiluted sake) before bottling. Sake is usually brewed at around 20 percent alcohol by volume; before bottling, it's cut with water to reduce the alcohol percentage. The type of water used has a significant impact on the sake that is readily apparent.

For centuries, water has influenced the way sake tastes. "People often say the quality of water in Nada directly contributed to the high quality of sake," says Aramaki. It did, of course. But he adds that the water from Mount Rokko, looming over the waterfront breweries, helped make better polishing ratios possible. The rivers running down the mountain past the breweries powered watermills that ground the grains. "The improvement of rice milling was one of the big reasons why Nada's sake was so good."

Then, that excellent Nada sake could be placed on *tarukaisen*, special ships designed to ferry casks up to Edo (present-day Tokyo). One of the reasons that Nada overtook neighboring Itami and Ikeda in

Osaka as the dominant sake region was that those areas didn't have easy ocean access for shipping.

## The Soft-Water Brewing Method

In the late 19th century, the most desirable sake was made with hard water, producing a rich, robust sake. In the 20th century things changed. Soft water became closely associated with ginjo sake, thanks to a low-temperature style of brewing that brought out delicate floral flavors.

Not all ginjo brews are made from soft water, but the low-temperature technique developed to brew with soft water has become a hallmark of the ginjo style. To make sake this way, regardless of water hardness, fermentation is carried out for 30 to 40 days at temperatures ranging from 43 to 50°F (6 to 10°C). "Because soft water doesn't contain many minerals, the point of this brewing method is to slowly dissolve the minerals in the rice before letting the yeast actively ferment," Kamotsuru Shuzo Brewery's Isao Aramaki explains. Low-temperature brewing also helps slow the vigorous fermentation that occurs with mineral-rich hard water. The process takes longer than traditional brewing because

Stopwatches help ensure that finely polished rice doesn't soak up too much water.

Senzaburou Miura transformed Hiroshima sake forever. His spirit of innovation is best understood by this quote that Hiroshima breweries hold dear: "Try a hundred things, and make a thousand improvements."

fermentation is slower at low temperatures.

Low-temperature brewing was originally developed out of necessity. In the 1870s, Hiroshima brewer Senzaburou Miura had been struggling to brew sake with soft water in the Akitsu area (present-day Higashi-Hiroshima). The water lacked sufficient minerals for strong fermentation, leading to rot-prone batches of sake. Not all Hiroshima water is the same. Saijo, home to Hiroshima's most famous brewing district, has medium-hard water, as do the Mihara and Takehara districts. However, the water in the Akitsu region is soft. Miura, who had traveled to Nada and Fushimi, knew the difference between brewing with hard and soft water. To make adjustments for the soft water in Hiroshima so that he could produce fragrant sake, he devised his signature brewing method.

"To prevent yeast from fermenting quickly, the ratio of koji and yeast starter added to the mash was lowered, while the ratio of water was increased at low temperatures. Of course, fermentation was controlled through low temperatures," says Aramaki. "Today, this has

become the basic method of making ginjo-shu, and it results in fine and delicate flavors." It doesn't depend on the water, though: this technique is also used by breweries with much harder water to make exquisite ginjo sake.

After Miura figured out that enzyme-rich koji brewed with soft water at low temperatures produced some truly elegant sake, his technique helped Hiroshima become one of the most famous sake regions in Japan, churning out award-winning results. In addition, his seminal 1898 work *Kaijouhou jissen roku* (A record of revised brewing methods) revolutionized best practices. Miura emphasized the importance of cleanliness, including the necessity of washing and sterilization. Also, he urged using a thermometer to check the temperature instead of simply going by feel as in centuries past. Today, this has become standard.

Others around Japan would apply low-temperature brewing techniques to create iconic sakes. One of these was Masatsune Hanaoka in Akita. After studying brewing at what is now Osaka University, Hanaoka arrived in Akita in 1918 to work as a tax bureaucrat. For the rest of his life, he dedicated himself to improving Akita's sake. Under Hanaoka's guidance, Akita sake makers began brewing at low temperatures for extended periods, which is ideal for ginjo-shu. This has since become the traditional Akita style.

Miura's ideas still live on, and sake makers recognize their debt to him. One of Hiroshima's most exciting breweries, Imada Shuzo, is located next to Miura's old residence. This association gave rise to the brewery's sake brand Fukucho, meaning "forgotten fortune." No one has forgotten Miura's contributions.

TOP LEFT Rice is inoculated with *koji-kin* spores. ABOVE Finished *koji* at Asahi Shuzo brewery in Yamaguchi Prefecture. LEFT Kazuki Usui of Senkin is famous for his well-crafted brews. "If we had kept making table sake, we would've gone out of business," he says. He and his brother turned around the family's brewery, switching to highly acidic sakes, which have become a hit with fans.

# KOJI

There's a Japanese saying that goes, *ichi koji, ni moto, san tsukuri,* or "first the koji, second the starter mash, and third the brewing." It explains which parts of the process are most important for good sake. Koji making is the foremost aspect of brewing, bringing depth, flavor and aromas that cannot be created with yeast alone.

Koji is steamed rice that has been inoculated with the *Aspergillus oryzae* fungus, which is called *koji-kin* in Japanese. "Mold" and "fungus" tend to have unsavory associations in the minds of Westerners. In Japan, however, where the climate is hot and humid in summer, people have harnessed beneficial molds and fungi to make good food and drink for centuries. In fact,

Tohoku University's Eiji Ichishima advocated for *Aspergillus oryzae* being named Japan's "national fungus," and in 2006, the Brewing Society of Japan took up his suggestion.

## The Fungus That Powers Sake

In English, the word "koji" is sometimes used to refer to the actual koji-kin or koji mold. In the sake-brewing world, though, koji refers to rice that has been inoculated with koji-kin. This is also called *kome-koji* (or rice koji), to differentiate it from other types of koji, such as the *mugi-koji* (barley koji) used in making the distilled liquor *shochu*. For making sake, however, only kome-koji is used, so in this context the word "kome" is typically dropped when referring to koji.

TOP LEFT A brewer at Daishichi inoculates steamed rice with *koji-kin*. TOP RIGHT Making *daiginjo* sake at the Yoshinogawa brewery in Niigata. CENTER Different breweries use different designs when cooling koji (Kenbishi on the left, and Imayo Tsukasa on the right), and this can denote the style of the koji. RIGHT Brewers at Kenbishi carry trays known as *koji-buta* that are used in the more work-intensive, traditional koji-making method.

Over the years, koji has been incorrectly compared with malted barley. In fact, James C. Hepburn's 1867 English-Japanese dictionary defined koji as "malt," a comparison made numerous times since. This is wrong. Malted barley is made from sprouted grain. Koji is not sprouted rice. Rather, koji is rice on which mold has been cultivated. For this reason, Tokyo University professor R. W. Atkinson, who described sake brewing in English in great detail in the late 19th century, championed using the original Japanese word instead. Interestingly, the first Japanese-to-European-language dictionary, the 17th- century *Nippo jisho*, defined koji as a yeast, which isn't correct, either.

We don't actually know how koji first appeared in Japan. It's possible that the technique was imported from China via Korea, but it's also possible that koji making developed naturally in Japan. Steamed rice that's left out will become moldy, inoculated by the wild koji-kin flying around in the air. At some point moldy rice was used to make booze, and the result ended up being good. The next time the brewer wanted to replicate that same tasty brew, they tried to recreate the same conditions, giving rise to a process. This is probably how koji making started in China and, if the technique wasn't imported from there, it could also be how koji making started in Japan.

In China, the first mention of *qu* (the Chinese word for koji) dates from mid-3rd century BC in the ancient Chinese text *Rites of the Zhou Dynasty*. Qu became a central pillar of Chinese food and drink making. Koji doesn't appear in Japanese texts until around 725, when a document called *Harima no kuni fudoki* (*Harima Fudoki: A Record of Ancient Japan*) recounts how an offering of rice for the deity Iwa-no-Okami accidentally got wet, causing mold to grow, and delicious wine was made from the moldy rice. This isn't a historical account, but is evident that by the 8th century, koji's general effect on sake was understood.

In the 10th century, cultured, stable koji starters known as *tomokoji* (literally "buddy koji") came into use, replacing the more unpredictable wild koji-kin. Wood ash was added to stabilize the starter and add minerals for healthy spore propagation. Around this time, the *koji muro* (koji-making room) came into use. At that time, it was an underground earthen room designed to trap heat. The contemporary cedar-lined koji muro wasn't developed until much later, and the stainless steel iteration is a 20th-century invention.

By the 14th century, koji-making guilds at Kitano Shrine in Kyoto dominated production. Buddhist shrines were more than religious institutions, but akin to universities, where academics studied new technology often imported during pilgrimages to China. The temple dried and preserved koji-kin for miso and soy sauce, as well as for sake.

## The Types of Koji-kin Mold

In Japan, there are four types of koji bacterium used. Generally, only one type is used for sake making, but there are some niche exceptions.

**Ki-koji-kin:** The microorganism fungus *Aspergillus oryzae* is known as *ki-koji-kin* or "yellow koji mold" due to its yellowish-green color. This is the standard sake mold. It's fragrant, but more sensitive than other koji-kin varieties used in hot and humid Kyushu in southwestern Japan for distilled liquors.

TOP LEFT *Tane-koji* or "starter koji" is used to inoculate steamed rice and make koji. Note that this is yellow *koji-kin*, which actually looks green. TOP RIGHT Tamanohikari president Tsuneo Maruyama shows finished koji. BOTTOM LEFT A brewer at Kobe Shushinkan closely examines koji. BOTTOM RIGHT *Nuruk* is the South Korean fermentation starter used to make alcohol drinks such as soju. Unlike koji, it's not a pure culture and is often formed into a hardened cake.

**Kuro-koji-kin:** This means "black koji mold." This variety, known as *Aspergillus luchuensis* (née *Aspergillus awamori*), is used to make shochu, Japan's domestic local distilled spirit, and *awamori*, the Okinawan distilled liquor. It can be used in sake brewing (see pages 96–97).

**Shiro-koji-kin:** A mutation of kuro-koji-kin, *shiro-koji-kin* (white koji fungus) is named

*Aspergillus kawachii* after Genichiro Kawachi, the researcher who spotted the mutated bacterium in 1924. Known as the father of modern shochu; his shiro-koji-kin helped improve the quality of the spirit and is now the dominant koji-kin for shochu. It is sometimes used in sake brewing to bring out more acidity.

**Aspergillus sojae:** *A. sojae* is yet another species of culinary fungus used in Japan. This variety is used to make miso and soy sauce.

## How Is Japan's Koji Different?

The basic concept behind the creation of koji is not unique to Japan. Similar saccharifying agents are used throughout Asia. China's version of koji, called *qu*, has been used for thousands of years to ferment Chinese food and alcohol. But although the Chinese were using the mold in food and drink production before the Japanese, qu and koji are not the same. Koji is *Aspergillus oryzae*, and is carefully propagated on rice in a way that discourages other microorganisms. Qu contains other microorganisms, like yeast. The Japanese insistence on the purity of the koji is singular.

In Japanese, the kanji character 麹, pronounced "koji," is a Chinese import that has been used since the Japanese adopted the Chinese writing system well over 1,000 years ago. However, in the late 19th century, a Japanese kanji character for koji, 糀, appeared. This kanji combines the characters for rice (米) and flower (花), which makes sense because up close the koji-kin spores actually do look like little flowers. However, the original Chinese kanji for koji (麹) includes the character mugi (麦), which means "barley," because Chinese koji has traditionally been grown on barley and not on rice. These days, the character 麹 is commonly used for koji, but there are those who insist on using the native Japanese kanji 糀 to denote koji instead.

In Japan, koji-kin spores are sprinkled directly on the rice. This technique, which creates exceedingly pure koji rice, is a hallmark of the Japanese style. However, in both China—as well as in South Korea, where koji-kin is called *nurukgyun*—individual grains are not typically inoculated. Rather, the koji-kin is propagated on hard blocks of rice mixed with grains like wheat. The microorganisms in this style run a wider range than just the *Aspergillus oryzae* typically used in sake production. For example, in South Korea and China, the fungi *Rhizopus oryzae* is also propagated. China in particular uses a whole host of microorganisms to make alcohol, including the genera *Absidia*, *Monascus*, *Mucor* and even *Penicillium*. The koji is typically pressed into the blocks or other hard shapes, unlike the loose molded rice grains used to make sake in Japan.

## How Does Koji Influence Flavor and Aroma?

Good koji makes good sake. If you visit a sake brewery, you're likely to be asked to try their koji. It should have a gentle chestnut aroma and taste slightly sweet. Simply put, koji is added to the mix because it creates sugars that the yeast eats and converts to alcohol. But like so many things in sake brewing, it's much more complicated than that. Koji can directly affect flavor and aroma. For example, koji produces amylase, which breaks down starch into simple sugars, and protease, which breaks down protein into amino acids. If too many amino acids are produced during the process, the resulting brew will taste heavy. If too few are produced, then the brew might not have enough body. It all goes back to the koji.

To help bring out aromas during fermentation and unlock flavors in the rice, brewers make different styles of koji. The Japanese word *haze* (pronounced "ha-zay," not like the English "haze") refers to the white spots that form over

# THE ART OF BLACK KOJI

**Japan's southwestern island of Kyushu is famous for the distilled spirit *shochu*. To make traditional shochu, you need *kuro-koji-kin* (black koji). It's perfect for shochu, but tricky for sake, which is why only a small number of breweries dare use it. One of those is Ikekame Shuzo in Kurume, Fukuoka Prefecture. "You can't just replace yellow koji-kin with black koji-kin and make delicious sake," says brewery president Teruyuki Kamachi. "You have to know exactly what you're doing."**

Founded in 1875, Ikekame Shuzo sits on the green shores of the Chikugo River, the longest in Kyushu. For most of its history, Ikekame had focused on sake, but around 1982, it began distilling shochu, the region's most famous tipple. That decade saw a shochu boom in which the drink, traditionally considered low-class hooch by polite society in Tokyo and Osaka, found a new generation of fans.

The acidity level of sake typically clocks in from slightly under 1 to around 2, with the average falling between 1.3 and 1.5 (the figure is based on the amount required to neutralize all the acids in a 10 ml [¼ oz] mash sample). *Yamahai* and *kimoto* styles have acidity levels of around 2, which is higher than typical sake brews due to longer fermentation times and higher lactic acid levels. "When yamahai and kimoto are heated, the lactic and succinic acids come through deliciously," says Kamachi. "However, it's a different story when they're chilled." In recent years, chilled sake has become increasingly popular, so Kamachi wanted to figure out a way to make chilled sake with acidity levels between 2 and 3.

"I got to thinking about the sourness in fruit, such as citric acid, and the malic acid in apples and was wondering if it could be used," he says. After graduating from university, Kamachi gained experience working in the drinks business, dealing with wine and Western spirits. When he returned home to Ikekame Shuzo, he started considering how he could bring some of the acidity found in wine to sake so it could better pair with the meat, pasta and cheese dishes that now commonly appear on Japanese tables. "That's when the citric acid made by kuro koji came to mind." The "kuro" apellation comes from the black color of the spores. "Black koji-kin has a unique characteristic that yellow koji-kin does not—the ability to produce citric acid." Though the spores are black, the mold-covered rice it makes is white, just like typical koji.

Unlike malt whisky, which is distilled two or three times, shochu is

**The seed starter for black *koji-kin* is actually black. However, the koji it produces is the standard off-white koji color.**

and fermentation won't progress smoothly," Kamachi says. "Precise control of the moisture, humidity level and temperature is even more essential with black koji-kin than with yellow koji-kin, making this extremely difficult work." Difficult, but the delicious results are worth it.

In May 2007, Ikekame Shuzo launched its kuro-koji-kin brew as Kuro Kabuto, or "Black Helmet." Says Kamachi, "It has a strawberry-like aroma that's different from your typical ginjo." The citric acid makes it an ideal partner for steak, especially wagyu, and other savory fatty foods. "The effect of the citric acid's is similar to the way sliced citrus fruit served with fish neutral-izes the fat and really enhances the flavor of the food."

Only a tiny number of breweries have dared to use kuro-koji-kin in sake brewing, because it's so compli-cated. But as Ike-kame Shuzo has shown, those who are able to pull it off can create something truly special.

typically distilled once. Its starch can come from an array of ingredi-ents: most often sweet potatoes, rice or barley, but also carrots, cactus or brown sugar. The grains, however, are not malted to make shochu—they're inoculated with koji-kin. "Kuro-koji-kin is good for shochu, because it produces large amounts of citric acid," says Kama-chi. "That drops the pH in shochu's main fermenting mash, and can protect it from contamination." This is key because shochu origi-nated in Kyushu, one of the warm-est regions in Japan, where distill-ers and brewers had long struggled with spoiled batches of mash in the days before air-conditioning.

In addition to promoting healthy fermentation, kuro-koji-kin also brings out robust flavors and aro-mas. "Using shochu koji in sake brewing gives it a similar acidity to wine. It also increases the flavors, amino acids, and bitterness, all of which move the brew very far away from typical sake," says Kamachi.

But Kamachi and his brewers could not simply use black koji-kin as is. It's a different mold from yellow koji-kin, the microorganism dubbed *Aspergillus oryzae*. Kuro-koji-kin is *Aspergillus luchuensis*. Ikekame Shuzo didn't want to cut corners and use a mixture of yel-low and black koji mold to make life easier. If it was going to make a brew with kuro-koji-kin, the koji would be made from 100 percent black koji-kin. This would require a different approach. The propaga-tion of the koji-kin spores would have to be kept in check, thereby reducing acidity to appropriate levels for sake. "When you hold back the acidity, there is a chance the enzyme balance will collapse

each grain. For the *tsukihaze* ("spotted *haze*") style, great care is taken to balance the temperature and humidity. The mycelia penetrate deep into the grain, and white dots of mold freckle the rice, creating koji that is low on enzymes, proteins and vitamins but high on starchy glucoamylase. This results in fewer undesirable flavors in fermentation and an environment in which the yeast can flourish, producing a lighter sake. The tsukihaze-style koji suits ginjo and daiginjo sakes. The other main style of koji making is *sohaze* ("encompassing *haze*") which covers the entire surface. This style results in vitamin-rich koji that quickly converts starch to sugar and produces a robust, quick fermentation. Sohaze is best suited to high-temperature fermentation and is often used for full-bodied sake, as well as mass-produced *futsu-shu*.

Brewers need to be careful during the koji process. Making rice with sticky, wet rice results in koji that's called *nurihaze-koji* (coated haze koji). The mold completely covers the rice, but only superficially, as if it's been painted on. The resulting koji is rife with nitrogenous compounds that produce unwanted flavors and aromas during fermentation. Another danger is *hazeochi* (literally "dropped haze"), in which the rice is improperly inoculated, and there isn't enough mold covering the grain, so the basic alcohol conversion fails or is impeded.

Since the vast majority of sake brewers use the same type of koji-kin, called ki-koji-kin (yellow koji-kin), it can be hard to understand how koji influences aroma and flavor. Yellow koji-kin creates fruitier and more floral aromas than black koji-kin, which produces highly acidic citrus notes. Since yellow koji fungus dominates, it can be difficult to identify its effects without another koji-kin variation to compare. Complicating the picture, there are now seemingly endless bioengineered aromatic yeasts creating sake scents that pop out of the glass. The proliferation and distribution of sake yeasts, which started in the 20th century, has allowed breweries to add a wider variety of aromas and flavors during fermentation.

## Kosozai

*Kosozai* is not a type of koji-kin; rather, it's an enzymatic substitute for koji-kin in brewing and cooking. (*Koso* means "enzyme" and *zai* is "material.") Enzyme preparations are also blended with traditional koji-kin. Kosozai bumps up enzyme activity and increases saccharification. It is used with low-cost futsu-shu as well as junmai, ginjo and daiginjo brews during low-temperature brewing. There are regulations regarding how much kosozai can be used. Among traditionalists, enzyme preparations are controversial, and are seen as a shortcut.

whole host of new aromas and flavors.

The role yeast plays in alcohol production is straightforward: Yeast consumes sugar and produces alcohol. But there things get complicated: in sake production a wide variety of yeasts is used, each with difficult effects on the final product. The signature esters for which *ginjo* sakes are famous—like ethyl caproate, which smells like apple, and isoamyl acetate, which is banana-flavored—come from yeast. Yeast can also add desirable acidic notes. Malic acid, for example, gives the brew a fresh bite.

Even though booze making goes back thousands of years, it wasn't until the mid-19th century that Louis Pasteur proved scientifically that yeast produced alcohol during fermentation. In 1895, researcher Kikuji Yabe first isolated the yeast strain used to make sake,

# YEAST

For over 1,000 years, sake was made without adding any yeast. Wild yeasts in the air would naturally convert sugars into alcohol, producing sake. In the late 1800s, with the influence of beer brewing, that started to change. Cultured yeast started being added, and in the following century a range of yeasts became available to brewers, helping to make the sake-making process more stable and opening up a

FACING PAGE, TOP TO BOTTOM Toji Masatsugu Fujino at Yoshinogawa brewery checks rice that will be used for *koji* making and sprinkles *koji-kin* over the rice. ABOVE Turning over the rice helps control the temperature and moisture during koji making. Paddles like this are used because steamed rice is so heavy. LEFT Inoculated rice is put into separate trays to aid control of temperature and moisture. The location of each tray is regularly changed to ensure uniformity.

THIS PAGE The association yeasts are sold in numbered glass vials. The top stem is easily snapped off so that the yeast can be propagated.

FACING PAGE Mitsuhiro Ban, toji at Hakutsuru, shows off a yeast sample. Hakutsuru has a massive R&D branch and even built a biotech research facility to develop its own yeasts.

*Saccharomyces cerevisiae*. This strain had been first observed by a German researcher in 1837. As Yoshikazu Ohya and Mao Kashima of the University of Tokyo explain, it was known in beer and wine production, but not as a sake yeast until Yabe's discovery. *Saccharomyces cerevisiae* is now usually known as *seishu kobo*, or "refined sake yeast." But yeast, one of the most important elements in making sake, isn't typically listed on sake labels. Stated ingredients typically include *kome* (rice) and *kome koji* (rice koji). If the brew isn't a *junmai*, then brewer's alcohol will also be mentioned. Usually, yeast is not.

"I think yeast isn't included on sake-bottle labels because it's difficult for people to understand," says Kiyoo Hirooka, the chief fermentation researcher at the Kyoto Municipal Institute of Industrial Technology and Culture. "People can understand rice and koji, but which yeast is used and what that means takes more explanation." By that, Hirooka means if a label reads "association yeast No. 6," customers might not understand what the heck is going on. "Association? No. 6? In *my* sake?"

## The Association Yeasts

Brewers order their yeasts directly from the Brewing Society of Japan. As of this writing, there are currently 28 association yeasts (*kyokai kobo*) available for breweries to order. Some, however, are low-foaming variations of the same yeasts. These yeasts are referred to by their numbers. In Japanese, for example, "association yeast No. 6" is Kyokai Kobo 6-go; the association refers to the Brewing Society of Japan, and the number 6 is the sixth numbered yeast it offers.

The Brewing Society of Japan began selling association yeasts in 1906, but it wasn't until 1917 that the original lineup of five association yeasts went on sale. The first association yeast was from legendary Nada brewery Sakura Masamune; the second was from Gekkeikan in Fushimi, Kyoto; and the other three, including No. 5 from the Kamotsuru Shuzo Brewery, hailed from Hiroshima. The selection of these five yeasts showed the importance and quality of Nada, Fushimi and Hiroshima sake. The goal in making the yeasts widely available was so breweries around Japan could make better sake instead of seeing batches go to rot. Good sake was taxable, while bad sake was not. Following Japan's victory in the Russo-Japanese War in 1905, the country's government needed all the yen it could get to continue building up its military, modernizing and industrializing.

Currently, the oldest yeast officially distributed is No. 6, which was isolated at the Aramasa brewery in Akita in 1930. No. 6 produces robust fermentation with a good alcohol yield, explaining why, five years after its discovery, it was in use throughout the country.

Association yeasts 1 to 5 are often grouped together, but No. 6 is seen as a landmark that changed sake brewing forever. The ones that followed No. 6, such as No. 7, No. 9 and No. 10, all seem to be related. You might think they are all derived from No. 6, but it's not that simple, according to researcher Takeshi Akao of the National Research Institute of Brewing. "It's easy to misunderstand that yeasts No. 1 to No. 5 were similar to each other," says Akao. "But No. 1 and

No. 2 are different, No. 1 and No. 3 are different, No. 1 and No. 4 are different and so on." It's not simply that No. 6 is unique, Akao contends; all of them were. However, the original five didn't hold up well in storage, and their outstanding sake-making qualities degraded. After No. 6, a series of excellent yeasts were discovered, most notably No. 7 and No. 9, both of which are still widely used today. There is a theory that No. 6 was the mother of the association yeasts No. 7, No. 9 and No. 10 (No. 8 is no longer offered). Could No. 6's widespread use during World War II have led to these other yeasts? The other theory is that all of these yeasts share the same as-yet-unidentified ancestor. "There is no proof or record to back up these claims, so we cannot make a scientific judgment," says Akao. It's true that for a period, only No. 6 was distributed, but many breweries did not even add yeast. "I don't think we can reach a simple conclusion," says

Akao. (For more about the Aramasa brewery, the home of association yeast No. 6, see pages 112–113.)

"Once we began distributing the excellent No. 6 yeast, the demand for the first five dropped, and we stopped releasing them," says Katsumi Nakahara, a researcher at the Brewing Society of Japan. Nos. 1 to 5 are not fragrant like modern yeasts, nor do they offer the robust fermentation and high alcohol yield of No. 6. Even though the yeasts are not officially available, the association has kept strains of them, as well as of the other yeasts it no longer sells. Says Nakahara, "We won't put them back on sale officially, but if there is a request, we do make those yeasts available." Yeast nos. 8, 12 and 13 are also no longer sold. (The Sakura Masamune brewery is now in possession of the yeast that it originally donated, No. 1).

The most widely used sake yeast is No. 7. The version available today is well balanced, promoting strong fermentation and giving off fruity ginjo aromas, all explaining why it's become the go-to choice. Around 50 percent of all association yeasts sold are No. 7. It was first isolated in 1946 at the Miyasaka brewery in Nagano Prefecture. That year, the brewery had racked up award after award, leading National Research Institute of Brewing researcher Shoichi Yamada to its doorstep, hoping to figure out how they did it. In the brewery's fermentation tanks, he discovered what was originally called "Masumi yeast," named after the brewery's most famous brand. The brewery didn't actually develop this yeast; it was a *kura tsuki kobo*, or a "yeast living in the brewery." The clean environment at Miyasaka enabled the microorganisms to thrive. Today a plaque marks the spot where No. 7 was discovered.

BELOW Association yeast no. 2 was isolated from sake made at Gekkeikan RIGHT This Masumi sake is called "Nanago" or "Number 7," after the yeast discovered at the Miyasaka brewery.

"I think the yeast spread throughout the country because sake that used it placed high in competitions. Compared to No. 6, its aroma was better and it was easier to work with," says Kenji Nasu, *toji* at Masumi. Because the brewery didn't develop the yeast, they haven't profited on it, but Masumi doesn't mind. "I don't think there is any point in fencing oneself off," says Nasu. Thanks to the Masumi yeast, breweries across Japan were able to produce even better sake. That's actually the point of the association yeasts.

The association yeast traditionally used most for ginjo sakes is No. 9. Researcher Kinichi Nojiro (later hailed as the "God of Ginjo" for his work) isolated the yeast at the Kumamoto Prefectural Brewing Research Center in 1953, and it was distributed from 1968. Its fermentation is strong and healthy and it produces fruity, rich brews with little acidity, making it ideal for the current ginjo flavor profile. By the mid-1980s, brewers entering the Annual Japan Sake Awards had devised what was considered the

The Miyasaka Brewing Co. was founded in 1662, but the Masumi name, which means "truth" or "transparency" wasn't used until the late Edo period (1603–1868). In the lower photo a plaque marks the spot where the No. 7 association yeast was discovered in 1946.

# REGIONAL YEASTS AND REGIONAL SAKES

Across Japan, researchers are meeting the needs of local brewers by developing their own yeasts. Kyoto is just one example. "In 1955, the association yeasts were causing lots of bad batches," says Kiyoo Hirooka, the city's chief fermentation researcher. Kyoto brewers needed better yeasts. The municipal government stepped in, and Hirooka's predecessors began work on more stable versions of association yeasts No. 6 and No. 7, creating what they called No. 1 and No. 2 respectively. The results were good, and by the 1970s, the municipal research institute was selling huge quantities to the Fushimi breweries. In the decades that followed, the city began working on its own original yeasts.

The lab of the Kyoto Municipal Institute of Industrial Technology and Culture is located in a modernistic glass and steel Japanese-style building in central Kyoto. There, at a mini table-top brewery lined with boxy laboratory equipment, Hirooka and his fellow researcher Tamami Kiyono use a variety of unique lab-made yeasts to brew sake in beakers. A small *sugidama*, the ball of cedar greenery often displayed outside breweries, hangs overhead.

"Our brewing is small-scale," says Kiyoo. "But we even do the three-step brewing process in order to make the most accurate lab version possible." The finished brew is run through a flame ionization detector to break down its chemical composition, so brewers can see, at least on paper, what's possible with the yeast. But does the lab-made stuff taste any good? "Of course, professional brewers will make much better sake," Hirooka says with a grin.

The goal isn't to make a Kyoto-style yeast. "Honestly, I don't even

believe a Kyoto-style sake exists," he says. "Within the prefecture and even just in Fushimi, there is so much variation. Every brewery is doing its own thing. That's probably why they all get along so well—they're not copying each other." Kyoto sake is typically stereotyped as a softer and more "feminine" style of sake. A trip around Fushimi breweries shows that this is simply not true. Wide variety and fierce independence are the modern-day hallmarks of the Kyoto style.

In the Fushimi district, brewers are making such a wide variety of sake that it is difficult to characterize the region. There's even a separation, albeit mental, between Fushimi and Kyoto city. For example, staff at Gekkeikan, one of Fushimi's (and Japan's) largest sake makers, will say they are going into Kyoto when they leave Fushimi for the city center, even though Fushimi is technically located within the city.

The variety around Kyoto Prefecture is even wider, with breweries like Kinoshita Shuzo (see page 127)

ABOVE The Kyoto Municipal Institute of Industrial Technology and Culture use a variety of unique lab-made yeasts to brew sake. ABOVE RIGHT Kiyoo Hirooka holds the lab's research brewing license.

and Mukai Shuzo (pages 84–85) in the far north region of the prefecture making some wonderful, atypical brews. "If I had a target, like a set style all brewers follow, then I could make a Kyoto yeast to suit that," says Kiyoo. "But it doesn't exist."

Instead, the lab focuses on making yeasts with good fermentation, high alcohol yield and desirable aromas and flavors. "I'd say yeast is responsible for 70 percent of a sake's flavor," he says. "That's not based on any particular data, and my conclusions could be biased because of my research expertise, but that's what I believe."

For a tasting note on a sake made with Kyoto yeast, see Tomio Tanshu Yamada Nishiki, page 228.

ABOVE In 2020, the Kyoto Municipal Institute of Industrial Technology and Culture released *kyo-no-koi*, a new yeast, overseen by researcher Tamami Kiyono.

magic formula: YK35: "Y" standing for Yamada Nishiki, "K" for "Kumamoto" or *kyu* (the number nine in Japanese, a reference to the No. 9 yeast), and "35" referring to a 35 percent polishing ratio.

The Kumamoto Prefecture Sake Research Center cultivates and distributes its own version of the No. 9 yeast, which it calls "Kumamoto kobo" (Kumamoto yeast). Why use the Kumamoto yeast instead of No. 9? Essentially, both yeasts are the same, but many breweries swear that the Kumamoto one ferments better than its association counterpart. The Kumamoto yeast has also been cultivated by other prefectures, such as Yamagata, to develop offshoots of the original. Until the arrival of strains that produce ethyl caproate in large quantities, it was the most widely used variety for entries in the National Japan Sake Competition. Now, that honor goes to the non-foaming No. 1801, a cross of No. 9 and the non-foaming No. 1601. For more on non- or low-foaming yeasts, see page 110.

## Ambient Yeasts

A small number of breweries in Japan do not add yeasts. Instead, they use ambient yeasts, which are called *kura tsuki kobo*, or "yeasts living in the brewery." Until the late 19th century, these yeasts were relied on to convert the sugar into alcohol. Even then, brewers were adding their own in-house yeast, but in a simple way: tools and tubs were not cleaned to the same degree that they are today. As a result, yeast microbes could be transferred via mixing pole from one batch to another. This would naturally ensure consistency between batches (which is considered a good thing). It could also easily spread harmful, rot-inducing bacteria around the brewery (which is considered a very bad thing). Today, good hygiene practices have made it easier to prevent the onset and spread of rot.

"Since 2017, when we switched to all ambient yeasts, we haven't had any trouble," says Teruaki

Hashimoto of the Miyoshino brewery in Nara.
Before the switch, Miyoshino was using
association yeasts No. 7 and No. 9. The ambient
yeast in the brewery is most likely descended
from those yeasts, but is much healthier and
stronger.

"It's the result of natural selection: the
toughest yeasts survive," say Hashimoto. The
result is a much sturdier sake with a far more
active fermentation. "For us, using ambient
yeasts is easier."

## Non-Foaming Yeasts

Typically, association yeasts come in foaming
and non-foaming varieties. Some "foamless"
yeasts do create a slight amount of foam despite
their name, but they are nowhere near the
bubbling heads on the foaming varieties. The
foamless versions have the figures written "01"
after the association yeast number. Thus, No. 7 is
the regular foamy yeast, while No. 701 is the
foamless version.

Foamless yeasts are mutated versions of the
regular yeasts. They have been spotted over the
years—the first one was recorded back in 1916 at
the Hiroshima Regional Tax Bureau. But it
wasn't until 1971 that the first non-foaming
association yeast was released, the aforementioned No. 701.

Pioneering work with low-foaming yeast was
done by Takao Nihei, a Japanese brewer at the
Honolulu Sake Brewery. In 1959, Nihei was
trying to overcome the difficulties of brewing in
Hawaii when he noticed the main mash foam
was not rising as expected. He had discovered a
mutant yeast strain, which he then quickly
adopted and used for brewing.

One of the most important reasons for using
low- or non-foaming yeasts is the yield. When
the foam builds up during the start of fermentation, space must be left in the tank so the
contents don't bubble over onto the brewery
floor. This means batches must be smaller. These

days, little spinning propellers are often affixed at
the top of tanks for foamy yeasts in order to help
prevent overflow. Another reason is manage-
ment. Foam rises and falls during the brewing
process, leaving residue on the side of the tanks
that has to be frequently be wiped off. If yeast
foam means a lower yield and more to clean,
then why do brewers even use their non-mutant
yeast strains?

"Foamless yeasts make the flavors in sake
thin," says Hideharu Ohta, president of the
Daishichi brewery in Fukushima. "For those
foamless or low-foaming yeasts, all the alcohol is
in the main mash. That means the fermentation
proceeds faster and produces more alcohol
before all the flavors have come out during the
brewing process."

In contrast, Ohta says, foam slows down
fermentation; the alcohol production is split
between the main mash and the frothy head,
creating a more flavorful sake.

Brewers traditionally used the foam to gauge
the progress of fermentation, with many
different Japanese words to describe all the
varieties of foam produced during sake brewing.

TOP LEFT The Miyoshino brewery in Yoshino, Nara uses ambient yeasts to make its Hanatomoe-branded sake. The area is also famous for Japanese cedar. TOP CENTER The ambient yeasts produce strong, sturdy sake. Pictured is a yeast starter batch. It had lovely pear notes. ABOVE *Kashi-dokkuri* flasks were for customers to fill, often emblazoned with a brewery or shop's name. These read "Miyoshino."

TOP A brewer stirs the mash in a *kioke* cedar tub. ABOVE Teruaki Hashimoto of the Miyoshino brewery in Nara holds a bottle of the *mizumoto*-stye Hanatomoe sake.

# ARAMASA: AN ICONOCLAST LEADING THE SAKE REVOLUTION

"Do you like *On the Road* by Jack Kerouac?" asks Yusuke Sato, following that up quickly with another query as to my thoughts on William Burroughs. These are questions I'd expect from an English lit major, not a sake brewer. In fact, Sato was a literature major at the elite University of Tokyo; he was also a journalist. He's now a brewer and eighth-generation president of Aramasa Shuzo in Akita. Sato is also an iconoclast, a dogmatic provocateur, a traditionalist and, among sake fans, a rock star. His family brewery, Aramasa Shuzo, is famous as the site where the Japan Brewing Association's No. 6 yeast, the oldest association yeast in general circulation, was isolated in 1935. Aramasa never received any money for it. "We did get a thank-you from the emperor, though." The yeast, with its gentle muscatel notes, had been eclipsed by far more fragrant modern yeasts—that is, until Sato revived it with a series of well-received releases with a big number six emblazoned on the bottles.

It's late 2018, and the 43-year-old Sato is decked out in a lab coat and a bandana. "The only yeast that was allowed to be used during World War II was No. 6," he says. It was distributed to thousands of breweries. Nos.1 to 5, he explains, were nixed because they didn't equal the robust fermentation and alcohol yield of No. 6. "Japan was fighting a war and needed money, right? A huge amount of that money was from sake, and the government wanted brewers to use the No. 6 yeast because it produces a lot of alcohol, and the sake won't go bad." No. 6, a naturally occurring yeast found in the Aramasa brewery, was so reliable that other yeasts fell from use. No. 6 might have been a little too good. "From 1939 to when Japan lost the war, the No. 6 yeast made the money that fueled World War II," Sato says. "If that yeast didn't exist,

the war might have ended sooner, Japan would've run out of money, and I don't think the nuclear bombs would've been dropped."

The vast majority of sake makers use the quick-starting *sokujo-moto* method in which lactic acid is added to the yeast starter. This cuts the time needed to make the starter in half—down to two from the four weeks needed for the natural, yet labor-intensive *kimoto* and *yamahai* methods. Using the sokujo method results in a clean and uniform brew, says Sato. This is because the rice dissolves much more quickly. The kimoto method used at Aramasa dissolves the rice much more slowly, which allows for a wide range of flavors, resulting in a complex, deep sake with appealing astringency, bitterness and umami. Sato invites me into the *shubo* room to take a whiff of the yeast starter that's only a few days

old. There's not much aroma. "Here, check this out," he says, opening the lid of a starter that's been fermenting for 25 days. There are lovely muscat notes, hints of yogurt and the sweetness of rice. It's a gentle bouquet that doesn't overwhelm, but impresses.

Back in the office, Sato admits he wasn't interested in brewing when he was younger. As a journalist, however, he started developing a taste for sake at drinking parties with other writers. "I started collecting sake," says Sato. "Then I wanted to start making it."

In 2007, Sato returned home to find Aramasa about to go under. The following year, he began brewing. He had specific ideas of what kind of sake he wanted to make, and over the course of several years, he began transforming the brewery. While his contemporaries pursued fragrant sakes, Sato set out to master yeast-starter methods. By 2012, Aramasa had stopped using the quick-start sokujo method and was switching gears to the kimoto method now used to make all the brewery's sake. "I use the kimoto method instead of the yamahai method, because kimoto is more stable," Sato says. The yamahai method leaves the microorganisms up to their own devices, but with kimoto, Aramasa can exert more control over the starter. "With

FACING PAGE Yusuke Sato. TOP LEFT A batch of *shubo* yeast starter made with the No. 6 yeast. ABOVE The discovery of the No. 6 association yeast here ensured Aramasa's place in sake history. FAR LEFT Aramasa explores traditional methods with *kioke* tubs. LEFT A flask of Aramasa's No. 6 association yeast. The yeast starter to which this was added had a lovely muscat grape note.

kimoto and yamahai, you cannot afford to screw up," says Sato. "If one batch goes to rot, then that bad bacteria will infect other batches." He also believes it's important to consider what these modern techniques really mean in a historical context. "In the sake industry, there's a lot of chatter about tradition," says Sato. But sokujo only dates back to around 1900. "The real sake tradition comes from the Edo period [1603–1868]," he says. It was during the Meiji era (1868–1912), in which Japan rapidly modernized and Westernized, that sake making changed. Methods like kimoto were cast aside in the name of progress.

"Since the Meiji era, sake making has entailed bioengineered yeasts, the addition of lactic acid or the sokujo method and the addition of enzymes in koji making," says Sato. He adjusts his skinny dark green necktie. "I'm a romantic, but the Edo style is better," he says. "The Meiji style is for factories. It's based on techniques developed for brewing beer, not sake."

Perhaps it's his experience as an investigative journalist, but Sato looks at his industry with skepticism. "I don't like the word 'ginjo,' and I don't put it on any of our sake," he says. *Ginjo*, he explains, is from *ginmi*, which means "to scrutinize." "In sake production, all it refers to is a rice-polishing percentage. That's it." You press a button, the machine polishes rice, and bam, instant ginjo. Have the machine polish it a bit more, and bam, *daiginjo*. "You don't need any skill whatsoever," he states. "I think real ginjo has nothing to do with polishing ratios." At Aramasa, wonderful sakes with 90 percent and 96 percent polishing ratios are produced.

I look at a sign on the wall that reads 新政厚徳 (*shinsei koutoku*) in beautiful brush calligraphy, which means "new rule, great virtue." It's a Meiji-era phrase dating from when the new imperial government came to power in 1868, not long after the brewery was originally founded, in 1852. Given Sato's aversion to sake innovations of that era, I'm surprised to see it displayed here. Then again, the phrase *shinsei*, meaning "new rule," was the name of the brewery until an alternative reading of the kanji characters, Aramasa, was adopted. I ask Sato how he feels about that history. "The Meiji government was doing what it thought was right for Japan," he replies. "Those sake-making techniques, such as sokujo, weren't designed by bad people. They were created with the hope of improving sake production." Sokujo, he continues, is ideal for a growing country with a high demand for sake. "But the population in Japan is declining," he says, "as is the demand for sake." The need for sokujo, he believes, has passed, and the older ways should be explored again.

# SOIL

Rice. Water. Yeast. In sake making, all of these influence the final outcome, but there's one important factor that's often overlooked: soil. The earth imparts different nuances to the rice that carry through to the final sake.

The Honda Shoten brewery in Himeji, Hyogo Prefecture, has been studying soil samples for decades. In 1977, the future-third-generation owner, Takeyoshi Honda, visited storied French wineries like Domaine de la Romanée-Conti and was bowled over by the quality and per-bottle price tag. At that time, Honda Shoten was selling its product to Ozeki to be rebottled and repacked into "one-cup" single-serving containers, but Honda wanted to shift to making premium brews. He realized that the winning sakes at the Annual Japan Sake Awards used Yamada Nishiki rice. At that time, smaller breweries like Honda Shoten were using table rice. The agricultural association wouldn't sell him any of the coveted seeds (their refusal, he later recalled, brought him to tears). But instead of giving up, the late Honda, who passed away in 2018, devoted his life to researching Yamada Nishiki, convincing local farmers to grow the grain and showing

ABOVE Honda Shoten released a line of sakes to show just how soil can impact flavor. BELOW These soil samples were taken from the Yashiro, Tojo, and Yokawa areas where Toku-A Yamada Nishiki was grown. Each area has its own flavor nuance, which comes through in the finished sake.

other small breweries how they, too, could use the most desirable brewing rice. In the process, Honda learned how Hyogo's soil influenced sake's flavors.

"Of course, Yamada Nishiki is suited to Hyogo," says Ryusuke Honda, fifth-generation brewery head. "It was developed here in Hyogo to be planted and grown here." But not all Yamada Nishiki in Hyogo is the same. There is

the Toku-A (special district-A) classification, which refers to areas in Hyogo where the most desirable Yamada Nishiki is grown. However, not all Toku-A is the same; there are two sub-categories: Toku-A-A and Toku-A-B. (There used to be a Toku-A-C category, but it has since been eliminated.) When researching Yamada Nishiki, the elder Honda discovered that certain areas in the Toku-A district had different soil properties. Convinced this affected the final brew, Honda not only sampled the rice, but also tasted the soil itself.

Differentiating the flavor profiles that soil creates can be difficult. To convey the impact soil has on rice, Honda Shoten released a series of three sakes brewed with the same water and the same association yeast No. 9 by the same brewers in the same brewery under the exact same fermentation conditions. The rice was all Yamada Nishiki; however, it was harvested from three different fields in Toku-A areas. These included the area formerly known as Yashiro in the city of Kato, what used to be called Tojo in Akitsu, and Yokawa in the city of Miki. Even though all three of these areas are still classified as Toku-A, the various Yamada Nishiki rice fields produce different-tasting sake. Because Honda Shoten paid such careful attention to brewing the three different Yamada Nishiki crops under the exact same conditions, the variations were even more noticeable.

All three areas have similar topsoil conditions. But what lies under those initial 12 inches (30 cm) makes a remarkable difference. The Yashiro rice fields, Ryusuke Honda explains, are filled with gravel from river

deposits, which prevents the roots of the Yamada Nishiki plants from extending deep into the soil. It is sandy, though, and absorbs water. "The result is a light and mellow sake," says Honda. The soil in the Tojo area is clay, and the roots of the Yamada Nishiki, which grow up to 5 feet (1.5 meters) can extend all the way down. This rice produced a fragrant and well-balanced sake. Most fascinating of all is the Yamada Nishiki grown in Yokawa. Below the topsoil, the earth is *haiao-iro*, which literally means "gray-blue colored"—a gunmetal hue. This sake tastes much more acidic, and the tongue-tingling finish lingers. "If you look at the chemical analysis, it's not actually more acidic than the other two sakes," Honda says. "All their data readings are the same, but the Yokawa soil has a lot of magnesium, and perhaps that makes it seem more acidic."

The influence of soil isn't unique to Yamada Nishiki or to the three areas that Honda used in his experiment. Wherever rice is grown, the soil has an effect on flavor. The magnitude of this effect, however, varies. For Honda Shoten, the local rice and soil just happen to be among the best-regarded in Japan, if not the world. "It was up to our brewery to not only pioneer the best sake rice in Japan, but also to show how the influence of the local soil can be tasted even in the final brew."

The current generation running things at Honda Shoten is the always upbeat Ryusuke Honda.

# JAPAN'S TOP SAKE-PRODUCING REGIONS

Does regionality in sake really exist? Absolutely. It exists all across Japan, with different areas specializing in different foods.

The process of sake making is a series of decisions. Brewers have an array of choices, ranging from types of rice and yeast to fermentation length and pasteurization. Ultimately, they decide the sake's flavor. Those decisions are often consciously and subconsciously informed by the food they eat.

Brewers in different regions grow up eating slightly different food. The most striking flavor difference is between Tokyo in the east, where basic soup stock is made from dried bonito, and Osaka in the west, where the basic soup stock is made from kombu seaweed. Instant-noodle maker Nissin sells variations of dehydrated udon for each side of the country, with the packaging marked "E" for east and "W" for west. There are other differences. In Osaka, the most widely sold nori seaweed is called *ajitsuke-nori*, or "flavor-added nori," made with soy sauce, sugar and mirin. It's savory and tasty, completely different from the bland nori sold in the east. The reason

TOP Nada-gogo's success has no doubt been helped by fertile Hyogo fields with top grade Yamada Nishiki. ABOVE The brewing district of Saijo is filled with white-walled breweries and red-brick chimneys.

was that the best nori sold in modern Tokyo Bay during the Edo period (1603–1868) didn't need any flavoring. In the Osaka region, nori wasn't widely eaten until flavoring was added. People in Osaka grow up eating flavored nori, while in Tokyo they eat plain nori. This discrepancy is so great that convenience-store chains in both regions sell *onigiri* (rice balls) with different nori. How does this influence sake?

"If a sake doesn't suit the local cuisine, it won't sell," says Toshio Taketsuru of Taketsuru Shuzo in Hiroshima (see page 13). "For example, our sake doesn't sell as well in Sendai, because people there eat heavily salted fish, which we don't in Hiroshima." Sendai brewers make lighter sake that pairs well with salty fresh fish, while Taketsuru Shuzo's heavy sakes go better with the Hiroshima region's savory food.

Regional flavors, however, are not static. The food eaten in Japan today is different than it was 100 years ago. Sushi wasn't widely eaten before the 19th century. Wagyu beef, as we know it today, is largely a 20th-century food. Within Japan, there are certain regional flavors that endure, although regional variations are shrinking. In November 1970, the first Kentucky Fried Chicken opened in Nagoya. The following year, the first McDonald's set up shop in Tokyo; in that same decade, family restaurants—Japan's versions of diners—started expanding. Food options were increasingly uniform in Japan, with nationwide food franchises and broader consumption of Western-style food. But regional differences still exist, and can be seen in sake.

## The Most Famous Sake Regions

Sake is brewed in all of Japan's 47 prefectures. Great sake is made across the country, but some regions are better known than others. Here are some of the most famous:

**Aichi:** Back in the 18th century, Aichi's sake was dubbed *oni goroshi*, or "ogre killer," for its high alcohol content, dryness and harsh flavor. Today, Aichi sake is famous for being soft and sweet—though in the Mikawa region, the local brews are full bodied. This suits the flavorful regional foods such as the dark-red Mikawa Hatcho miso.

**Akita:** Here, excellent water and delicious rice make some of Japan's most desirable sake. Winters are cold, but not severe. Akita's copper and silver deposits brought mining, and breweries opened so miners could quench their thirst. Recently the region has had a renaissance, with styles varying from brewery to brewery.

**Fukuoka:** With good access to soft water, Fukuoka was one of the three largest sake-producing areas until the 1970s, following Nada and Fushimi. Fukuoka sake used to be on the sweet side but modern Fukuoka sakes are often fruity and light (especially the brews aimed at the Tokyo market), or dry and refreshing.

Along with local dishes, this eatery in Yamagata city lists the sake brands it serves, which includes local brew Juyondai from Takagi Shuzo in Murayama, Yamagata Prefecture.

RIGHT The Nada district used to ship sake to modern-day Tokyo in vessels called *tarukaisen*. BELOW Established in 1791, Matsumoto Shuzo is one of the most iconic-looking breweries in Fushimi and all of Japan. BELOW RIGHT Kumamoto and the Kyushu region aren't exactly synonymous with cold weather, but the region's more mountainous areas do see snow.

**Fukushima:** This region is home to a variety of consistently excellent styles. After the 2011 nuclear disaster, Fukushima sake producers went to great lengths to ensure safety. Japanese sake fans rushed to support Fukushima's brewers, as well as those in the surrounding areas.

**Fushimi:** Located in Kyoto Prefecture, Fushimi has a variety of breweries, all keen to do their own thing. Kyoto sake has been called "feminine" due to its soft water and its contrast with "macho" Nada sake. However, these preconceptions are outdated. Half of all of Japan's sake is made in Fushimi and the nearby Nada region.

**Ishikawa:** The 16th-century lord Toyotomi Hideyoshi, who united Japan in the 16th century,

enjoyed sake brewed in the southern part of Ishikawa Prefecture. Today, that region, known as Hakusan, has a geographical indication (GI) to distinguish its products. The area's sake has a gentle fruity aroma and a flavor reminiscent of rice. Many Ishikawa brews are excellent warmed.

**Kumamoto:** Though the home of famed Kumamoto yeast No. 9, this prefecture doesn't have a strictly defined style. Prior to the 20th century, it brewed a style of red sake or *akazake*, made with an added wood-ash preservative. Today, this red beverage is still imbibed and also used for cooking. In the 20th century, Kumamoto invented new techniques, presenting the sake world with the discovery of its local yeast, which is still one of the best for fragrant and fruity brews.

**Nada:** The *Nada-gogo* (five villages of Nada) area stretches nearly 7½ miles (12 km) from Nada Ward in Kobe to the Izumi area of Nishinomiya City. The region is home to many of the country's biggest breweries, including Hakutsuru, Ozeki and Kenbishi. Around 25 percent of all the sake in Japan is produced here and the region has been awarded a geographical indication (GI). Traditionally, Nada sake is called masculine, thanks to the hard water that encourages robust fermentation. But there are also light, fruity and floral brews to be had.

**Niigata:** The area is famous for the *tanrei karakuchi* (clean, crisp and dry) style, thanks to its soft water, hard Gohyakumangoku brewing rice and long fermentation times. Niigata's sakes are among the most clearly defined in Japan. Some breweries have been moving away from tanrei karakuchi to just a clean, crisp tanrei style.

**Saijo:** In Japan, the phrase *sandai sakedokoro* (big three sake spots) refers to Nada, Fushimi and Saijo. This region's sakes are generally gentle, with lots of wonderful, classic ginjo brews.

**Shizuoka:** In the ginjo kingdom of Shizuoka, ginjo-shu comprises over 27 percent of all sake (the national average is around 15 percent.) Shizuoka ginjo is characterized by its refreshing but soft mouthfeel, fruity but modest aroma, and fine flavor without unwanted off-flavors. It's ideal for pairing. The birth of the Shizuoka-type ginjo was motivated by the need to survive in an unforgiving and shrinking market.

**Yamagata:** One of Japan's best-known ginjo regions, recipient of a geographical indication (GI), underscoring the importance of its regional products. The Yamagata brewing industry slumped as the sake market shrank after World War II. But in 1985, a host of Yamagata breweries started churning out award-winning daiginjo.

The prefecture's sake-brewing research institute had developed new rice varieties, yeasts and *koji-kin*, and the breweries had stayed in close contact to swap info. The typical Yamagata *junmai* ginjo sake is soft.

## Jizake: The Local Stuff

In the Edo period, the term *jizake*, or "local sake," as well as terms like *inakazake* (rural sake), implied cheap, low-quality brews. Jizake was seen as less desirable than the national brands from Nada and Fushimi. But that sake, like most, was made only from rice. That changed.

From 1937, Japan was fighting a war with China and four years later, it was fighting the US. Besides obvious human costs at home and aboard, war put a strain on resources, making rice scarce and expensive. New techniques were developed so that brewers could make sake with less rice or, in the case of *goseiseishu* (synthetic sake), no rice at all. *Sanbai-jozo-seishu*, also called *sanzo-shu*, means "tripled sake," referring to how brewing alcohol was doubled for the main mash, resulting in three times the yield. To create the flavors in sake, sweeteners, lactic acid and MSG were added liberally. In the following years, as the country recovered from war, sake that got you drunk was good enough. During the decades that followed, though, it was not.

Sake sales peaked in 1973, and then sales of mass-produced sake started going downhill. During the 1970s, customers learned the scandalous news that national brands were secretly buying sake from smaller producers and rebottling it as their own. Jizake started taking on a positive meaning. Japanese National Railways had launched a "Discover Japan" domestic tourist campaign, and people ventured out of the city to the countryside, where they encountered handmade sake from small breweries that didn't have enough yen for automation. That decade saw the first jizake

The shutter for a liquor store in Niigata city reads 地酒 (*jizake*), meaning "local sake."

tastes in Tokyo," says Masataka Shirakashi, president of Kenbishi, Japan's oldest sake brand. "The result is that many types of sake from different regions become similar because they're reacting to trends so they can compete. It's like how all the cars in F1 racing look the same."

If it's real jizake, shouldn't sake contain local rice? Some breweries use local rice, but others import their rice from other regions. Premium *daiginjo* is typically made from Yamada Nishiki rice, and the best of that breed hails from Hyogo Prefecture. Because the big Nada breweries have a long-standing close relationship with nearby farmers, they can secure the best Yamada Nishiki. Even though they're national brands, could this mean they're also making jizake?

Furthermore, many brewers come from other regions for the seasonal work. So even if they're not locals, can they make local sake? What about yeasts? Sake made with an association yeast (see page 105) won't be local, unless it's made in the brewery where that yeast was originally discovered. Of course, using the yeasts growing naturally in the brewery helps ensure that the brew is regional, but that can also restrict the range of sake the brewery wants to make. Water, of course, can be local or, if necessary, trucked in. If a sake maker wants to talk up how good their local well is, more power to them.

In many ways, the obsession over regionality is fairly recent. In other ways, it's not. Caring about which rice is used and where it was grown is a modern postwar phenomenon; contemporary sake fans have the luxury of being discerning about grains. In the past, sake drinkers weren't as fussy about sake rice. But that doesn't mean brewers weren't aware of which rice made good sake. Hideo Kuroda points out in his 1984 book *Nihon Chusei Kaihatsushi no Kenkyu* )

boom, with another following in the 1980s. Sake fans lusted after premium small-batch regional brews. In a country with widely available food and drink, the phenomenon of searching after rare *maboroshi no sake*, or "phantom sake," was a postwar luxury made possible due to Japan's rocketing economic growth.

It is possible that views on jizake have overcorrected too far. Some serious sake drinkers turn their noses up at widespread national brands—whose success, it should be noted, comes from hard-won experience. These purists are missing out on some excellent sake.

There is no official definition of jizake. For some, it means everything but Nada and Fushimi. For others, it refers to handmade sake from small regional breweries—but success can change that. Some brands, like Kubota and Dassai, which started out as jizake, have grown and gone nationwide. So the word "jizake" itself is ambiguous and problematic. What exactly does it mean? If sake is local, then should it be consumed mostly in the area where it's brewed? But if that's a small rural town, the brewery might have a tough time surviving in such a limited marketplace. Shipping its brews to Tokyo or Osaka puts the brewery in a better position financially and helps it stay in business. Success might turn the sake maker into a national brand. "A lot of breweries end up trying to appeal to

(Research of development history of the middle ages in Japan) that as early as the Kamakura era (1185–1333) certain rice suited for brewing were identified and even named, such as koizumi-wase. But it really wasn't until the late 19th century with the discovery of Omachi, that the stage was set for modern brewing rice.

The term "jizake" is all about perception and image. Many sake fans would describe sake made by a small brewery with a limited staff producing small batches as jizake, even if the brewery had to automate parts of its production because it didn't have enough brewers, or it wasn't using local rice or had to outsource its rice polishing. Conversely, those same fans wouldn't call sake made by a large nationwide brewery jizake, even if it carries out many steps by hand and uses rice that's grown a short drive away and polished in-house. In the world of jizake, the smaller and more obscure a sake is, the better. That doesn't necessarily translate to quality, however.

## The Return of Individuality

The Japanese word *kosei* means "individuality." For much of the 20th century, sake lost its kosei and became homogenized. However, smaller makers also face a loss of individuality because many of them make sake for larger markets, such as Tokyo, rather than for local customers; their branding is designed to win awards in national or international contests, appealing to trends and tastes of the day.

Until the 1900s, all sake made in Japan had kosei. This wasn't a choice; it was due to circumstances, such as a steady supply of uniform yeasts, high quality, polished sake rice and mastery of empirical brewing science. In the 20th century, breweries switched from their local, often wild, yeasts to dependable Brewing Association yeasts that promised delicious sake. They exchanged stability for individuality.

Large breweries in Fushimi and Nada grew larger, pumping out more sake than ever in the decades following World War II. At the time, jizake was not popular, and national brands ruled the liquor shops. As they couldn't make enough, the larger brewers contracted smaller ones to make sake that was blended and sold under the national brand. This practice was known as

LEFT Shoki Tokubetsu Junmai (page 244) is a *jizake* from Nagano. CENTER Kenbishi is Japan's oldest brand. This Kuromatsu Kenbishi is reviewed on page 228. RIGHT Kubota (page 215) is a brand that started local then spread nationwide.

*oke-uri*, meaning "selling a tub" (this referred to the *oke*, the tub or vat in which sake was brewed), or *oke-gai*, meaning "buying a tub." Many brands got hooked on the practice: during the 1970s, over one third of the sake bottled and sold by the country's biggest brand names was outsourced.

During the 1990s and 2000s, with sake sales lower than ever, many breweries lost their oke-uri contracts. Some no longer had brands or followers, and were forced to shutter. Others retooled and were resurrected as popular makers of local sake. The practice of oke-uri contributed to the loss of kosei in the sake industry that continues to this day.

That doesn't mean oke-uri was all bad, though. "Oke-uri has its merits," says Teruaki Hashimoto, *toji* at his family's Miyoshino brewery in Nara, where the excellent Hanatomoe sake is made. "You can get brewing techniques from the experts at the big breweries and that's a huge plus," says Hashimoto, who worked at Kenbishi, one of Japan's biggest sake makers, before heading up his family's brewery. "To be honest, small breweries don't have advanced brewing techniques, but they can learn them through the oke-uri process when brewing to a famous maker's exacting specifications."

The Miyoshino brewery stopped oke-uri in 2010 when orders dipped and it became unprofitable for them. It began brewing for itself, and now offers a line of wonderfully acidic brews.

When they outsource, the big breweries have smaller producers make sake to their exact specifications. This sake is then blended with in-house sake for the brewery's signature flavors. "The country's largest makers have high-level blending know-how, which is how they release a consistent product," Hashimoto says. But blending in the sake world isn't held in the same regard that it is in the world of whisky, which also has a long tradition of sourcing from a variety of producers and relying on the skill of blenders to create the flavors and aromas that customers have come to expect.

At the end of the day, broadly speaking, uniformity has led to better sake. Today you can walk into a liquor store in Japan and grab pretty much any sake off the shelf and be assured you'll have something drinkable (the same cannot be said of wine or other distilled spirits!). On the down side, uniformity has also meant a lack of kosei. The pendulum began swinging back at the end of the 20th century, when an increasing number of breweries set out to distinguish themselves from the competition. They're focusing on kosci as a way to stand out, drum up publicity, make interesting sake and, most importantly, to survive.

## Regionality in Sake

Is it possible to categorize all Japan's sake regions by flavor profile? One could try. But blindly attempting to classify sake into codified regions shows a misunderstanding of sake, its brewers and its history. Breweries in sake regions throughout Japan—even on the same street or right next door to each other—often make wildly different sake. They have to, because they need to differentiate themselves from others.

Yes, certain brewing rices or water classifications might lend themselves better to particular styles more easily. Of course, the sake should pair with the local food. And yes, in some areas, brewers have become synonymous with distinct types, or for making those types famous. However, trying to pigeonhole iron-clad regional flavors and shoehorn all local brews into that construct overlooks how tastes and styles have developed over time and, more importantly, the brewers' skill and the sake-making process itself. For example, Niigata is now known for its clear and crisp tanrei style, but during the 1960s, it was making a heavier and sweeter Nada style of sake that was popular at the time. What this does show is how once a particular style becomes popular, other breweries are quick to change production in hopes of cashing in. (They are running businesses after all!) But tastes change and so does sake. Even in Nada, where the flavor profile is stereotyped as "macho," there is a wide variety of flavors. The deep, savory sake of Nada icon Kenbishi is nothing like Kobe Shushinkan's fruity brews—and these two makers are only a 10-minute walk apart! The young generation in charge over at Kobe Shushinkan wanted to make a totally different style of sake than the brewery had previously produced. An unwavering belief in regionality can do a severe discredit to that region.

With rice being imported from different prefectures, with water being treated (and even blended!), with a wide variety of yeasts and with breweries using cooling and refrigeration, brewing possibilities are seemingly endless. Brewers today are freer than they've ever been. Throughout the history of sake, new technology, whether new yeast starter methods or improved rice polishing, has changed how stuff tastes. The Japanese diet isn't static either and new food and flavors have impacted what people want to drink. The sake of today is different from the sake of 100, 200 and 500 years ago. This is not a static drink. It never has been. It never will be.

## Advice for Visiting Breweries:

There are nearly 1,500 breweries in Japan, scattered across the country. Visiting breweries throughout Japan is possible, but make sure to check each brewery's website to see if tours are offered or if they have onsite shops or tasting areas. Some breweries have them; some do not. This can be due to compact brewing spaces that are not designed for visitors, or because the brewery employees are already spread thin. Check before you go! Make reservations if necessary.

If you go on a tour, go easy on cologne and perfume, as strong aromas can disturb the tasting experience for other visitors. Also, because microorganisms are a key part of sake production, do follow your guide's directions about washing your hands, sanitizing and, depending on the brewery, wearing protective garments. Many breweries are old buildings with steep staircases, so watch your step. But above all, please enjoy your brewery tour!

**Fukushima:** fukushima-sake.com/
**Fushimi (Kyoto):** fushimi.or.jp/ sake_guide/
**Ishikawa:** ishikawa-sake.jp/eng/
**Kumamoto:** kumamoto-sake.com/
**Nada (Hyogo):** hanshin.co.jp/ global/en/nada/
**Niigata:** enjoyniigata.com/en/special/ sake.html
**Saijo (Hiroshima):** saijosake.com/town/index. html

For more breweries, search: japansake.or.jp/ tourism/contents/en

A sake barrel is sealed at Hakutsuru Brewery. The brewery's museum is a great place to learn about sake history and serving styles.

# HOW TO ORDER AND ENJOY SAKE: SERVING TEMPERATURES, FLAVOR PROFILES, FOOD PAIRINGS AND MORE

## DRINKING GOOD SAKE

Sake is the most versatile alcoholic brew on earth. It tastes good whether warm, hot, chilled, cold or at room temperature. A major part of the fun with sake drinking is seeing where on this spectrum a particular sake shines. The label on the back of the bottle may give advice for recommended serving styles, but don't let that limit you.

Sake drinking is most enjoyable with food and with others. Specifying how you want the sake served shows an awareness of the season, the cuisine and what you are ordering. It's also a bit personal, like ordering a steak. How do you like yours done?

There are a couple of basic rules of thumb. *Daiginjo* and *ginjo* sakes are usually good chilled or cold. Full-bodied *junmai*, *honjozo* and table sake can work well warm or hot. However, this isn't always true. If it were, what fun would that be? The following sections in this chapter describe how sake is served.

### Kan: The Hot Stuff

*Kan-zake*, or "heated sake," has been enjoyed for centuries. *Honcho shokkan* (A look at this country's food), a compendium of food and drink from 1697, sang the praises of warm sake, stating that chilled sake was fine for a drink or two, but for more extending drinking sessions, warmed sake was easier on the body. However, philosopher Kaibara Ekken, later called "the Aristotle of Japan," recommended neither hot nor cold sake in his 1713 work *Yojokun* (The book of life-nourishing principles), saying they were hard on the stomach. Instead, Ekken recommended lukewarm sake. This became the preferred way of drinking sake.

Warming sake opens up an array of aromas that might not emerge otherwise. During the 1960s and '70s, it was assumed that sake should be warm, and it was often served piping hot, but not necessarily for the best reasons. Sake shipped abroad contained added alcohol and sugar, and heating them would burn off some of the

Sakes from Kinoshita Shuzo (see facing page) are versatile and sturdy and work well at a range of temperatures. See page 238 for a tasting note review.

rougher flavors. Kan-zake has therefore become associated with poor quality, and in the past few decades, chilled sake is assumed to be the premium stuff. This, unfortunately, has caused kan-zake to get a bad rap. When the weather is cold, Japanese people enjoy eating hot food. Why get chilled by drinking cold sake? Likewise, when the temperature gets warm, chilled sake is perfect. Japanese food is seasonal, and Japanese booze should be, too.

Restaurants and bars that serve sake in Japan have the necessary equipment to easily serve up kan-zake. Japanese microwaves also have dedicated setting options to heat up sake. Lacking such facilities, the easiest way to heat sake is to place a *tokkuri* flask in a water-filled pot on the stove and heat it up. Check the temperature often to gauge heat and, if necessary, use a thermometer. For more on how to heat sake, see pages 146–147.

Below are some of the different styles of heated sake. Keep in mind that people perceive temperatures differently and that these are basic rules of thumb.

**Hitohada-kan**, 95–104°F (35–40°C): Basically, "heated to the temperature of skin." At these temps, aromas can start to open up. As a rule of thumb, pretty much everything from daiginjo to table sake works at *hitohada-kan*.

**Nurukan**, 104–113°F (40–45°C): *Nuru* means "lukewarm." With this style, more aromas open up, but some daiginjo starts to fall apart when served this style. Ginjo, junmai, honjozo and table sake typically perform well in this range.

**Jyokan**, 113–122°F (45–50°C): While this isn't the hottest of the hot, this steamy sake is, well, up there. Junmai, honjozo and table sake are generally delicious. In Japan, this is often the default temperature for warmed sake because it makes for pleasant drinking.

**Atsukan**, 122–140°F (50–60°C): "Hot sake." You probably want to stick to honjozo and table sake at these temperatures because the added brewer's alcohol evaporates well when heated. Hearty kimoto and yamahai junmai brews can be excellent atsukan sakes. Note that some sakes are better at 158°F or even 176°F (70–80°C).

# RECLAIMING DELICIOUS HOT SAKE

**"I'm one of the last to go through the old *toji* system," says British-born Philip Harper, toji at Kinoshita Shuzo in northern Kyoto Prefecture, home of the Tamagawa brand.**

After arriving in Japan in the late 1980s to teach English, Harper fell in love with sake, cutting his teeth at the Ume no Yado brewery in Nara, thanks to a friend. The work was—and still is—hard. During his first season, Harper only got one day off, and it was for his wedding.

"I think it was pretty daring of the owner to let me in," Harper says, taking a sip of green tea in a small side room. "Later, he said he thought I'd be there for only a few months." Instead, Harper worked there for years. "The owner didn't expect me to last, because most Japanese people didn't." He did more than last. In 2001, he became the first Westerner to pass the Nanbu toji guild examination. Questions covered brewing science; an essay is included, and there is a tasting section. "They round it off with a terrifying interview with the bigwigs of the union," says Harper. Only about 50 percent of candidates pass, and Harper says he "scraped through."

The initial novelty of Harper's nationality has long worn off, and he is producing some of the most interesting and delicious sake in the country. He focuses on more traditional, if not long-lost, flavors while challenging preconceived notions. "When I started drinking sake, I was told you drink the good stuff cold and the bad stuff hot, which is complete nonsense," says Harper. "A whole generation of people learned that. Sadly, the same idiocy has been taken overseas."

Harper's sake is versatile and sturdy and works well at a range of temperatures. He excels at *kimoto* and *yamahai* brews, using the yeasts and other microorganisms that live in the brewery instead of cultured yeasts. The brewery also has a massive refrigeration setup for unpasteurized sake, and has repurposed an old rice warehouse into a bottle-aging cellar. The variety at Kinoshita Shuzo is staggering—not bad for a brewery that had nearly shut down before Harper arrived.

While other brewers chase more fragrant yeasts and increasingly wine-like brews, Harper champions the styles that play up sake's strengths. "We have to compete with beer and wine," he says. "You have to have reasons to drink sake." For Harper, one of those reasons is versatility. "If you list all the things sake is good for, one is that you can drink it at all these different temperatures," he says. "So, it seems to be a complete own goal to focus on something you can drink only at one temperature." While many of the more floral and fruity *daiginjo* sakes fall apart when heated up, Harper's daiginjo actually tastes better warm.

"For me, it's a sad thing that the industry has let hot sake become marginalized and unhip," Harper says. "Maybe that's the single biggest job we have—to bring that back."

**TOP** Before coming to Japan, Harper studied English literature at Oxford University. **LEFT** Kinoshita Shuzo's vintage *yamahai* is excellent warmed.

## Room Temperature

The baseline for tasting most sake is room temperature, except for unpasteurized and *nama* brews, which are usually stored in the fridge. For everything else, start at room temperature and go from there, either hot or cold based on the season. Heat or cold can mask flavors, so drinking a sake at room temperatures is a way to kick the tires and see what's really under the hood before taking it out for a spin.

Note that in Japanese, *hiya* (冷や), meaning sake that's not warmed, refers to room-temperature sake. However, the character 冷 (*rei*) on its own refers to "cold." This can cause confusion. *Jouon*, which means "room temperature," can also be used when ordering sake. It might be the safest way to order room-temperature sake.

## Reishu: The Cold Stuff

In Japan, *reishu* (cold sake) might seem like a relatively recent trend, but history indicates that it's not. *Nihon Shoki* (The Chronicles of Japan),

BELOW Sake is poured into an *ochoko* with a *ja-no-me* (snake eye) design. BOTTOM LEFT Cold Ozeki was a cutting-edge idea and ahead of its time in many respects. BOTTOM RIGHT An alley in Omoide Yokocho ("Memory Lane") in Tokyo's Shinjuku. Note the *sugidama* cedar ball hanging at the top of the photo, indicating that the pub serves sake.

an official history compiled in 720, recounts how Prince Nukata no Ohakatsuhiko, son of Emperor Ohjin (200–310), spotted a himuro (ice house) in Nara while hunting. The local governor showed the prince how snow was stored and stayed cool even through summer. According to W. G. Aston's 1896 translation, the governor added, "As to its use—when the hot months come it is placed in water or sake and thus used." The prince had the frozen stuff brought to the emperor who liked it enough to make a rule that winter ice would be stored to use later. Ancient wooden tablets also show that Prince Nagaya (684–729) owned a himuro in Nara. Modern-day excavations appear to support these records. Scholars speculate that Prince Nagaya also drank sake with ice to help beat the heat.

Summertime cold beverages were more widely available during the Edo period (1603–1868), thanks to urban icehouses, but the plebes really started enjoying cold drinks and shaved ice in the late 1800s when a merchant, Kahe Nakaga-

wa, started importing ice from Hokkaido. During the Meiji era (1868–1912), the labels on exported Kiku Masamune sake bottles read, "May be used either cold or moderately heated." But sake was still usually served hot or warmed.

In 1932, Nada brewery Ozeki released "Cold Ozeki," intended to be consumed cold. With the Japanese economy in poor shape due to the Great Depression, it might not have been the best time to release such a forward-thinking sake. There were other challenges. For one, its label had English on it, which wasn't unique for export sake, but was unusual for a domestic sake. Also, it was sold in what looked like a whisky bottle, not a traditional sake bottle. Finally, Ozeki wanted folks to drink Cold Ozeki, well, cold. In a world dominated by kan-zake, this was an anomaly. But the 1950s brought refrigerators to middle-class homes, which led to widespread consumption of cold beverages, with beer leading the charge. Japanese people became more and more used to drinking iced drinks. All of this created the necessary conditions for cold sake to become more popular.

In Japan, a common term for "chilled" or "refrigerated" sake is hiyashite. This refers to sake that has just been pulled from the fridge and has been cooled to around 50°F (10°C), depending on how the sake is stored. Within reishu, however, there are several distinct subcategories:

**Suzu-hie**, Meaning "refreshing chilled," this is served at 59°F (15°C). It offers a good balance of a lush, thick mouthfeel with chilled drinking experience and aroma.

**Yuki-hie**, "Snow chilled." Served at 41°F (5°C), the sake is on its way to being frozen. This slows down the compounds, resulting in muted flavors and aromas. Excellent on a blistering day, though.

**Mizore-zake**, "Sleet sake." This frozen sake slushy is another terrific summertime treat.

## HOW TO TASTE SAKE

There's drinking and tasting. Both are important and enjoyable, but tasting involves thinking deeply about the sake and structure of the sake. As with all tastings, don't wear cologne or perfume and be sure not to wash your hands with scented soap. Also, steer clear of coffee, spicy food or any other food or drink with strong aromas. You don't want anything that gets in the way of tasting the sake as fully as possible. Also, be sure to drink a chaser of water, called *yawaragi-mizu* (soothing water), to lower the alcohol level in the bloodstream. One sake-bar master told me that whenever customers request yamaragi-mizu, he knows they want to appreciate sake and not just get drunk.

In Japanese, tasting sake is called *kiki-shu,* or *kiki-zake*; the sake is usually at room temperature. Traditionally, a *kiki-choko*, a white porcelain-tasting cup with a two indigo rings inside forming what's known as a *ja-no-me*, or

snake eye, is used for tasting sake. The first step in tasting is to examine color and clarity. The blue rings in the kiki-choko are used for judging clarity, while the white helps assess color.

Next, nose the cup or glass. If the vessel is large enough, swirl gently to jostle the aromatic compounds. The scents experienced through the nose are called *uwadachika* in Japanese. What do you smell? There are no wrong answers; it's your nose. Think about whatever pops in your head. Don't force it. Keep in mind that the aromas in sake are much more compact than wine or whisky aromas. If you find yourself losing the aromas and are unable to discern any scents, take a short break and smell your hands. This will reset your nose. Floral and fruity *daiginjo* and *ginjo* sakes will typically have strong top notes, though many great sakes will not. Some aromas will be muted. Don't judge a sake by its top note alone. This is one way sake tasting differs from whisky and wine tasting.

Now take a sip. Let the sake gently move over

FAR LEFT Pouring and receiving are key parts of Japanese drinking culture. It's polite to pour and receive with two hands. LEFT Sake warms in a water-heating contraption called a *shukanki* or "hot sake machine."

the tongue and throughout the mouth, thinking about the mouthfeel. Is it sharp? Silky? Sweet? Acidic? Astringent? Breathe in through your nose. In Japanese, the aromas that travel through the nose to the mouth are called *fukumika*. Many sake flavors and aromas come through with the fukumika. In some sakes, this is more noticeable than the subtle top note. Think about the aromas and the flavors. Are they different? The same?

Swallow, and observe the finish. Was it long? Short? Crisp? Clean? Short, quick finishes are held in high regard, but thanks to the influence of wine and spirits, long aftertastes are getting a second look.

Take a brief moment to think about the sake, taking stock of the experience. There are fairly uniform standards for sake taste in Japan, with emphasis on balance, harmony, smoothness and whether not a particular expression is emblematic of its style. The term *zatsumi* is used to describe any roughness that interferes with those factors. However, sometimes zatsumi is good! It

might not win points in an official tasting, but those rough edges can give a sake personality and complexity.

The most important thing is whether or not you liked the sake. Make your evaluation, and if you enjoyed it, have another cup or glass, trying it warmed, hot, chilled or cold.

## The Flavors of Sake

A typical question for sake lovers in Japan is whether one prefers dry (*karakuchi*) or sweet (*amakuchi*) sake. This is the most basic differentiation in sake flavors.

On the back label of a sake bottle, the *nihonshudo* (sake meter value, which is the specific gravity of the fluid) is generally listed with either a plus or minus number. It will usually fall somewhere between -3 and +8. The easiest way to decipher this is that a sweet sake with a higher glucose content will have a minus number, because sugar is heavier than water, while a drier sake would have a plus value. Neutral readings hover close to zero. Simply put, very sweet sake is -10, while quite dry sake can be +10. However, those numbers can go higher! For example, Amano Sake in Osaka released an old-style sake with a nihonshudo of -100!

While the nihonshudo is the clearest indicator of sweetness or dryness, factors like alcohol percentages and acidity levels can affect flavor, as can each individual's perception of taste. This is why nihonshudo is not always the an accurate way to predict how a sake will taste. Speaking generally, sakes on either end of the nihonshudo scale will be very sweet or very dry. As of 2016, the average for table sake was +3.7, ginjo was

# THE DEEP FLAVORS OF UEHARA SHUZO SAKE

**Do you like *amakuchi* (sweet-tasting) or *karakuchi* (dry-tasting) sake? This question is typical for sake drinkers, but it overlooks the complex in-between flavors. "Truly tasty sake isn't just amakuchi or karakuchi," says Isao Uehara, owner of Uehara Shuzo. "Truly tasty sake has the umami of rice." Located on northwest side of Lake Biwa, the largest lake in Japan, the brewery is surrounded by fertile rice fields. You can taste those flavors in the sake it makes.**

While other small breweries have turned to automation to either streamline processes or produce very pure flavors, Uehara Shuzo makes its sake the old-fashioned way. The rice is steamed in a wooden *koshiki* tub—a rarity today. For some batches, the standard rice-cooling machine is used, but for others, the rice is cooled in the winter air. Wooden *kioke* brewing tubs sit alongside ubiquitous standard-use enamel tanks. The automatic press sits forlorn, as everything the brewery makes, from super-premium *daiginjo* to budget-priced *futsu-shu*, is pressed by a *sakabune* with the *tenbin-shibori* method, in which the weight of stones is used to gently press the sake. *Koji* is still made in small

wooden trays, and between 75 and 80 percent of the sake is made from yeast that lives naturally in the brewery. Even modern methods of making *yamahai* starter, such as using a power drill for mixing, or adding yeast, are eschewed for traditional techniques such as ramming the brew with a bat-like pole and the use of ambient yeast. Stepping into the brewery is like going back 100 years in time.

The rise of Niigata's *tanrei karakuchi* light, crisp and dry style of sake shifted the emphasis from umami to easy drinking, Uehara says. "Because there wasn't a focus on flavor, this simple contrast of sweet-tasting and dry-tasting sake arose." But recently, that divide is falling,

thanks to the rising popularity of umami-rich sake from breweries like Uehara Shuzo. "In the past, easy-drinking sake that was like water was seen as desirable," he says. "That's changed. Personally, I get tired of drinking sake that tastes like water." Uehara Shuzo aims to make sake that doesn't get dull by the second glass.

The brewery's Furosen-brand sake is made in the yamahai style, and the slower and lengthy fermentation results in rich, deep flavors. The previous *toji*, Hiroshi Yamane, started brewing in the yamahai style back in 1992. At that time, barely any brewery in Shiga was making yamahai sake. Yamane retired and has since passed away, but the style continues under the present toji, Yasuo Yokosaka. "When Yokosaka started, I just told him that Furosen was deep and has a quick finish," says Uehara. "That's it. I don't micromanage him— I entrust the brewing to him. He's the toji. He understands better than anyone how to make that

LEFT **Photos of the previous *toji* Hiroshi Yamane and the current one, Yasuo Yokosaka.**
ABOVE **A line-up of Furosen-brand sakes.**

happen." Although the equipment is the same, the water is the same, and yeast is the same, the sakes brewed under Yamane and Yokosaka differ slightly, showing that the toji has an ineffable influence. "Of course each toji has his own flavor. Yokosaka's newly brewed sake is beautiful and well-defined, while Yamane's was robust," says Uehara. "But what's interesting is that after aging, Yokosaka's sake becomes closer in character to that of his predecessor. With time, his sake is bound to become even closer to Yamane's." In the current sake world, many toji are more than happy to take center stage and show off sake they really want to make. Yokosaka's approach is much more in line with the world of the *shokunin* (artisan), deferring to the inherited house style. "Our toji is generously brewing to that style," says Uehara. "He's not trying to shine a light on himself." Instead, he shines it on the umami-rich flavors for which the brewery has become famous.

It's those deep flavors that, in 2019, led the world-class Noma restaurant in Copenhagen to select Uehara Shuzo's Soma no Tengu sake for its pairing menu (see tasting note on page 247). "Suddenly, I

got a call from my sales agent, who said, 'Congratulations!' I said, 'For what?'" Uehara had never heard of Noma, but after looking up the famed restaurant online, he was bowled over and delighted that such an internationally renowned restaurant was carrying the hand-crafted sake made at this little brewery in Shiga.

 "We're not focused on how our sake pairs with food," says Uehara. "Every year the variables change: the rice is slightly different, the

TOP *Sugidama* hang outside Uehara Shuzo. ABOVE Using a chalk drawing, Isao Uehara explains how a *tenbin shibori* (balance press) works ( for more, see page 60).

weather is different . . . So you can't pinpoint specific flavors in certain meals. If pairings emerge, great," he says. "But we're not thinking about that at all." At Uehara Shuzo, they're only thinking about how to make delicious sake.

TOP LEFT TO RIGHT Sanshoraku Junmai is ricey (see p. 232); Tamagawa Shizen Shikomi Junmai Yamahai is milky (p.246); Fu has apple nuances (p.216). CENTER LEFT TO RIGHT Denshu Tokubetsu Junmai tastes of melon and banana (p.231); Ishizuchi Junmai Ginjo Green Label tastes of orange (p.227); Honjozo Kita no Nishiki Houmon is flowery (p.219); BOTTOM LEFT TO RIGHT Honjozo Muroka Nama Genshu has notes of Asian pear (p.217); Yuki no Bosha Yamahai Junmai is creamy (p.231); Junmai Koshu Yamahida Genshu 2002 tastes of nuts, mushrooms and honey (p.238).

+3.9, *junmai* was +4.4 and *honjozo* was +4.6. Average nihonshudo readings also vary with region. For example, as of 2016, the average for Niigata was +6.0, while Aomori averaged –0.3. This could be interpreted as meaning Niigata sake is typically quite dry, while Aomori's sake is on the sweeter side. It's more accurate, however, to think of flavor profiles beyond the long-standing "sweet" and "dry." But as my co-author

Takashi Eguchi points out, typical sake aromas and flavors can be divided into five basic categories. First, those derived from ingredients such as rice, rice flour, cooked rice, rice bran, hay, marshmallow, mochi, chestnuts (in the case of koji rice), minerally nuances from the water, cotton candy, evaporated milk and other sweet milky notes; second, fruity and flowery aromas produced by the yeast, such as apple, Asian pear, lychee, muscat grape, banana, melon, apricot, orange or mandarin, green citrus, strawberry, lily and lavender; third, sharp nuances from the alcohol, such as pepper, rosemary and grass; fourth, nuances created during fermentation like cheese, butter, yogurt and fresh cream; and fifth, matured nuances that come through aging such as dried fruits, chocolate, maple syrup, caramel, honey, dried mushroom, Japanese cedar or oak from casks, nuts, soy sauce, Darjeeling tea, wax and even vanilla.

Some of these tastes would be considered "off-flavors," such as any yogurty, grassy, or caramelized notes, and in the country's nationwide sake competition, the Annual Japan Sake Awards, points would be deducted for their presence. But that certainly doesn't mean they're bad—anything but!

## Off-flavors

These are aromas and flavors predominately viewed as undesirable. But not all off-flavors are the same for every brewer, nor are they unwanted. Some off-flavors fill out the flavor of a sake, offering a wider range of tastes. For most, a desirable sake aroma is the *ginjoka*, or "ginjo aroma," of apple, banana and pear. Fresh, elegant and often fruity aromas are ginjo signatures. The clean smell of rice junmai-shu or the clean crispness of *honjozo-shu* are also well regarded.

While off-flavors won't get high marks on sake entered into the country's biggest sake contests, some brewers—and customers, especially those outside of Japan—are open to off-flavors that smell and taste rather pleasant. For example, *koshu*, or "aged sake," which has been purposely allowed to break down and degrade, can smell nutty, which is an off-flavor; also, some *taruzake* smells like a cedar forest (for more on taruzake, see page 30). Breweries aiming for these aromas do not consider them off-flavors.

Bad off-flavors would include moldy smells or smells that indicate unhygienic standards or sloppy brewing. Many off-flavors are precursors or indicators of spoilage. Diacetyl, a lactic acid that grows in the main mash, will ruin the batch if it over-propagates. High quantities of this natural compound, which has a buttery smell, can turn into *tsuwari-ka*, or "morning sickness stink." Caproic acid causes unappetizing soapy or cabbage aromas. Cork taint, the bane of wine drinks, also appears in sake, even though corks are not used in production or in bottling. In sake brewing, the cork-taint compound, 2,4,6-trichloroanisole, can originate from the wooden trays used during koji making.

While aromas of fiber, paper and cardboard, as well as rubbery notes, which happen when sakes are left out too long, are unwanted aromas, certain off-flavors can make a drink delicious. The most important thing is understanding the brewer's aim. If you get a bottle of Dassai, a sake that is famous for its freshness and elegance, and it smells like sneakers, then you've got a bottle that's gone bad. But if you get a Tamagawa that is rich, savory and brown, then you are drinking some excellent aged sake.

Funky notes can be generated by the rice or even the koji. High levels of lactic acid can create yogurty, buttery or cheesy notes. Aged sake can smell like nuts, caramelized sugar or soy sauce, or have notes similar to the raisin aromas in brandy. "If sake with these flavors is paired correctly with food, then it's no problem," says Atsunori Takeshima, director at the Emishiki brewery. "But with putrid off-flavors, no matter what you do, it's no good."

# RAISE A GLASS TO ONE CUP SAKE

**It was 1964. The Tokyo Olympics turned the entire world's eyes on Japan for the first time since World War II. That year, one of the giants of the Nada brewing district, Ozeki, would release one of the most influential and revolutionary postwar booze products: One Cup Ozeki.**

Go to any convenience store or any supermarket in Japan and you'll see those glass cups with blue and white labels. The iconic One Cup Ozeki is everywhere. This isn't fancy sake, but honest, well-made *futsu-shu*. The One Cup Ozeki brand was the pioneer of the cup-sake segment and has spawned many imitators.

"We can bottle 1,000 One Cup Ozeki per minute," says bottling-plant manager Hiroshi Ogura. "We're aiming for 160,000 cups today." This plant, which specializes in the classic 180ml version, has two machines each churning out 500 cups. Another plant bottles the mini and jumbo cups, which require specialized machines.

In Japan, it's hard to imagine a time when the ubiquitous One Cup didn't exist. You can thank beer for that. Through the 1950s, sake sales were slumping and, in 1959, beer consumption overtook sake. The country's youth were drinking more beer, especially women. Those 1.8-liter (4-pint) glass sake bottles looked old-fashioned next to modern-looking canned beer. Ozeki was feeling the hop-scented heat and wanted to change the way people consumed sake. For centuries, sake was poured from a bottle to cups. This became the natural way people interacted with sake. Beer could be consumed in a similar matter but with the advent of beer cans in the late 1950s, it

could now be enjoyed privately. The president of Ozeki wanted to put sake in a cup, slap a label on it and sell it as is. R&D began in 1960.

Knowing that the Olympics would bring foreign visitors to Japan, Ozeki wanted to make an international splash. When One Cup Ozeki went on sale in 1964, coinciding with the Olympics opening ceremony, the label, created by graphic designer Joji Matsukawa, featured big English letters. The blue background and stylized English font were cool. A fuddy-duddy drink, this wasn't. Ozeki wasn't just trying to appeal to foreigners, but to hip Japanese youth.

New products have their problems. The cup was not airtight like today, leaking all over the place and infuriating shop owners. The labels (now paper with white backs) were painted directly on the glass. Looking at the label face on was fine, but from the back, the sake appeared blue, causing further complaints. A screw lid would've been the easiest for Ozeki. But the extra grooves on the glass would be right where the consumer's lips touched, causing an unpleasant drinking experience. So, instead, Ozeki decided to do the most difficult thing possible and create a ring-pull lid, designed to appeal to beer can drinkers. But Ozeki got the cup shape right from the get-go, with the original design done by industrial designer Iwataro Koike. In 1966, the brewery created a booze vending machine for One Cup. Kirin had tried selling beer in vending machines in 1962

but didn't find much success until the 1970s. But in 1967, Ozeki rolled out 100 One Cup vending machines in Tokyo. The one-100-coin price point and easy availability in a time before round-the-clock convenience stores made the ready-to-drink sake a hit, especially among construction workers who wanted to grab a drink at the day's end. In the decades that followed, especially as some got increasingly snobby about sake, that blue-collar image became hard to shake.

Throughout the years, Ozeki has continued to refine and perfect its One Cup. "A few decades ago, we were using imported Chinese glass to save money, but it kept breaking, so now we only use made-in-Japan glass," says Ogura. The glass is not UV treated, the idea being that One Cup Ozeki probably won't be on store shelves long enough to be damaged by sunlight. The current iteration is just about perfect. The pull-top comes right off and

the lip fits comfortably. The compact glass is easily held in the hand, while the mouth is wide enough to accommodate the bottom part of the nose, so you can smell the sake while taking a sip. Like Coca-Cola in a bottle, this iconic glass cup makes an everyday sake better.

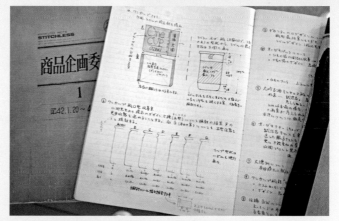

FACING PAGE One Cup comes in a variety of sizes. See page 221 for the tasting note. TOP Glass cups wait patiently to be filled with Ozeki sake. ABOVE Notebooks used during the design of One Cup. As these drawings illustrate, Ozeki thought in great detail about the lip of the cup, one of the factors that makes Ozeki such a comfortable drink. LEFT A bottling-line employee checks One Cup Ozeki.

Sake drinkers in Japan are so accustomed to clear, fresh-smelling sake that any sort of mature notes are instantly characterized as off-flavors. The country's National Research Institute of Brewing has set definitions that differentiate between *hine-ka* "old smell," and desirable aged-sake scents, called *jukusei-ka*. Hine-ka is often compared to the strong smell of rotten cabbage. During the first year or so of maturation, the amino acids and sugars are starting to react and the sake hasn't settled into aging on a smooth path. But after several years of aging, the round, caramel-like aromas take hold.

Dismiss all off-flavors as bad and you'll miss some truly interesting sake. Just stay away from brews that smell noxious, like mold or vomit.

## Crisp, Clean and Dry Sake

For decades, Niigata sake has been described as *tanrei karakuchi*; "tanrei" meaning crisp, clean and smooth, and "karakuchi" meaning dry. This style generally has relatively low acidity.

"Hard rice and soft water are hallmarks of Niigata sake," says Satoshi Murayama of the Taiyo Sake Brewery, noted for its immaculately clean, dry sakes. "This is how we make the tanrei style." Niigata hasn't always made refreshing sake. In the years after World War II, when the sweeter full-bodied sakes from Nada dominated, Niigata breweries tried to replicate those brews. "We had no choice, because that's what was selling," says Murayama. Even Taiyo used to make sweet sakes. "The brewing process had a fourth stage where sweet *amazake* was added."

By the 1970s, the Niigata Prefectural Sake Research Institute pointed out that the region's light, crisp sakes were starting to garner more and more praise. Niigata brewers were moving away from trying to replicate the Nada style and instead starting to make sake that suited their water and rice. Taiyo was hitting its stride with the tanrei karakuchi style, which it used to make one of the first widely available daiginjo sakes, Daiginjo Taiyozakari, released in 1972.

Niigata brewers often refer to the theory that sweet, heavy sakes predominate during periods of economic downturn, as people don't have enough cash to fill their bellies with flavorful sweets, and conversely, in periods of economic prosperity, dry and crisp sakes dominate. No sakes better suited the 1980s and the heady Bubble Era than Niigata's. This was a decade of

FACING PAGE, LEFT Satoshi Murayama displays recent awards the Taiyo Sake Brewery has won. FACING PAGE, RIGHT Taiyo was one of the *ginjo* pioneers, releasing Daiginjo Taiyozakari in 1972. THIS PAGE, LEFT This cup sake release might look familiar. THIS PAGE, RIGHT Taiyo's sake is also sold abroad under the Hiro brand.

white wine, vodka, shochu and healthy, light food. Niigata sake was the perfect fit.

In the 1970s, key infrastructure projects, like the Kanetsu Expressway joining Niigata and Tokyo, were completed. This proved beneficial when Niigata's brews started making waves with Tokyo drinkers, as it was easier to ship sake to the capital. In 1982, the Joetsu Shinkansen, the bullet train connecting Niigata and Tokyo, made it easier than ever for Tokyoites to jaunt up north to the land of rice and sake.

In 1985, Niigata's Asahi-Shuzo (not to be confused with Yamaguchi's Asahi Shuzo, makers of Dassai) launched its Kubota-brand sake in the mid-1980s, capitalizing on the country's ravenous demand for Niigata sake spearheaded by the delicious and highly desirable Koshi no Kanbai from Ishimoto Shuzo. Asahi-Shuzo, long a cutting-edge brewery, was one of the first to ditch *kioke* (wood fermentation tubs) for enamel tanks. Today, the inside of the brewery looks like something out of Stanley Kubrick's *2001*. The Kubota brand helped lead the tanrei karakuchi charge, making its way into supermarkets and liquor stores across the country.

The word "karakuchi" must have caught the imagination of beer makers too. In 1987, Asahi Breweries released Super Dry, featuring the characters *karakuchi* (辛口) on the label. The beer was a big hit, by 2005 outselling the heavier Kirin Lager, the nation's favorite beer until then. Kirin, however, coopted the "tanrei" moniker for its low-malt beers. Even so, when sake drinkers hear "tanrei" they automatically think of Niigata.

I remember spending a Sunday afternoon at Yoshinogawa, Niigata's oldest brewery (dating from 1548), tasting their full lineup of sakes. Every brew, from the excellent (and dry) *honjozo-shu*, its wonderfully earthy *junmai-shu* or its slowly aged and luscious *ginjo-shu*, had its own distinct arrival—whether subtle, brash or rich—but they all wrapped up in a clean and crisp fashion.

Still, not all Niigata sake makers are doing the dry style. "The Niigata style started with tanrei karakuchi, but we've been moving away from karakuchi," says Yosuke Tanaka of Imayo Tsukasa, who's been aiming for more umami in his brewery's sake with a nice tanrei finish. That crisp and clean finish is the most appealing part of the traditional Niigata style.

# PAIRING SAKE AND FOOD

The standard line is that, since sake is made from rice, it goes with anything. This is not true. Some brews pair better with certain dishes. There are several good rules of thumb regarding sake and pairing (see page 213.) Of course nothing is 100 percent certain, and you will always find exceptions. That said, here are some things to keep in mind.

### Brewing Style

The way a sake is made can provide hints at how to serve or order.

Fruity and floral *daiginjo* and *ginjo* sakes tend to perform best around lighter food. They're usually best chilled and are lovely in summer.

*Kimoto* and *yamahai* styles are nuanced and versatile, and hold their own with a wide range of food. They're not ideal for a dessert drink; they go better with the main meal. Both shine in the cooler seasons, because these brews typically are good at room temperature and heated.

*Bodaimoto* (*mizumoto*) style sake is highly acidic and tends to go well with cheesy dishes.

*Sparkling sake* is best served like champagne. It works well as part of the meal or with crackers and cheese, fruit and white chocolate.

*Nigori* is usually terrific with spicy foods.

*Koshu* can be paired in a similar fashion to sherry. Depending on the koshu's sweetness, dark chocolate might go well. It's usually brilliant with cheese.

*Kijoshu* was designed to be a sake that could be served with a full-course meal. It's sweet and often acidic, which is something to keep in mind when pairing.

### Polishing Ratio

Sakes made from finely polished rice—that is, daiginjo and ginjo brews—are typically fruity and floral. Meats, pasta and fish all tend to work well, as does spicy food, but be careful with

At an annual Dassai event in Osaka, Dassai 23 is paired with a fish dish.

TOP A test release of Dassai made with American-grown Calrose rice. BOTTOM Dassai 23 also pairs well with beef, at a Dassai event in Osaka.

highly aromatic sakes around fish as they can often overpower the food. They can hold their own with flavorful dishes, such as BBQ!

Sake made from less polished rice, especially the barely polished brews, tend to have more body and oomph. Pair them with steak, burgers and savory Japanese food like chicken teriyaki.

## Added Alcohol

*Junmai* sake tends to have more body than *honjozo* brews. The added alcohol in honjozo makes the sake lighter and sometimes even smoother. Junmai can be a bit chewier, which should be kept in mind.

But honestly, the best way you know what sake goes with what food is to try, taste and experiment. Nothing beats a taste test! Try not to pair blindly unless you have no alternative. A sake might seem to have certain characteristics on paper, but it will be an entirely different beast when poured into the glass. Sake is a drink that goes well with food, so be adventurous!

## Serving Sake the Noma Way

The two-Michelin-star Noma topped the World's 50 Best Restaurants in 2010, 2011, 2012 and 2014. Reservations for chef René Redzepi's new Nordic cuisine is among the most coveted on earth. The multicourse seasonal menus are paired with a wine-heavy beverage selection that has also included champagne, beer and sake.

"I don't recall my first sake," says Mads Kleppe, head sommelier at Noma in Copenhagen. "But I do remember the first one that really opened my eyes." That sake was Ine Mankai, made by Mukai Shuzo in northern Kyoto (see page 241).

When Noma moved to Tokyo for two months in 2015, Kleppe gave sake another try, visiting some breweries. "It was a real revelation to see sake as a cultural drink, an artisanal product and something to serve with food in different settings." At Noma Tokyo Kleppe served Ine Mankai with roasted wild duck. "When we returned to Copenhagen, it was only natural for

As with many great restaurants, it's not only the approach to food that makes Noma so interesting, but also its thinking about drinks. The current Noma is located in an old naval warehouse where the Danish military stored mines and built ships. The location has space for the restaurant to grow more food and experiment with fermentation.

us to bring sake back," he says. "People were excited because the sake was so different from the sake that had been served in Europe before."

Sake then began appearing on Noma's pairing menu in Copenhagen. While the restaurant doesn't serve Japanese food, it has its own fermentation lab and serves up fresh, local ingredients—and fermentation and freshness are hallmarks of Japanese cuisine. Sake is a natural fit. Noma's decision to pair sake like any other drink, instead of only with Japanese food, shows an understanding of universal flavors that isn't limited solely by cultural constructs.

"In Europe, when working with wine and beverages, you only get exposed to very generic, average commercial sake," says Kleppe. "That's one reason it never really took off here." For many years, since sommeliers outside Japan didn't have access to a range of sake, working with the drink either felt limiting or didn't meet their needs. The rise of sake with floral aromas and higher acidity has interested more sommeliers. However, at Noma, the sake-pairing process is approached intuitively, free of simplistic pairing "rules" such as "junmai is good with beef" or "daiginjo goes well with chicken." Sake is versatile, but pairing depends on the brew, season and food.

"I've been here at Noma for a long time, where our way of thinking about food and cooking is quite unique." Kleppe's approach isn't simply to mix and match basic flavors. "You have to learn a new language," he says. "That's why working with sake felt really natural. There were no boxes to tick." One of Kleppe's go-to sakes is Daigo no Shizuku from the Terada Honke brewery. Terada Honke makes what it calls *shizen-shu*, or "natural sake," from pesticide-free organic rice and ambient yeast. "It's a sake that changes so much from brew to brew," says Kleppe. "At Noma in

Tokyo, it was the first drink in our pairing menu, but at our new Noma here in Copenhagen, it was served for dessert. That's how versatile sake is."

## Choosing a Serving Vessel

At Noma, Ine Mankai was served in a wineglass, while Kleppe served a chilled nigori sake from Akishika Shuzo in Osaka in beautiful chilled ceramic cups. The cup or glass can affect the way sake tastes. The best choice of vessel depends on the sake, how it is served, and what drinking vessels are available. The key factors below may help you choose.

The saucer-like *sakazuki* is uncommon in daily use. Lacquered or made from porcelain, it's typically reserved for weddings or other ceremonies, as it has been for centuries, and not judging sake. Interestingly, prior to the 1300s, unglazed earthenware *kawarake* saucers were used at ruling class banquets for boozing. These were analogous to modern-day Red Solo Cups and were pitched after use. These days, Jingo-ji Temple in Kyoto lets visitors throw kawarake saucers to ward off evil.

While the sakazuki was still used for formal ceremonies, the *ochoko* or *choko* started being used for informal drinking in the Edo period (1603–1868). Today the ochoko is the default sake vessel, easier to drink from than the saucer-like sakazuki. Historically, the choko was not exclusively for sake: there were soba choko

ABOVE LEFT Wooden *masu* or *kimasu* are often used at festivals where sake is served. While iconic, they are not ideal. The lip is not designed for drinking, and the wood can affect flavor. ABOVE Ceramic jugs could be easily refilled, cleaned and reused.

used for noodle sauce. Once sake drinking became a daily activity for the masses, the choko were likely repurposed from food to booze. According to the *Morisada manko* (Morisada's sketches, 1837–53), a catalog of contemporary Japanese culture, choko were made of porcelain but not usually lacquered. At Japanese restaurants, sake is traditionally enjoyed via the ochoko or the *gui-nomi* ("chug" as in to "chug a drink"), which is typically larger. Not all sakes work in an ochoko or gui-nomi, especially highly fragrant brews.

Daiginjo and ginjo sakes often need wine-type glasses rather than sake cups. The extra space at the top of the glass traps the aromas for nosing enjoyment. However, sake pros in Japan do still taste ginjo sakes with kiki-choko vessels.

Since kimoto- and yamahai-style sakes aren't usually highly fragrant, they can get lost in wineglasses. Instead, try an earthenware cup, an ochoko, a *kiriko* (small cup of cut glass), a small porcelain cup or, in a pinch, a whisky tumbler. Heavier, richer sakes feel more at home in earthenware cups. Japan's first sake was most

likely made in an earthenware pot, and the first serving cup was probably fired, unglazed clay.

Modern junmai and honjozo sakes can run the whole gamut of flavors, complicating things. It's best to test a pour in whatever cup or glassware is available. If the sake has a strong top note, go with a wineglass. Otherwise, use a traditional sake cup is best, if available, or a smaller cup.

In Japan, sake is sometimes served in a *masu*, a small cedarwood box that was traditionally used for measuring rice. According to legend, it became a sake-drinking vessel when punters wanted to make sure they weren't getting swindled out of a proper pour. These days, sake is sometimes served in masu at religious festivals. Restaurants may offer sake in a brimming masu, or put a small cup in a masu and fill it to overflowing so that it spills over into the little cedar box. Drinking from a masu can be awkward and uncomfortable at best. Restaurants that use it to serve overflowing cups might be demonstrating that they're not stingy on the sake, but that style of serving makes a fair mess.

If serving hot sake, you want a cup that holds heat, such as earthenware and porcelain. Some swear by tin (*suzu*), which conducts both heat and cold well. Generally, earthenware, porcelain, tin and glass all work well when sake is served

ABOVE LEFT Sake is often served with light eats or snacks. ABOVE Sake is an essential part of Shinto weddings with the couple imbibing nuptial cups three times during the ceremony. BELOW Some restaurants and bars let patrons pick their own sake cup. Which one would you choose? And why?

LEFT A selection of sake cups and a *katakuchi* pitcher. BELOW This style of glass, called a *seishu* glass, was designed by renowned designer Sori Yanagi at the sake industry's request to help promote chilled sake. Since its release in 1975, the now iconic seishu glass has been widely accepted and praised for its design, practicality and shape that evokes the traditional saucer-like *sakazuki*.

cold, but because of wine's influence, glassware has become increasingly prevalent.

As for serving vessels, the common ones are the traditional *choshi* pot-style server and the iconic *tokkuri* flask (the terms "choshi" and "tokkuri" can be used interchangeably). The *chirori* (sake warmer) can be also be used.

## How to Warm Sake

Warm sake is delicious and recommended. Ordering it in a restaurant should be no biggie, but what about enjoying it at home? Not a problem. Here are the most common methods:

**Hot water bath:** If you want a single serving of hot sake, put some hot water in a small dish then put in a sake cup filled with sake. Check the temperature with a thermometer or by tasting.

Experiment with methods and times to find the one that works best for you. Everyone experiences flavors and aromas differently.

**Stovetop:** Fill a pot with water and put in your tokkuri flask so that the water level reaches the flask's halfway point or slightly lower. Remove the tokkuri (this is important!), bring to a boil, and turn off the heat. Put the tokkuri back in. The longer you leave it, the hotter the sake. A minute and a half in the hot water gives warm sake (*nurukan*). Niigata's Kikusui brewery recommends covering the top of the tokkuri with plastic wrap to trap the aromas. You can check the temperature with a thermometer or remove the tokkuri when the sides feel warm.

**Sous vide:** Professionals might want to use the sous vide water heating technique, which circulates hot water in a pot at an exact temperature, using sous vide equipment like Anova, which clips right onto a pot or pan and

heats up water to precise temperatures.

**Microwave:** Try zapping your tokkuri in the microwave for about a minute, on the lowest setting (around 500 watts). If you want it hotter, heat for another 10–15 seconds. If it's still not hot enough, repeat the last step until you are satisfied. Some recommend wrapping the tokkuri's top with plastic wrap. This is not required. Some purists are against heating sake in a microwave, claiming that the intense heat strips nuances from the brews. (In Japan, many microwave ovens have convenient sake settings options, making heating up sake a cinch.) But please, don't put sealed mini bottles of sake in the microwave as the metal caps could spark and become hazardous.

If you don't have a tokkuri, use a coffee mug. It performs well when heated and actually makes for a nice sipping vessel.

## Freshness and Storage

Ideally, sake should be stored out of sunlight. If it's unpasteurized or needs chilling, chuck it in the fridge. Either way, don't leave it for too long. Sake generally doesn't get better in the bottle and you can't store it and expect it to stay the same. Think of sake like fruit: it will go bad, and you need to drink it while it's still fresh, generally within the first three to six months after shipping. Many daiginjo sakes simply fall apart the longer they're kicking around. *Nama* sakes

LEFT Tin *chirori* (sake warmers), originally intended for warming, are increasingly used for serving. ABOVE *Kiriko* (cut glass) cups are excellent with chilled or room-temperature sake.

are even more fragile; think of them like raw fish. You won't want to leave them around, even in the fridge, for extended periods of time.

However, if you get a robust kimoto or yamahai, a hearty junmai or honjozo, or even a durable ginjo, it could be possible to leave the brew aside for an extended period before opening. The Daishichi brewery (page 48) says its sake gets better with age, and Philip Harper at the Kinoshita brewery (page 127), recommends buying the oldest bottles you can find. If you do plan to age sake on your own, it's a good idea to taste before aging to see how it changes during the do-it-yourself maturation process.

# THE BEAUTY OF CLAY VESSELS

**"I've always found that 85 to 90 percent of people just want to drink," says ceramics dealer Robert Yellin. "It could be in a paper cup. They don't care." That remaining 10 to 15 percent do care, Yellin adds. "Those quirky few want to drink the proper way with the utensils that were meant for sake. That's what *shuki* were all about." Shuki means "sake vessel," or "sake set," the traditional cups and flasks that have been used for centuries.**

Yellin's gallery is tucked away in a beautiful old Kyoto teahouse. Jazz plays over the stereo speakers; Yellin tells me that Chick Corea once lived in this house. The tatami room on the first floor is filled with Japanese pottery, or *yakimono*.

"I particularly love sake vessels," he says. "That's how I got started in the pottery world." Yellin is one of the world's leading authorities and dealers in Japanese ceramics, specializing in contemporary artists. He moved to Japan in 1984, and "like everyone" thought he would only stay a year. He stayed longer. Much longer.

Everything changed for Yellin after seeing photos of shuki in Hiroshi Kondo's book *Saké*. "I thought, look at all these cool things. I got to find out more." He threw himself into learning as much as he could. "One day, someone gave me a Bizen cup," he says. Bizen is a region in Okayama famous for its distinctive pottery style that's over 1,000 years old. "That cup turned my whole world upside down. It was this dirty brown looking brick thing. But that was my Western aesthetics looking at it, and I had to turn that off."

Western ideas of beauty are still firmly rooted in Renaissance no-

tions of symmetry and perfection. Traditional Japanese concepts of beauty are not. "It's the Zen Buddhist *wabi-sabi,* if that's what you want to call it." The idea of wabi-sabi is that nothing is perfect, nothing is finished and nothing lasts forever. "It's nature working with human endeavor and the idea that there are things you cannot control." In yakimono, that means cracks, pits, asymmetrical fissures and the like. Pots, bowls and cups that are not perfect, and that is why they are beautiful. Bizen pottery is the epitome of wabi-sabi.

That cup became his teacher, Yellin says, adding that he might not be able to explain the exact moment Japanese aesthetics finally clicked. "Maybe it was when I put some sake in the cup, and that made the vessel's walls glisten. The colors became richer. "That cup also taught me about the history of Japan," Yellin says. "I thought, boy, wow, there is a whole lot of history and culture in that little cup."

Yet, in recent years, there has been a move away from shuki to wineglasses. "I know people who say they'll never drink sake out of a ceramic cup," says Yellin. "It has to be something with a rounded base, like a Riedel glass. That's fine—

everyone has their own personal preferences, and the main thing is that you enjoy the beverage." Yellin says that he, too, occasionally drinks sake out of a glass. Of course, glassware has been instrumental in helping sake expand internationally, because Western restaurants aready have wineglasses on hand. "I get it," Yellin says. "People want to see the clarity and the viscosity."

With the increased use of glassware, something is being lost and something is being gained. Sake can reach more tables across the world. Yet, the traditional way it was imbibed is being pushed aside in the name of progress. "I just love the feel of clay—the earth," says Yellin. "I love going into the kitchen and thinking about which cup I want to use. It's like picking out

music. It adds to the ambiance and the mood."

Traditionally made clay sake vessels have an even deeper meaning. These are pieces of earth formed by hand and then put into a blazing hot kiln. "I call them 'clay jewels,' because they're made of the materials of nature and the elements of life itself—water, fire, air, clay and the human spirit," says Yellin. "Each piece is unique. You will only get one that way in the kiln. It's different from mass-produced glass." The way the inside of each cup reflects light depends on the time of day and the sake. This is why there is a long tradition in kabuki plays of characters seeing reflections and visions in their sake cups. Unlike glass, which strips the sake bare, exposing everything, ceramic ware unlocks the imagination. You contemplate the sake in a way that isn't possible when drinking from an all-revealing glass.

"I think for a Western audience, glassware makes for an easier approach," says Yellin. "Like I said, the majority of people just want to drink; they don't care if it's from a paper cup." But those who are interested in experiencing how sake has been traditionally enjoyed for centuries are in for a real treat.

The Robert Yellin Yakimono Gallery has a wide range of sake cups and *tokkuri* flasks. If you are visiting Kyoto and interested in purchasing *shuki*, the gallery is highly recommended. Keep in mind that these vessels are made by some of Japan's most venerated potters, which is reflected in prices.

# THE SWEET SAKES OF EMISHIKI

*Kijoshu* is super sweet sake. "Your typical kijoshu is made quite sweet with a high alcohol percentage, but then brewers drop that percentage down to 13 to 14 percent," says Atsunori Takeshima, the 39-year-old director at Emishiki Brewery in Shiga. "We don't. We release our kijoshu as undiluted *genshu* at 17 percent alcohol." Cutting the brews with water makes them lighter, but Emishiki's sake is so smooth and round that the subtle, yet high alcohol percentage doesn't smack you in the face. Instead, it sneaks up. "Kijoshu should be sweet, and it should be strong," he says with a wide grin. Otherwise, what's the point?

Emishiki bottles its brews with avant-garde labels and beautiful art. "I didn't study design in college," says Takeshima, who met his wife, whose family owns the brewery, at Tokyo University of Agriculture. "If you just notice what's on the billboards in Tokyo, you can pick up a good design sensibility." Newly wed Takeshima arrived at Emishiki in 2007. For decades, the company had survived on selling its sake to Gekkeikan to be blended and resold, but in the year 2000, that contract had not been renewed. There was no local following and no fans. Emishiki needed a complete overhaul.

"Up until then the dry *tanrei kara-kuchi* style of Niigata had dominated," says Takeshima, himself a Ni-igata native. "I thought there was going to be a shift to fragrant, sweeter sakes and so it would be beneficial to change our style."

During the third stage of the brewing process, Emishiki adds its junmai-shu sake instead of water. This stops the fermentation and makes the brew sweet. The added sugar overwhelms the yeast, causing it to emit even more acidity. Typically sake is not that acidic, but kijoshu is at least twice as acidic due to this process. In Emishiki's case, because its sake is so sweet and so strong, the acidity is beautifully balanced. "We're still making ginjo style sake, so it has to be balanced," says Takeshima. Any more acidity, he explains, would ruin that interplay.

BELOW, LEFT TO RIGHT Rice steams at Emishiki during morning brewing. A brewery worker scoops out steamed rice with a shovel. The bags used for pressing sake are meticulously cleaned. Bags filled with sake are folded and carefully laid on top of each other for pressing. The weight of the bags prevents the sake from spilling out. Atsunori Takeshima holds an isshobin (1.8-liter [4-pint] bottle) of Emishiki's Sensation brand (see page 236). THIS PAGE, RIGHT Lab equipment that is used to analyze sake.

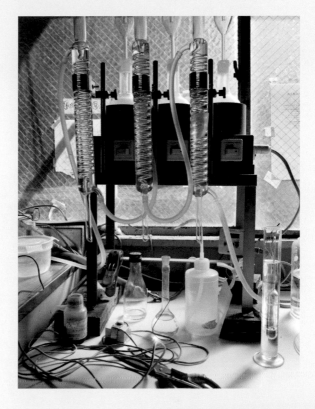

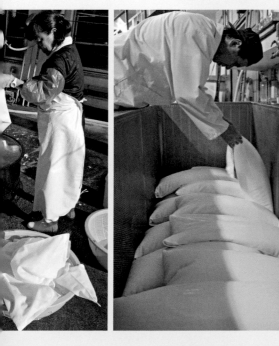

殿斎酒造

At its heart, sake is about the people who make it, and the people who drink it. The yearly *doburoku* festival at Zenkonji Kasuga Shrine in Higashi-Osaka is a chance for locals and sake makers to mingle.

# FROM SACRED BOOTLEG BOOZE TO BIG BUSINESS: A BRIEF HISTORY OF SAKE BREWING

## THE ORIGINS OF SAKE

Japan's first alcoholic drink wasn't made from rice, but more likely, fruit. It was a wine produced thousands of years ago, possibly from wild grapes and berries. Archaeologists have found carbonized traces of fruit seeds in pots from the Jomon period (14,000–300 BC) that were apparently designed for fermentation.

The theory that wine was the first alcoholic drink made in Japan is supported by the fact that rice wasn't introduced from China and Korea until 2,500 or 3,000 years ago. With the advent of rice farming in the late Jomon period, Japanese rice booze was born. But proper sake came much later, once rice production stabilized. According to the *Kojiki*, Japan's oldest official historical text (711–712), a visitor named Susukori from the Baekje Kingdom in modern-day Korea brewed excellent sake that got the emperor hammered. In the 8th century, the imperial court in Nara established its own brewing department called

Miki-no-tsukasa (aka Sake-no-tsukasa). It wasn't until the Muromachi period (1333–1573) that privately owned breweries came into their own, and commercialized sake production firmly established itself outside Buddhist temples and Shinto shrines. By 1580, the three-step brewing process, which continues today, had already been established. But before all that happened, the conversion of rice to alcohol arose in a far more primitive tradition: mouth-chewed sake.

### Brewing by Mouth

*Kuchikamizake*, or "mouth-chewed sake," was one of the earliest alcohols made in Japan. The brew is exactly what its name says it is: sake made by chewing rice. Here's how it works: the amylase enzyme in human salvia saccharifies the rice starch, resulting in a sugary, watery paste that was spit into an earthenware vessel. Once this chemical breakdown occurs, naturally occurring yeasts in the atmosphere consume the sugars, producing alcohol. It's thought that the word *kamosu*, meaning "to brew," is related to the word *kamu*, meaning "to chew."

This primitive process flourished from around 400 BC, or perhaps even earlier. In the early centuries, kuchikamizake probably wasn't made just with rice, but most likely millet and nuts, too. The same process developed elsewhere in Asia, such as the Pacific Islands, as well as South America and Africa. In China, however, a multistage brewing process was already being used to make liquor.

The widely held belief is that women, especially virgins, made kuchikamizake, but according to *Osuminokumi fudoki* (The records and customs of Osumi), both men and women in what is now eastern Kagoshima Prefecture would gather to chew and spit rice for brewing. While *Osuminokumi fudoki* was written in the early 8th century, the customs it mentions date back earlier. In Okinawa, which was another kingdom entirely back then, and among the indigenous Ainu people of Hokkaido, making a type of kuchikamizake continued until the mid-7th century. For example, there are mentions of kuchikamizake made from rice in Okinawa as late as the 15th century, and there are stories of it being made in a shrine in the northern city of Akita as late as the 1940s. Locals say, however, that it ended there after World War II. When contacted about this, the shrine denied having any records of kuchikamizake being made there. (As of this writing, the mouth-chewed brew is currently not made at any shrine in Japan.) However, the 2016 hit anime *Your Name* featured kuchikamizake as a pivotal story point, showing shrine maidens making it for a rural ritual in contemporary Japan. This is unlikely, but faux kuchikamizake—not actually chewed by mouth—went on sale in an effort to capitalize on the anime's success.

While drinking spit sake probably doesn't sound appetizing, the biggest limitation is actually production. Making kuchikamizake in large quantities is difficult, and the practice was discarded once better brewing techniques were imported from China via the Korean Peninsula. Over 9,000 years ago, China was already making a variety of wine from wild grapes, honey and, yes, rice. The Chinese didn't have a recorded tradition of kuchikamizake. Instead, they made highly concentrated yeast starters to brew booze using biochemical techniques that were highly advanced for their time.

In 2007, fermentation researcher Takeo Koizumi recreated kuchikamizake in a Tokyo University of Agriculture lab for Japanese TV. The professor had four female students he dubbed the "Kuchikami Girls" chew on steamed rice for four minutes before spitting it into laboratory flasks. Afterward, the students complained that the lengthy chewing made their jaws and heads hurt. A week later, the porridge-like mixture had fermented into a brew with a 5.2 percent alcohol content—considerably lower than that of refined sake. However, the kuchikamizake had four times the sugar and acidity of sake, making for a sweet-and-sour yogurt-like concoction.

For modern tastebuds, used to a range of flavors, the idea of spit sake might not be appetizing, but for people several thousand years ago, it probably was a guaranteed good time, chewing headaches aside.

## The Ancient Doburoku Method

*Doburoku* is the oldest surviving method of making sake. There are a variety of ways to brew it, but the basic premise is simply this: steam rice, mix it with *koji* and mash it up in water. In a couple weeks, you'll have something that will get you drunk. It is unfiltered and unrefined.

This is a drink with a complex history. Since the Meiji period (1868–1912), breweries could get a license to make unfiltered sake. But doburoku is not just unfiltered booze; it can also be *omiki*—sacred sake. Omiki is used as an offering to shrine deities, and Shinto priests use it in purification ceremonies, such as during groundbreaking ceremonies for new buildings. In Shinto weddings, the bride and groom both drink sake to purify themselves. (They usually don't drink doburoku, but refined sake that has been brewed outside of the shrine and then blessed.) Traditional omiki is not pressed, however, as doing so would force the hand of humans on to this religious brew. Not filtering the brew keeps all the sacred grains in the sake.

Among farmers, doburoku has traditionally been a drink they make from their crop. Just as they cook and eat rice they grow, they brew it and drink it. Sake used to be more expensive, so it was cheaper just do make it yourself. For centuries, farmers were making doburoku while professional brewers across the country were using the latest technology to create their booze.

In 1899, home brewing was made illegal after a series of restrictions of the centuries-old practice. This wasn't merely because the Japanese government was filled with killjoys, but because they ran a country that increasingly needed revenue sources. At that time, sake taxation was increased to pay for the military, and it's estimated that home brewing, which may have amounted to a fifth or more of the sake being made in Japan, was also on the rise. In 1880, the restrictions on home brewing had begun. Two years later, home-brewing licenses were required, and doburoku sales were prohibited. After the first Sino-Japanese War, doburoku for home use was taxed, and in 1899, it was banned altogether. This wasn't the first crackdown on home brewing, nor would it be the last:

A print depicting the myth of the serpent-dragon, Yamata-no-Orochi. The Shinto God Susanoo left sake for the dragon, who drank it, passed out and was slaughtered by Susanoo.

in AD 646, for example, folks were asked to limit consumption (then, probably homemade doburoku). Refined sake has also experienced crackdowns, such as in 1252 when the Kamakura shogun temporarily halted sales. Fifty years later, sake was banned in Kyoto, but according to Suzanne Marie Gay in *Moneylenders of Late Medieval Kyoto*, it's unclear whether the ban was enforced.

In Japan, it is illegal to make any beverage with an alcohol content greater than 1 percent at home. So forget homebrewed sake and do-it-yourself beer. Homemade *umeshu*, a liqueur made from *ume* fruit (a type of apricot often mistakenly called a plum), is legal. However, people in Japan are not actually making the alcohol; they buy spirit that is already distilled—and taxed—to mix with the fruit and sugar to make umeshu. Before 1962, when liquor tax laws were changed, even making umeshu was illegal in Japan.

At the time when personal brewing was outlawed, the country's slogan was *fukoku kyouhei*, "rich country, strong military." By 1897, liquor taxes accounted for over 30 percent of the country's national tax income. (By comparison, this number was barely 2 percent in 2017!) The government wasn't just taxing booze, but soy sauce, sugar, salt, kerosene and textiles—whatever it could to raise revenues and pay for the

modern naval warships, guns and troops that made its growing war machine. Taxes had been going up since the 1880s, putting pressure on brewers and driving many out of business. Doburoku had been a way rural folks could enjoy a brew without having to pay extra to the taxman. But with more 20th-century wars on the horizon, the Japanese government needed every last yen it could get.

Today, making doburoku is illegal without a license. Dozens of Shinto shrines have the license, but a small number actually brew it themselves. They pay alcohol tax—not on what they sell, because legally they can't sell it, but on what's brewed. For shrines, making doburoku is a financial loss. But those that still brew aren't doing it for money, but to preserve culture.

Starting in March 2003, the government began recognizing doburoku "special zones," areas in which the unfiltered brew could be made. These licenses are for farmers who want to make their

FACING PAGE At Zenkonji Kasuga Shrine, *doburoku* is brewed in a small structure called Zoshu Saiden (Sake Brewing Sanctuary). Brewers remove their shoes and don slippers inside. BELOW, LEFT TO RIGHT Making doburoku; cooking rice to pound into rice cakes; cooling the rice; braiding ropes for Shinto decorations.

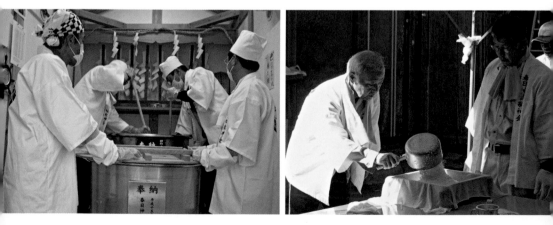

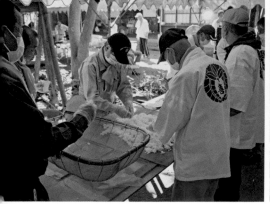

# THE DOBUROKU BOOTLEGGER

**"All the farmers made *doburoku*," says 83-year-old Isonobu Kawasaki. "Sake used to be too expensive, so rural people made their own. My grandmother was a doburoku master."**

Kawasaki flashes a big mischievous smile, while his eyes dart around his farmhouse in rural Toyama Prefecture, looking for something. I take inventory of the room, noting two calendars, two clocks, multiple jars of glue, and shelves stacked with portable radios. "This is my doburoku brand," he says, holding up a label. It reads "Yakunin Goroshi" (役人殺し), or "Bureaucrat Killer." Kawasaki is Japan's most infamous doburoku brewer, creating hooch that has a balanced sweetness and acidity. Doburoku might be unrefined sake, but that doesn't mean it's not good.

It's all done right here. "That over there is where I make the *koji*," he says, pointing to a box that resembles a portable cooler. It's outfitted with a heating lamp, which allows him to control the temperature.

He'll wake up in the middle of the night to check on the koji. "Here's what I'm brewing now," Kawasaki says, walking into the adjacent room (which is lined wall to wall with books) and lifting the lid off a small tub. And that brings our brewery tour to a close.

When locals stop by, Kawasaki is quick to offer a glass of doburoku. He's not brewing to make money; rather, it's because he's a farmer. But brewing has got Kawasaki into a heap of trouble. In October 1996, tax authorities raided Kawasaki's Toyama home and his Tokyo rice shop. A case was filed against him for violating Japanese liquor tax law, but Kawasaki argued that the charges were "nonsense" because doburoku was a traditional farming beverage and he was brewing his for personal consumption.

ABOVE The Kawasaki family shop, which was raided in 1996 and a case filed against Kawasaki for violating Japanese liquor tax law for brewing his own *doboroku* sake. In his defense, Kawasaki argued he was brewing for his own personal consumption. BELOW The bootleg booze improves during the cold weather, Kawasaki says.

This wasn't the first court case involving doburoku. Toshihiko Maeda, author of the 1981 book *Doburoku o tsukurou (Let's make doburoku)*, was also charged with violating Japanese liquor tax laws. Maeda's defense was that, since he had the right to brew for himself, the charges violated his constitutional right to the pursuit of happiness. The case went all the way to the Japanese Supreme Court with a ruling handed down on December 14, 1989. Maeda lost and had to pay a fine amounting to several thousand dollars.

With that legal precedent, perhaps Japanese tax authorities thought Kawasaki would be an easy mark.

He was not. While acting as his own attorney, the bootlegger did everything possible to grind the wheels of justice to a halt. Kawasaki would turn in legal documents written in pencil. Instead of using kanji characters, he would write things out phonetically in katakana. Since Japanese is rife with homonyms, the authorities would have to continuously check with Kawasaki to clarify what he wrote. Taking Kawasaki to court turned into a major pain in the ass.

On December 12, 1997, Kawasaki was found guilty of violating the Liquor Tax Law, with the presiding judge saying that the way in which the defendant ignored the law was "remarkable." Even with a fine of several thousand dollars and a four-month prison sentence (with a two-year stay of execution), Kawasaki asserted that it was only remarkable because the law was bad. He added that he was going to keep brewing doburoku—as he has. "But don't you have a dobu-

roku brewing license now?" I ask. Kawasaki laughs, "Nope!" Even after the court case, Kawasaki sold sake home-brewing kits. Was that legal, I venture. "It was just the actual kit, not the ingredients, so yes," Kawasaki replies. "Which means it wasn't much fun."

I look closely at the label for his Bureaucrat Killer brand. In Japanese, it reads, "Mr. Taxman, this is doburoku." The label acknowledges that the doburoku was brewed without a license and clearly spells out the Liquor Tax Law it violates and that doing so could mean up to five years in prison. Kawasaki is picking a fight. But for the past several decades, the authorities have left him alone. "I think they got tired of me," he says with a grin, adding that he thinks the post-1990s doburoku liberalization was probably thanks to his battle in court.

ABOVE Isonobu Kawasaki shows off the "Bureaucrat Killer" label that he slaps on his bottles.
BELOW Besides brewing *doburoku*, Kawasaki also makes delicious miso.

TOP LEFT Bags of rice straw to be turned into sacred Shinto ropes. ABOVE A tray is filled with bottled doburoku. The Zenkonji Kasuga Shrine label is affixed to each bottle by hand. RIGHT Doburoku is completely unfiltered. Here, buckets are filled from the brewing tank and then bottled directly.

own doburoku from their own rice and offer the unfiltered drink at their inns and restaurants. The brew is taxed, of course, and has a minimum production requirement of 6 kiloliters (1,595 gallons), which comes to about 3,300 1.8-liter (4-pint) bottles. As of 2019, there were around 176 recognized doburoku areas in Japan.

The closest modern relative to doburoku is *nigorizake*. This type of sake, which didn't exist prior to the 1960s, is filtered and, while cloudy, it's still refined. Nigori's ancient, unrefined ancestor, doburoku, with its chunks of rice, is more of a porridge—and a boozy one, at that.

## Experiencing Japan's Sacred Sake

It's a few minutes after 8 am on October 1. We've just arrived, but the villagers started setting up hours ago. Yesterday a typhoon passed through, and there were fears of rain today. But here at Zenkonji Kasuga Shrine in Higashi-Osaka, it's a beautiful, clear morning, with mosquitos already buzzing around—perfect weather to make the unfiltered sake known as doburoku. The villagers are brewing it as sacred sake.

"Everyone making doburoku here has to be at least 60 years old," says the shrine's head priest, Yukichi Takamatsu. Turning 60 in Japan is a big deal because, by the old calendar, it marks a person's rebirth. The villagers are decked out in festival *happi* coats which are emblazoned with the shrine's name and emblem. Men are doing all the brewing, wearing yellow towels wrapped around their necks to denote their 60-plus years. A red towel means the participant has just turned 60. One man fanning steamed rice has a blue towel, which Takamatsu explains means he is 59 years old and will be able to brew starting next year.

Even among the small number of Shinto shrines with doburoku brewing licenses, Zenkonji Kasuga Shrine, which has records of making doburoku back to the 1700s, is increasingly a rarity. Ohmiwa Shrine in nearby Nara, possibly the oldest Shinto shrine in Japan, has stopped brewing doburoku as of the time of this writing; Kasuga Grand Shrine, also in Nara, has outsourced its brewing to local sake brewery Harushika Shuzo, which makes the doburoku at its *kura* and then brings the brew to the shrine. "If the doburoku is brewed outside of the shrine, it has to be blessed by a Shinto priest to become omiki [sacred sake]," says Takamatsu. "But since we are brewing at the shrine, it doesn't need to be blessed. It already is sacred."

Soaked rice is placed into wooden trays and then steamed over an open flame. "We know it's done by how much steam it emits," a villager tells me. The rice is then cooled in the early October air and then taken to the *Zoshu Saiden* (Sake Brewing Sanctuary), where it is brewed with water drawn from mountain spring known as the "dragon's mouth."

"We're now using Gohyakumangoku sake rice with a 70 percent polishing ratio," says Takamatsu. "What we are brewing is getting closer to refined sake." Closer, maybe, but it's still doburoku, with unfiltered clumps of rice carrying over to the finished drink. Unlike the cloudy nigorizake, which is filtered, doburoku is bottled directly from the fermentation tank. In

decades past, the shrine's libation was made without any of the refinements of modern sake, using table rice polished to 90 percent (the same ratio as rice used for eating), wild yeasts and miso koji instead of rice koji, resulting in a lively, tart brew.

"We could make doburoku without adding any yeast," says Takamatsu. "Whatever was in the air or living in the Zoshu Saiden converted the sugars into alcohol." While the chemical process is clearly understood know, imagine how the shrine's parishioners must have felt centuries ago upon seeing mashed steamed rice in water turn into booze.

The quality of that old-time doburoku made from miso koji and wild yeasts varied wildly from year to year. The local tax office recommended stabilizing the brew, and in the late 2000s, Zenkonji Kasuga Shrine began adding lactic acid and a brewer's yeast from Takara Shuzo under the supervision of Yagi Shuzo, a Nara sake maker. The standard three-step process is used, plus an extra step in which the brew is fortified with amazake to help round out the flavor. The brew still varies from year to year, depending on the weather and the temperature. The fermentation time is only 15 days, which is on the short side. Brewing starts on October 1, after the harvest, so the doburoku is ready for an October 15 festival dedicated to Emperor Jimmu, the country's legendary first emperor who settled the Japanese people in the Yamato Plain in nearby Nara. The doburoku is a sacred offering.

Yet, like many Shinto events, making it is a lively, fun affair. The villagers drink and eat as they spend the day steaming rice and brewing doburoku. This is about community, about people coming together and expressing gratitude for the fruits of the real world and the spirit world. The smoke from the fire fills my nose, and I watch as a brewer uses a small ladle to fish out a couple of mosquitos that have gone belly-up in the brew. They chat and laugh, and it's the most

fun I've seen anyone have making sake, ever. It's also the only time I've watched brewers working and thought, "Yeah, I could do that." —And this is exactly the point of doburoku.

"Anyone can make doburoku, which is why it continued to exist after the advent of professionally brewed refined sake," says Takamatsu. "Doburoku is the easiest sake for regular people to make." When the history of sake is discussed, it is often stated that doburoku evolved into modern-day sake. That's true. But doburoku didn't vanish; it still exists, even if the Japanese government attempted to eradicate home brewing, making it illegal and punishable by fines and even prison. Shinto shrines have special doburoku brewing licenses (in Zenkonji Kasuga's case, the Takamatsu priest, not the shrine itself, has the license) so that they can brew for religious reasons.

Two weeks later, I return to the shrine to see the doburoku removed from the kura. Even though the shrine can't sell the doburoku, it still must pay a 75,000-yen tax on the alcohol production, causing understandable grumbling among the villagers who wonder why the government must get a piece of everything. While men brew the sake, wives, mothers and grandmothers stick labels on 1.5-liter (3-pint) plastic bottles to be filled once the doburoku is ready. A total of 160 of these bottles are divvied

ABOVE LEFT A rare opportunity to see rice for sake steamed outdoors at Shoryakuji Temple's bodaimoto festival. ABOVE After steaming, the rice is spread out in the open air to cool.

up among participants, and another 500 smaller 500 ml (1-pint) bottles will go to locals.

The brew is thick, a bit like the rice gruel I eat when I'm under the weather, but one that packs a boozy punch. The doburoku is 16 percent alcohol (and has gotten as high as 19.4 percent!). I take a sip, chewing on the grains of rice. It's tart, earthy and frank, more like a food than a drink. "It's good, right?" a villager asks, slapping me on the back with a grin. It certainly is.

## How Buddhist Monks Changed Sake

Shoryakuji Temple is one of the most important spots in the history of sake. Walking around the Buddhist temple grounds, you might not realize that fact. There's only a stone marker proudly proclaiming this as a birthplace of modern sake.

"This is the only Buddhist temple in Japan with a license to make sake," says Chobei Yamamoto, the *toji* and president of the Yucho brewery and maker of the excellent Kaze no Mori–branded sake. "Because of this temple's history, the government issued it a brewing license." We're at Shoryakuji in early January, a few days after the New Year's holidays. A handful of breweries from around Nara have gathered to make *bodaimoto* (aka *mizumoto*), the yeast starter the temple made famous. Built in 992, Shoryakuji used to be a massive complex with 86 subtemples. Today, only a few structures still stand and only one priest, the head priest Koshin Ohara, now lives there with his family.

In the Nara period (710–794), a brewing department was established in the country's ancient capital so that, possibly, brews like refined sake and white sake could be made for ritual celebrations. By the Heian period (794–1185), Buddhist priests studying abroad in China were bringing back advanced brewing techniques and fermentation know-how to make cutting-edge sake. By the first millennium, around 15 different types of sake were recorded. *Soboshu*, or "monks' sake," debuted during this period. Shoryakuji was not alone in making it; other large temples began brewing it too.

This special sake, along with martial training and Buddhism's religious teachings, helped the temples become a powerful economic and political force. While the warlord Oda Nobunaga

Warlord Oda Nobunaga enjoyed the monks' sake, but he wasn't a fan of their power. In this print Nobunaga defends himself during a coup at the Kyoto temple Honnoji on June 21, 1582. The temple was set ablaze and Oda ultimately died by *seppuku* ritual suicide.

Buddhist monks and brewers pray for good *bodaimoto* at Shoryakuji Temple in Nara.

might have enjoyed the monks' sake, he wasn't a fan of their power, and he moved to suppress Buddhism, thus weakening the temples, in his quest to unify Japan at the end of the 16th century. Nobunaga didn't hate sake (according to one lurid and probably unsubstantiated story, he drank sake from his enemies' skulls!), nor did he hate religion (contrary to another myth, Nobunaga did not persecute Jesuit missionaries). But he did hate threats to his power, and the massive temple complexes that brewed sake and housed warrior monks represented just that. Weakening the temples brought soboshu's heyday to an end, while a rising merchant class in the Edo period (1603–1868) supported the opening of thousands of privately owned sake breweries across the country.

Shoryakuji was torched in 1180, and saw strife during the Warring States period in the 16th century, but its greatest destruction and neglect occurred during the late 19th century, when the newly elevated imperial government denigrated

Buddhism, a Chinese import, to elevate the indigenous Shinto religion and, in turn, the Meiji emperor, in a consolidation of power that brought the shogunate to an end.

But this is where modern sake started. The most advanced monks' brew of all, called *bodaisen* after the mountain on which this temple sits, was made right here, using the pure water of the mountain and the sophisticated knowledge that its monks possessed. ("Bodai," which means "enlightenment" or "nirvana," is a word rich with Buddhist associations.) Initially, the sake was brewed for religious offerings, and was made from rice grown by feudal tenant-farmers. The yeast starter that characterizes it is called *bodaimoto* (known elsewhere as *mizu-moto*, or "water starter").

"Come here and take a look at this," says Yamamoto. He shows me where they've soaked raw rice for three days and drained the lactic acid–rich water into smaller tubs. The damp January air smells sour and like yogurt. That's the scent of lactic acid, which is essential in fending off harmful bacteria so that the desired yeast can propagate. "You can taste that sour sweetness in the final sake," Yamamoto says. At Shoryakuji, sake isn't being made, but *shubo* yeast starter. "More Nara-grown rice is then steamed over here," Yamamoto adds, pointing to a large *koshiki*. The steamed rice is spread on hemp blankets and placed outdoors to cool. Once cooled, it's then mixed with the lactic acid–rich water as well as koji and left for 10 days. The result is a starter with a heavy and healthy lactic acid concentration. The starter is divided up among eight Nara breweries, which then use it to brew special bodaimoto releases.

It's easy to think of Buddhist temples as mere religious institutions, but during their day, they were centers of learning and research, more like universities. Part of what was studied there was the modern equivalent of biotechnology. The temples were staffed not only by monk academics who were experts in religious studies and biochemistry, but also by *souhei* warrior-monks Temples like Shoryakuji sat on land that wasn't taxed, and made extra cash selling sake. By the early Muromachi period (1336–1573), Shoryakuji had entered a golden age, thanks in part to its innovative bodaisen sake—the Japanese analogue to the Trappist beer made by Catholic monks in Europe.

Other Buddhist temples were known for their sake, but the Shoryakuji monks were some of the most advanced brewers of their time. They used white rice both to make their koji and in brewing, resulting in sake known as *morohaku*, or "both white." (The standard style at the time was *katahaku*, or "single white," which used brown rice for the koji and steamed white rice for brewing. Using morohaku was revolutionary, and its effects were felt for centuries later. The

late 17th-century food encyclopedia *Honcho shokkan* listed *nanto morohaku* (Nara style morohaku) at the top of its list of famous sakes, showing just how important this technique was.

But morohaku wasn't the only innovation at Shoryakuji. The three-step mashing process known as *sandan jikomi*, which is now a standard part of sake brewing, was also pioneered here. Dividing the mashing process, when all the raw materials were mixed together, into several stages ensure healthy and highly concentrated yeast propagation as well as helped prevent spoilage. Chinese brewers had been using multistep mashing processes since at least the Song dynasty (960–1279), so it's possible that Buddhist monks from Shoryakuji saw it while they were studying (and boozing) in China.

Another innovation at Shoryakuji was that the monks stabilized the sake after brewing by heating it with the *hi-ire* process—hundreds of years before Louis Pasteur "invented" pasteurization in France. This technique was also originally Chinese, and may have been encountered by Japanese monks during their trips abroad. In any case, the final result was a filtered sake that is closest to today's *seishu*, or "refined sake." Before bodaisen, sake was cloudy and unrefined. This is why this small Buddhist temple in the rural Nara calls itself the birthplace of modern sake.

The bodaimoto-making method is recorded in the first sake-brewing guide, *Goshu no nikki* (The sake journal), written between the 14th and 16th centuries. Originally, bodaimoto was made during summer, because the lactic acid would propagate rapidly at temperatures between 68° and 95°F (20–35°C). However, compared to the later *kimoto*, *yamahai* and *sokujo-moto* starters, the risk of spoilage was high, and even before the sokujo-moto quick-starter method was developed in 1909, bodaimoto had largely fallen out of use. But since the 1930s, it has been used in Nara to make a style of doburoku for Shinto shrines.

The starter was resurrected in the mid- to late 1990s, thanks to scholars at Nara's Tenri University and local sake brewers like Yucho Shuzo, after an in-depth study of the *Goshu no nikki* brewing text. It was the first time in around 500 years that bodaimoto had been made at Shoryakuji. Now it is brewed shortly after the New Year's holidays in Japan, because the cold air quickly cools the steamed rice and brewers can squeeze in a moment to make the starter. Bodaimoto gives a sake unique yogurt and aged cheese notes, so while it might be trickier to use compared with other methods, it produces flavorful and mellow brew. In 1999, the Yucho brewery trademarked the term "bodaimoto" for Japanese sake, Western and Chinese alcohol, medicinal booze and fruit juice, while Shoryaku-ji trademarked it for food products, including dairy products, soup stock and even curry. A handful of brewers, however, do make bodaimoto outside of Nara prefecture and away from Shoryakuji. Trademark or not, bodaimoto is indelibly connected with this temple.

## Shinto Purity and the Divine Drink

As the above accounts show, sake has deep connections to both Shintoism and Buddhism, Japan's two dominant religions. Both have left an indelible mark on sake brewing in Japan.

ABOVE LEFT An early morning prayer for the sake gods. Offerings include fruit, vegetables, eggs, and the celebratory sea bream. ABOVE Izumo Taisha Grand Shrine in Shimane Prefecture is one of Japan's oldest and most sacred Shinto spots.

Shintoism, the country's indigenous beliefs, has the closest spiritual connection to the drink, with *omiki* (sacred sake) being offered to the gods. Shinto offerings are made to thank the gods for protection from calamity. At ancient Shinto festivals, sacred sake was brewed at shrines and then imbibed by the locals. As the brewing process developed during the 16th and 17th centuries, the Shinto deities remained integral to the process, as they are even today.

"Every morning when I come in, the first thing I do is go to the small shrine in the brewery and pray," says Mototsune Aikawa, toji at Gekkeikan's Uchigawa brewery. "This is standard at breweries here in Japan." Brewers offer thanks for the good sake they've made, and pray for safety. In the past, breweries were much more dangerous places, with perilously narrow staircases and open vats of bubbling booze. An accidental fall could mean death. Moreover, microbiology wasn't understood then, so turning rice into delicious sake seemed miraculous.

But Shintoism also places a huge emphasis on

cleanliness and protection from disease. Visitors to shrines wash their hands before praying (some even wash out their mouths). Salt, a natural disinfectant, is used to purify things as well, which is why sumo wrestlers throw a handful into the ring. (Sumo, a sport created for the entertainment of the kami, also has strong ties to Shintoism). Because sake can be susceptible to harmful microorganisms that cause batches to rot, cleanliness is paramount. Sake is strongly connected with certain Shinto sites like Ohmiwa Shrine in Nara, considered the birthplace of sake; Matsuo Taisha in Kyoto, famous for its water and revered by brewers; and Umenomiya Taisha, where Oyamazumi-no-kami, the first god to brew sake, is enshrined.

Shintoism is not a religion in the traditional sense. It has no holy text like the Bible, and there are no commandments or rules. It doesn't even focus on good versus bad; rather, it contrasts dirt, disease and death with purity and cleanliness. Shintoism is deeply connected to nature, and shrines dot the mountains across the country. The largest mountain, Mount Fuji, is sacred. Shintoism is so deeply embedded in Japanese culture that it wasn't even defined until Buddhism was imported in the 6th century and began took hold over the centuries that followed. Prior to that, the religion was nameless.

TOP LEFT A shrine at the Eigashima Shuzo brewery dedicated to Kyoto's Matsuo Taisha Shrine.
TOP RIGHT Sake barrels stand outside Mitate Shrine, next to Matsuo Taisha in Saijo, Hiroshima.
ABOVE Ohmiwa Shrine isn't only important to sake brewers but to any company that makes alcoholic drinks. Next to the sake casks are offerings of Asahi beer and Yamazaki whisky.

167

# THE OLDEST BREWERIES

A handful of locations claim or have claimed to be the birthplace of sake. The problem with dating the oldest brewery still in production is that not all sake makers have records of when they began brewing. Furthermore, over the centuries, breweries have gone out of business. Around three-quarters of Japan's sake breweries are less than 200 years old. Out of those dating further back, which is the most ancient?

Shimane Prefecture, on the Sea of Japan coast, claims to be where sake originated. As of this writing, Shimane's official website calls the prefecture "the birthplace of sake." In Japan's oldest text, the *Kojiki* (Record of ancient

TOP LEFT Many steps in sake production are still done the old fashioned way: by hand. TOP RIGHT Japanese celebrity Daigo is Saburo Takeshita's great nephew. He has his own sake line. ABOVE LEFT Saburo Takeshita with a portrait of his brother Noboru, former Japanese prime minister. ABOVE RIGHT The banners outside the brewery say "Izumohomare," the brewery's representative brand. FACING PAGE Konishi Shuzo's remake sakes, based on ancient recipes.

matters), from AD 711–712, there's the myth of Yamata no Orochi, an eight-headed, eight-tailed serpent-dragon. The Shinto god Susanoo left a vat of strong sake for the booze-loving Orochi, who drank it and passed out. Susanoo drew his blade and hacked the serpent-dragon to bits.

"This area in Shimane, the Izumo region, was the setting for the *Kojiki*," says Saburo Takeshita, owner of the brewery Takeshita Honten. (His brother, incidentally, was former Japanese prime minister Noburo Takeshita, one of the most influential politicians of the late 20th century.) "Because of that story of the Orochi, it's said that this is where sake originated." According to some, the legend might actually might have some basis in reality. "Even now, there's this big winding river nearby, the Hii River, that twists and turns like a snake," says Takeshita. "In the past, it was a source of flooding and caused damage, so perhaps ancient people based the story of the serpent on that winding river."

In any case, the area is rich in history. "Shimane was the world of Japanese myth," says Masayuki Imanishi, the 14th owner of Imanishi Shuzo. "That's certain. Here in Nara is where the authentic accounts of the origins of Japanese culture started." It's also the birthplace of sake, says Imanishi. His award-winning brewery is in Sakurai, Nara, which was the capital from 457 to AD 479. The brewery sits at the foot of Mount Miwa, home of Ohmiwa Shrine, one of the earliest (perhaps *the* earliest) Shinto shrines in Japan. In olden times, Mount Miwa was also called Mount Mimuro; *mimuro* referred to the origin of sake. Today, brewers from around Japan visit Ohmiwa Shrine to pray for good sake.

Since the entire mountain is sacred, there's no main shrine where a deity is housed. The mountain's religious significance predates the building of shrines to house kami. "Besides sake making and the country's first Shinto shrine, this is where Buddhism first took root in Japan. Also, you can find the oldest road in the country here," Imanishi says, taking a sip of warm tea. He's sitting on tatami at a low table in family's century-old house. I tell him the house, and its garden, are beautiful. "The upkeep isn't easy," he says with a grin, and takes a bite out of a mochi snack.

The Imanishi brewery dates itself from 1660. There are nearly 50 sake breweries in Japan that

LEFT Konishi Shuzo was founded in 1550, and today, the family still manages the brewery. BELOW Konishi also brews Belgian-style beer, making the company one of the first craft-brewers in Japan.

RIGHT These Konishi sake barrels bear the name Shirayuki, or "White Snow," a brand name that dates from 1635. Konishi Shuzo claims that this makes it the oldest sake brand in Japan. In 1995, Konishi launched Shirayuki-branded beer.

are even older, including Kenbishi and Konishi Shuzo. For years, Sudo Honke in Ibaraki Prefecture has been hailed as the oldest. It has been run by the Sudo family ever since it was established in 1141. However, in a 2015 interview with Japanese magazine *Shukan Asahi,* the 55th head of the brewery, Yoshiyasu Sudo, said that Sudo Honke wasn't the oldest sake maker in Japan. "It's a brewery in Nara, not us," he said, adding that he didn't want Sudo Honke called "the oldest brewery in Japan."

The brewery in Nara he's apparently referring to is Imanishi Shuzo. "The owner of the brewery in Ibaraki says we're the oldest," says Imanishi. "We only list our founding as 1660 because that's as far back as we can trace it," he adds. "We're certain it goes back further, but can't say that unequivocally, so we have to use a date we can prove." Furthermore, Imanishi says, there are no surviving records of why the brewery was created. "Maybe it was to make sake for Ohmiwa Shrine, the oldest in shrine in Japan," he says. "We don't know."

There are clues that hint at an answer. Ohmiwa Shrine is called the oldest Shinto shrine, and much Japanese history and culture can be traced back to Sakurai City, Nara. The country's oldest road, Yamanobe Road, runs from Sakurai to Nara City, and the first historical mention of sake brewing placed it here. Both the *Kojiki* and the *Nihon Shoki* recount that in the 3rd century,

ABOVE LEFT Masayuki Imanishi stands in front of the brewery that bears his family's name. CENTER Imanishi Shuzo brewery can trace its ancestry back to 1660. ABOVE RIGHT Bottles of Imanishi's award-winning Mimurosugi.

a plague struck the land. The Ohmiwa Shrine deity Omononushi visited Emperor Sujin in a dream. To help placate the deity, the emperor had a brewer named Ikuhi whip up a batch of his best sake as an offering. It worked, the plague ceased and the brewer is now enshrined at Ohmiwa as a sake-making deity. Further evidence of the connection between Mt. Miwa and sake is the fact that the brew that Ikuhi made for Omononushi—and sake offered to the deities even now—was called *miwa.* The *makura kotoba* (poetic epithets used in Japanese ancient poems) for the word *miwa* is "umazake," meaning "delicious sake."

Sakurai is not only significant for Shintoism. The city is also where an envoy from Baekje (now southwest Korea) landed, bringing Buddhist teachings that won over the emperor and later spread throughout the country. With Buddhism came increased contact with China and, as a related benefit, increased brewing knowledge. At the Buddhist temple complex Shoryakuji, also in Nara, that know-how would later be put to great use. It's also the home of

Japan's oldest recorded mention of sake brewing.

The slopes of Mount Miwa are covered with sacred Japanese cedar trees. Traditionally, Japanese cedar, or *sugi*, was used to fashion the tubs, casks and tanks that sake was made in. The round ball of cedar greenery called a *sugidama*, or *sakabayashi*, which is associated with sake brewing, originated in Nara. Sake brewers from across Japan visit Ohmiwa Shrine every November to pray and to receive a sugidama made from the branches of the mountain's sacred trees. It will be hung in front of the brewery to announce that sake is in production.

"Originally, sake was a sacred communication tool," says Imanishi. "People would drink it and then go into a trance when they were inebriated and then communicate with a deity." The sake that was made for religious festivals at Ohmiwa Shrine at that time wasn't like the refined sake of today, but unprocessed sake akin to doburoku.

## The Advent of Wood

Today, the overwhelming majority of sake is brewed in tanks made of either stainless steel or enamel. For all the talk among small brewers regarding "tradition" and "old techniques," this is rather recent, dating back to the 1950s. Before then, all sake was brewed in wood. When sake makers switched to steel, enamel and resin, the change in flavor was so noticeable that brewers received complaints.

The first mention of using an *oke*, meaning "tub" or "vat," for sake making dates from 1582 in the *Tamon-in nikki*, a detailed diary of sake brewing written at a Buddhist monastery in Nara known as Tamon-in. It only became possible to make the large wooden tubs known as *kioke* after the carpenter's plane was imported from China. The technology to make big tubs meant that large-scale sake production was also possible. Prior to this, sake had been brewed in ceramic

jugs, which were never large enough to make massive batches for sake to satisfy thirsty customers.

Big tubs meant big sales, and the sake industry started to take off. This also created a symbiotic relationship between brewers in different industries. After around 30 years, a sake brewery would sell its kioke to miso or soy-sauce brewers (miso brewers would sell their kioke to soy-sauce makers, but not the other way around; soy sauce left too much flavoring in the wood). Miso and soy-sauce brewers could use the wood sake tubs for another hundred years or more. Much of the umami in soy sauce was due to micro-organisms living in the wood over the two-year fermentation process. Before World War II, there was a similar relationship wherein soy-sauce brewers would buy old sake bottles for their savory sauce. Today, some miso makers and soy-sauce brewers are starting to use kioke again.

The wooden tubs affected the flavor of sake—to the point that when breweries switched from wood to enamel tanks by the mid-1950s, there were complaints. The wood's astringency can come through the final brew, giving more depth to the flavor. "The difference between sake brewed in wood and sake brewed in an enamel tank is the difference between a record and a

FACING PAGE A *torii* gate leading to Ohmiwa Shrine, which is said to be the oldest Shinto shrine in Japan. BELOW Ohmiwa Shrine is the location for a yearly sake festival, with sacred dancing by shrine maidens and offerings to the gods. Among these offerings are eggs, to honor an ancient tale in which the Ohmiwa Shrine deity Omononushi once appeared in the form of a snake. Since it's believed that snakes love chicken eggs, these edibles are often left as an offering to the god.

compact disc," says Toshio Taketsuru, whose Hiroshima brewery uses wooden fermentation tanks for its premium *daiginjo*. Typically, sake brewed in kioke does not have wood aromas or flavors (though it can have a certain astringency, depending on the brewery). The kioke are coated in *kakishibu* (persimmon juice) to waterproof and protect the wood. There are exceptions to this, however. "Whether it's a new or old kioke, we don't coat them with kakishibu," says Yosuke Tanaka, CEO of Niigata's Imayo Tsukasa. "All we do before use is wash the kioke and fill them with hot water to check for leakage." This explains why Imayo Tsukasa's kioke-brewed sake has distinct Japanese cedar notes. Furthermore, the wooden casks used to make cedar-scented *taruzake* (see page 30) are not coated with kakishibu; rather, they are shaved inside to bring more wood aromas and astringency into the sake.

ABOVE This old woodblock print is believed to depict a cooper working in what is modern-day Nagoya. Note how the tub frames a distant Mount Fuji. BELOW LEFT Branding irons at Imayo Tsukasa's brewery museum. BELOW Yosuke Tanaka, CEO of Imayo Tsukasa stands in front of metal brewing tanks.

Generally speaking, however, because of the kakishibu coating, kioke-brewed sake will generally have only a hint of wood aroma, if any at all. The appeal of kioke brewing is the layered, mellow sake the casks produce. Unlike the hermetically sealed enamel and resin tanks, kioke are open at the top, allowing the brew to interact with the brewery's microorganisms as well as microorganisms that reside in the wood. The result is sturdy, versatile brews with character and individuality that are good at any temperature.

In the old days, during the summer, when brewing had to stop, the wood vats were left out in the breweries' main yards and taken apart. Shortly before the brewing season began, locals would hear the thump and clank of hammers as the kioke were assembled. In the present day, not even 20 of the country's working sake breweries use kioke. This may be partly because they are not easy to use. The tubs are harder to clean than the metal tanks, and if hygiene is overlooked, can become home to rot-inducing bacteria. It's also more difficult to control the temperature for kioke than enamel- or resin-lined tanks. During the 1950s, brewery after brewery began ditching wooden vats in favor of modern tanks, at the recommendation of the Japanese government.

For a time, it seemed as though kioke making would die out. Starting in the late 1990s, US-born Sarah Marie Cummings, previously managing director of Masuichi-Ichimura Sake Brewery in Nagano, started sounding the alarm that the kioke craft could be lost. Cummings even founded a nonprofit group called the Committee for the Preservation of Oke Brewing. In 2018, the country's most famous kioke cooper, Takeshi Ueshiba of Fujii Wood Work in Osaka, said he was planning to retire in 2020. During his last few years of work, there was a mad rush among sake brewers—and even whisky distilleries keen to use Japanese cedar fermentation tanks—to place all their orders. Ueshiba crammed years of work into that final stretch to fill all the orders. He's not Japan's last kioke cooper, however. Soy-sauce brewer Yasuo Yamamoto, owner of the Yamaroku Soy Sauce brewery, apprenticed with Ueshiba in 2012. That same year, Yamaroku brought back kioke to his brewery. Furthermore, Yosuke Tanaka, CEO of the Imayo Tsukasa brewery in Niigata City, went with two other brewers to study with Ueshiba in fall 2018. Kenbishi, the oldest sake brand in Japan, set up its own cooperage in that same year, staffed by coopers able to make and repair kioke, while the Aramasa brewery in Akita was in the process of switching all of its enamel-lined tanks for wood ones, adding to its already large kioke collection.

# JAPAN'S OLDEST SAKE BRAND

**"Kenbishi has been making sake since 1505," says current president Masataka Shirakashi as we walk through the brewery's employee parking lot. The multistory brewery towers overhead, and on the roof sits a giant sake cask, its instantly recognizable logo evoking a rich history. The brewery was initially established in 1505 in Itami, Hyogo Prefecture, under the name Inaderaya, and later took its current name, Kenbishi. Since the late 1920s, it has been located in the Nada district of Kobe.**

The enormous cask bearing the Kenbishi logo is easily visible from the highway. Branding is key in Japanese sake and has been for centuries. With so many different brews released, people need an easy way to spot—and remember—brands. According to the 1849 text *Nisen-nen sodekagami* (2,000-year pocket guide), Kenbishi has been using the same logo since its early days, making the design Japan's oldest existing brand logo. That would also make it one of the oldest logos in the entire world, predating most European branding, which took off during the 18th and 19th centuries. Furthermore, it shows how savvy 16th-century Japanese consumerism was. "Sake before Kenbishi was sold as Mr. So-and-So's sake," says Shirakashi.

"Ours was the first sake to be sold under a product name with a logo." During the Edo period (1603–1868), Kenbishi was one of the most expensive and desirable sakes available. Samurai, in particular, enjoyed Kenbishi, Shirakashi notes. Thanks to a line from an old kabuki play, there's a theory that the 47 ronin, the famed masterless samurai out to avenge their unfairly convicted liege lord, drank Kenbishi before their assault on the compound of court official Kira Yoshinaka. After the raid, which resulted in Kira's decapitation, 46 of the ronin were ordered to commit ritual suicide. The 47th ronin, however, was issued a pardon.

"The top of the logo refers to the male form, while the bottom part represents the female one," says Shirakashi, pointing to each part of the design. The logo is akin to the *in-yo*, as the Japanese call the yin-yang symbol. "The logo means there are two different parts, and thus it is balanced." While the logo now indicates the way the sake tastes, its original purpose had a simpler meaning. "A long time ago, many people couldn't read, so using a logo was a way to make sure they would recognize Kenbishi."

It was because of the history and legacy of Kenbishi that Shirakashi's great-grandfather, Masao Shirakashi, bought the brewery in 1924, when it had fallen on hard times. The Harley-riding Masao was well aware of Kenbishi's importance in the history of sake when he purchased the brewery. The Shirakashis became the fifth family to own Kenbishi, guiding it through the difficulties of the 20th century. During the rice shortages of World War II and the years that followed, the government ordered sake makers to dilute their product with

FACING PAGE, TOP Kenbishi president Masataka Shirakashi. FACING PAGE, BOTTOM Four of the 47 *ronin* drink from a Kenbishi-branded cask as they prepare to carry out their revenge. This image is from a pre-World War II pamphlet published by the brewery. LEFT A row of traditional *dakidaru* canisters, made by Kenbishi.

brewer's alcohol and additives like amino acid and glucose. "During the war, we stopped making Kenbishi," says Shirakashi. The Kenbishi sign out front also came down. The brewery was making a wartime brand of sake called Senryoku. "The sake made and sold during World War II wasn't any good because of the rice shortages," says Shirakashi. "It didn't taste like Kenbishi, so it wasn't sold under the Kenbishi name." Even right after the war, the government still wanted brewers to churn out sake, and dilute it with additives. "My grandfather wasn't going to make sake like that," Shirakashi says. So he phoned up the government offices and said the war was over, this was a free country and asked why he had to make sake like that. "During the war, he would've been arrested for that, but what could the government do once it was over?" Kenbishi sake returned in 1948, made as it had been prior to WWII, and once again became a big hit.

Kenbishi brings in 80 seasonal workers every fall. These *kurabito* work through the winter to make its robust and savory sake. By comparison, most modern breweries have fewer than ten kurabito. According to Shirakashi, since so much of the sake production is

done by hand, the large number of kurabito is necessary. "We put all our money in the sake. To keep costs down, we don't have any office staff, we don't advertise, and we don't have Kenbishi stores or restaurants," he says, pausing with a chuckle. "I take that back—there is one office worker: me. My wife also helps out.

"My great-grandfather felt that the Kenbishi name was incredibly important and needed to be cared for. That's why he bought the then-struggling brewery," says Shirakashi. "This isn't a brand my family made, but one that has passed through various hands before we were entrusted with it. Others before us protected the Kenbishi name, and it's something we must protect as well."

ABOVE CENTER A brewery worker wraps a *taru* cask. ABOVE Cleaning koji trays with hot water.

# THE ANCIENT EIGHT

These breweries are Japan's oldest, as catalogued by researcher Tsuneo Kita for the Brewing Society of Japan. The years given are not necessarily founding dates; often production can be dated years, decades or even centuries prior.

### 1. Sudo Honke*
**Ibaraki Prefecture, 1141**

The exact founding date is unknown, but this brewery is reportedly mentioned in a prayer that dates to 1141. The sake made by the Sudo family, a powerful local clan, was collected as yearly taxes.

*There is some debate about whether this is actually the oldest brewery in Japan. In the *Weekly Asahi* in December 2014, Sudo Honke declined the title. "We're not the [oldest] one. That would be a brewery in Nara," said Yoshiyasu Sudo, Sudo Honke's 55th-generation owner. It's believed he was referring to Imanishi Shuzo, whose records only go back to 1660.

### 2. Hiraizumi Honpo
**Akita Prefecture, 1487**

Originally founded as sea merchant, this company brewed sake as a side gig until the early Meiji era (1868–1912). In the 1990s, the brewery became well-known for its acidic, full bodied yamahai brews made with hard water.

### 3. Kenbishi
**Hyogo Prefecture, 1505**

Kenbishi, which lays claim to Japan's oldest sake brand, was originally established in Itami. It later moved to Nada to be on the coast so it could easily ship its sake to Edo (modern-day Tokyo).

### 4. Yamaji Shuzo
**Shiga Prefecture, 1532**

Located up the street from Tomita Shuzo, this brewery is known for its dry sakes and mulberry-leaf liqueur. It wasn't uncommon for sake breweries to sprout up on heavily trafficked roads, ready to sell to a continuous stream of customers.

### 5. Shusen Kurano
**Nagano Prefecture, 1540**

In 1561, the Battle of Kawanakajima was fought on Nagano's Kawanakajima plain, several miles away from Shusen Kurano. The brewery speculates that battling samurai even drank its sake.

### 6. Tomita Shuzo
**Shiga Prefecture, 1543**

The Tomita brewery was founded along the Hokkoku-kaido, a road traveled by Buddhist pilgrims bound for Nagano and gold miners

The Kenbishi logo.

Tomita Shuzo. Its Shichinoyari logo is visible on the brewery.

RIGHT Yoshinogawa *toji* Masatsugu Fujino takes a sip of sake. BELOW RIGHT A glimpse of the interior of Hiraizumi Honpo, known for its excellent *yamahai* brews.

headed to Sado Island. Its best-known brand is Shichinoyari, meaning "seven spears." For more, see page 17.

### 7. Yoshinogawa Shuzo
### Niigata Prefecture, 1548

Yoshinogawa Shuzo is the oldest brewery in Niigata Prefecture, the region of the country where there are now the most sake breweries. The brewery is modern and makes a range of styles, from mass produced to painstakingly handcrafted.

### 8. Konishi Shuzo
### Hyogo Prefecture, 1550

This company began making sake to supplement its pharmaceutical business. According to company lore, Konishi began producing clear sake after ash was accidentally dropped into cloudy brew, creating clear *sumi-zake* (ash sake), which began fetching high prices by the end of the 16th century.

The Yamaji Shuzo brewery gift shop.

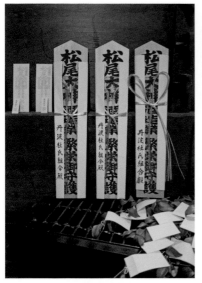

Inside the Tanba Toji Sake Brewery Museum. The photo on the left shows Shinto talismans called *ofuda* from Kyoto's Matsuo-taisha Shrine, which has a long-standing connecting to sake breweries. Throughout Japan, breweries have amulets from Matsuo-taisha Shrine to protect brewers and pray for good sake.

## The Rise of the Brewers

Buddhist monks might have invented modern sake brewing, but it was the emergence of merchant-driven sake business that took the drink to the masses. During the Kamakura period (1185–1333), Kyoto emerged as a powerhouse. The city was filled with samurai, its storehouses were filled with rice collected as tax from domains across Japan, and its Buddhist monks were making and selling koji. No wonder Kyoto became home to 342 breweries.

But by the first half of the Edo period (1603–1868), the breweries of Ikeda in Osaka and Itami in nearby Hyogo dominated. This did not happen in a vacuum. The region had access to high-quality rice, whether from merchants or

fertile fields. Osaka also had Buddhist temples filled with the latest brewing knowledge; it also bordered Nara, the home of Shoryakuji Temple, known as the birthplace of modern sake.

Monks made the change from religious to secular life, getting involved in a variety of business, including moneylending and sake brewing. Located on Mount Amano, the Osaka Buddhist temple Amanosan Kongoji, which is part of the esoteric Shingon sect, was lauded for its sake, called Amano-zake. It had fans among the samurai elites, including Hideyoshi, the warlord who built Osaka Castle and unified Japan in 1588. Hideyoshi also held what could be called the first *jizake* (local sake) tasting in spring 1598, when only the best sake from around Japan was served, including brews from modern-day Fukuoka, chrysanthemum sake from Kaga, monks' sake from Nara and Amano-zake from Osaka.

In the 1600s, Edo's growing middle class was thirsty, as were the samurai who had been relocated to the swampy backwater town that was the new capital. Entrepreneurs jumped into the brewing business, sending their sake up to

Edo by pack mule. Itami in modern-day Hyogo became famous for its *morohaku* white-rice sake, a style that was invented in Nara but perfected in Itami.

Monks were only able to brew in earthenware pots, with one batch about 540 liters, a pittance compared to today's fermentation tanks. As mentioned, mass production was only doable once carpenter's planes and large saws known as *ogabiki* were imported from China during the 15th century. These tools made it possible to construct tubs large enough to ferment big batches to meet the increasing sake demand.

What caused the number of brewers to increase was the liberalization of sake-brewing licenses called *sakekabu*, literally meaning "sake certification." In 1754, the price of rice dropped and the shogunate relaxed the sakekabu system. The deregulation led to more breweries setting up shop and thriving, especially in Nada.

Mass-produced sake required teams of brewing experts. As the breweries grew larger,

they hired teams of brewers, headed up by *toji*, to make the sake. The Tanba toji guild, hailing from a region in Hyogo Prefecture, dates from at least the late 18th century. The other two famous toji guilds are the Echigo toji from Niigata and the Nanbu toji from Iwate. During the 19th century, these secretive guilds came to dominate sake making, hiring teams of breweries and traveling to the *kura*, where they'd live during brewing season.

Sake was shipped to Edo on dedicated vessels called *tarukaisen*. These faced greater competition from steamships in the late 1800s. By 1907, the railroads had been nationalized, making it easier than ever for sake makers in areas like Hiroshima to get their sake to Tokyo.

The exterior of the Tanba Toji Sake Brewery Museum. The museum documents the guild's history, and includes sake-making equipment. It also catalogs the breweries that use Tanba *toji* as well as the guild's current members.

Tsunekichi Okura, then 39 years old, sits in the second story executive lounge at Gekkeikan's Okura Sake Brewing Research Institute. The photo dates from 1912, and the cabinet to Okura's right is on display at the Gekkeikan Okura Sake Museum.

# THE FIRST MODERN MAKER

In November 1928, Tsunekichi Okura stood in front of his company, next to a car, posing for a photo in his finest tux and tails, top hat slightly cocked to one side. He looked proud—rightly so. He turned Gekkeikan into a sake powerhouse.

It was the dawn of the next generation. Japan's new emperor, Hirohito, had ascended to the throne after his father the Taisho emperor passed away, ushering in the Showa era. Gekkeikan, the most modern sake maker in the country, commenced construction on a cutting-edge brewery it named Showagura (Showa brewery) in honor of the new Showa emperor. It was the most advanced brewery of its day.

At that time, there was nothing like the Showagura. The multistory reinforced concrete brewery had a German-built freight elevator. To control temperature, the second floor's fermentation room was outfitted with air-conditioning ducts—Gekkeikan had imported a York air-conditioning unit from the United States. At that time, air-conditioning was a rarity in Japan.

It was also a novelty in the United States, where there wasn't a fully air-conditioned hotel until the mid-1920s (that was the St. Anthony in San Antonio, which was outfitted with a York unit). Showagura became the blueprint for how modern sake breweries built before World War II and in the decades after should look. Three years after it was constructed, Gekkeikan installed an ultra-modern bottle line that could automatically wash and sterilize the glass bottles and fill 1,000 of them per hour. But Showagura wasn't only a high-tech factory; it made sake that met the expectations of the most discerning palates in the country. For this reason, in January 1928, Gekkeikan began brewing special sake at the brewery for the Showa emperor's official coronation ceremonies that fall. This wasn't a first for Gekkeikan; as makers of *goyoshu*, or "sake for imperial use," they had also brewed sake for the enthronement of the previous ruler, Emperor Taisho.

For the Showa emperor's coronation, Gekkeikan loaded up a Chevy with celebratory sake barrels. A Shinto priest had blessed the vehicle, which was decorated with *shimenawa*, sacred ropes of twisted rice straw. A wooden placard that read "Coronation Sake" was erected in the truck's flatbed; "Gekkeikan" was painted on the sides. You couldn't buy this kind of advertising. The photo of Okura shows him at the moment before the sake was driven from Fushimi to the imperial palace in central Kyoto.

One might assume that Okura was just another landed gentry that had taken over a successful business, cruising on his family's name. This was not the case, however. In 1886, 13-year-old Tsunekichi took over after his father's death. The brewery, then named Kasagiya, dated from the 17th century, when the family forebear Jiemon Okura moved to Fushimi from the southern Kyoto town Kasagi. In 1657,

there were 83 breweries in Fushimi, but in the wake of a 1868 battle between pro-shogunate and pro-imperial forces, only two breweries were left. One was Kasagiya; the other was Kitagawa Honke, brewers of the Tomio brand.

Fushimi was a port city with around 50 ships traveling down the Yodo River to Osaka during the late 1860s. A decade later, trains connected Osaka and Kyoto, increasing the flow of goods and people, and more breweries began setting up shop in Fushimi, breathing life back in the

*Jikkokubune* or "ten koku boats" (one *koku* is 48 gallons) transported sake and rice during the Edo period (1603–1868). From spring to autumn there are boat tours in Fushimi, with lovely views of Gekkeikan's Uchigura brewery.

TOP In 1911, Gekkeikan launched salicylic acid-free sake. The company used special paper seals from the Osaka Hygiene Laboratory on the bottles, which have been reproduced in this painting, to state that its sake contained no preservatives. ABOVE A window into a brewing tank gives a peek at fermentation on the 12th day.

district. Tsunekichi's mother had him work in the brewery to learn the family business, something owners and their offspring generally didn't do at the time. He might have been young, but under his leadership, the company went from being a small local producer making 23,775 gallons (90,000 liters) annually in the 1890s to making 2.37 million gallons (9 million liters) a year during the 20th century.

What made Okura such a revolutionary figure was his modern approach to making sake. In 1905, he changed the brewery's name to Gekkeikan, meaning "Laurel Wreath," after a general suggested the moniker due to its associations with victory in classical Greece. Unlike typical sake breweries, which embraced traditional Japanese motifs or iconography, Gekkeikan conveyed a regal, even foreign air. For early 20th-century Japan, modernity was represented by the Western world. This brewery reflected that. Science and data were embraced. Western-style bookkeeping was adopted to track expenditures and pinpoint wasteful spending. Okura set up a brewing research center in 1909, only five years after the National Research Institute of Brewing had been established in Tokyo. Around a year later, Gekkeikan released a preservative-free sake that was did not contain salicylic acid, which had been added to keep sake from going bad despite its toxic effects (it was finally banned in 1969). Each bottle had a seal from the Osaka Hygiene Laboratory as proof the sake was entirely preservative free. Around that same time, Gekkeikan started selling small bottles with attached cups at train stations. *Ekiben* (bento-box meals sold at train stations) had been around since 1885, but since sake was sold in large casks, there wasn't a way to market it to the increasing numbers of railroad passengers until Gekkeikan's *kopputsuki kobin* (small bottle with attached cup) went on sale in 1910. Two years later, Gekkeikan was selling 33,286 gallons (126,000 liters) of sake at 71

stations. In 1913, that number jumped to 119,828 gallons (453,600 liters) at 88 stations. Gekkeikan wasn't only pioneering for its use of small bottles; it was also the first brewery to bottle sake in brown glass, which cuts out UV light and prevents spoilage. As early as 1915, for the San Francisco World's Fair, Gekkeikan was selling its sake in the now-ubiquitous brown bottles. It took most breweries until the late 1960s to switch from light-blue bottles to brown or green bottles.

In 1961, 11 years after Tsunekichi's death, Gekkeikan became the biggest sake company in Japan, producing 4.75 million gallons (18 million liters) annually. That same year, the company became the first modern Japanese brewery to produce sake year-round. The spirit of innovation and rapid growth that began under Tsunekichi Okura was carried forward.

TOP This photo, from around 1920, shows the Okura Sake Brewing Research Institute on the left. This Western-style building shows Gekkeikan's dedication to scientific research and was, for its time, a rarity among sake breweries. ABOVE LEFT A cask and branding irons, including one reading *ginjo* (吟醸) meaning "carefully brewed." At that time, the term didn't refer to polishing ratios. ABOVE RIGHT A bottle of Gekkeikan sake. The brewery's logo was registered in 1905 and the laurel wreath design evoked the ancient Greeks.

# AKITA JOZO: AN APARTMENT-SIZED MINI BREWERY

**It's not every day you enter a brewery that's on the ground floor of a modern apartment-building complex. Among the breweries in Japan, Akita Jozo is a rarity. "There's another Kyoto brewery that's in an apartment building," I tell Tadahiko Kobayashi, the company owner and *toji*. "Oh yeah?" he replies. "I've heard there is one in Hiroshima, too. It's definitely not common, though."**

Tadahiko Kobayashi, the *kuramoto-toji* of Akita Jozo.

There are stacks of data charts and pipettes spread messily all over the main office table. Machines and equipment are shoehorned into a tiny lab that is barely bigger than a closet. "It's very compact in here," Kobayashi says. "We can't make more sake because of the lack of space." He wishes he could make more, though. "But there's no room to expand here; the size of

**BELOW, LEFT TO RIGHT** The brewery's *koji* room; A metal mesh walkway above the brewing tanks; brewing tanks under the metal walkway, an economical use of space. Here are the brewing tanks under the metal walkway.

the brewery is fixed. There are lots of things I'd do differently if I was able to."

Kobayashi might have regrets about the brewery's size, but he certainly doesn't have any about the sake he's making. His elegant Yuki no Bijin (Snow Beauty) brand *junmai* sakes are the pride of Akita. To keep up with the constant demand, the brewery is selling sake as fast as it can make it. "People rush me into selling my sake," Kobayashi says. "So I speed up the production process, even if it could probably use a few more months of maturation. Ideally I'd prefer to age my sake for a little while longer,

around six months or so, so it's at its best."

At the turn of this century, it was a different story. The brewery was in a conventional brewery building, focusing on table sake, selling what it could to larger breweries. In 2000, Kobayashi tore down the old brewery that his grandfather had

established in 1919 and in its place built a multistory apartment building with a small brewery on the ground floor. "Are there any sake-themed events for people who live in the apartments?" I ask. "Oh no, nothing like that," Kobayashi replies with a chuckle.

With this new and more compact brewery, Kobayashi set out to reinvent the brews his family had been making. "I wanted to make a quality product," he says. "I didn't think it would be possible for this brewery to continue as had in the past." By 2004, Kobayashi was the toji, aiming to make the best sake possible. "I've had a lot of sake in my life and have never felt, like 'Oh wow,'" says Kobayashi. "In my mind, I have this idea of what a delicious sake should taste like. I'm going after that ideal sake." I press him on how such a sake would taste. Kobayashi pauses for a moment, then replies, "I can't put it into concrete words because I've never tasted it."

This small brewery is not aiming for perfection, however. Kobayashi is quick to acknowledge that not every batch is the same. "There is bound to be variation because we are not blending batches," he says. "But in the world of wine, variations are expected. They are part of the enjoyment." Throughout much of the 20th century, variation in sake was edged out by the desire for uniformity. "But our customers understand that there will be some variation in the sake we produce," says Kobayashi. "If they don't, well, there's not much we can do about that." The brewery's mission is an ideal product rather than a perfect one.

We leave the office and enter the brewery, which makes remarkably economical use of its space. Unlike many breweries, including modest-sized operations, it contains no dead space. Every nook and cranny has a function. Inside the temperature-controlled brewery is a dedicated area for washing the rice and another dedicated area for steaming and cooling it. There's a full-on cedar-lined *koji* room and a separate room for the *shubo* yeast starter. There are nine compact fermentation tanks, and there's a pressing area. It's hard to believe that crammed into this space that is smaller than the 18-yard penalty area of a football field, this brewery is making some of the best sake not just in Akita, but in Japan.

Kobayashi points to a wooden box at the bottom of the shubo tank, saying, "See

The brewery sits at the bottom of an apartment complex. Residents have every right to be very proud. Kobayashi did mention that getting trucks to and from the brewery is tricky, however.

that? There's a heating lamp in there we use to heat the shubo." Instead of putting in *dakidaru* canisters filled with hot water or ice to control the temperature, Kobayashi heats his yeast starter from below or lets the air-conditioning cool it down.

"Can you make that ideal sake?" I ask later. "I want to," Kobayashi answers with a smile.

"Do you think you will?"

"Not yet," he says. "Not yet."

The Paris location Dassaï Joël Robuchon offers *daiginjo* sakes with a uniquely Parisian twist.

# SAKE GOES INTERNATIONAL: EXPORTS BOOM AND SAKE BREWERIES OPEN WORLDWIDE

## FOREIGNERS DISCOVER SAKE

Early impressions of sake overseas were overwhelmingly favorable. Sake was first mentioned in English in 1687 in the translated *Travels of Monsieur De Thevenot*. Globetrotter Jean de Thévenot wrote of the Japanese, "Their ordinary drink is a kind of beer (which they call *saque*) made of rice . . . a Hollander gave me some of it to drink out of curiosity, and I found it to be pretty good."

In his 1721 work *Hyakusho bukuro* (Farmer's satchel), scholar Joken Nishikawa wrote that a Dutchman praised sake, crying, "This land's alcohol is the best on earth!" The Dutch came to Japan in 1609, and were the only Westerners given exclusive trading rights with the Japanese. This arrangement ended in 1854, after the Americans' black ships rolled up in Tokyo Bay with their big guns. But before casks of sake ever ended up in the hands of Holland's sailors, the Portuguese were describing it—and drinking it.

The Portuguese first landed in Japan sometime around 1543, only to be kicked out during the first half of the following century. Sea captain Jorge Álvares, not to be confused with the similarly named sea captain who was the first European to visit China, issued a report in December 1547 about his visit to Japan that, according to Portuguese scholar Clive Willis, helped inspire the Jesuits' decision to come to Japan. Besides insights into local culture and customs, the report mentions that the Japanese drink sake, correctly adding that it was made from rice. Álvares wrote that he never saw any Japanese drunk out of their minds, because when they got too tipsy, they would sleep it off. Portugal's Jesuit missionaries brought Christianity and wine as well as an eagerness to record what they saw. In January 1552, Francis Xavier described their daily drink as "arrack" that was "made from rice." The word "arrack" refers to a spirit that is distilled, not brewed. Since Xavier landed in Kagoshima, a region famous for shochu, it's possible he was not writing about sake, especially as shochu can be made from rice. Or perhaps he really was calling actual sake "arrack." Fellow Jesuit Luís Fróis, who published a treatise in 1585 comparing Europe and Japan, also wrote about sake, calling it "vinho" (wine) and explaining that Japanese wine was made from rice.

It 1603, the first Japanese-language dictionary for a European language was published. Called *Nippo jisho*, it defined sake (written "saqe") as *vinho*, which means "wine" in Portuguese. The dictionary also contained over 50 sake-related terms, which included words related to the different types of sake, such as *koshu, nigorizake*, etc., and words related to the sake production process, including *koji, moto* and *morohaku*, the latter of which the dictionary indicated originated in Nara). These words are still commonly used today in sake production, which is remarkable considering how much the Japanese language, like most others, has evolved in the past 400 years. In most languages, certain words—water, road, man, woman—have staying power throughout the centuries. In Japanese, sake words have persisted, too.

João Rodrigues, another Jesuit missionary, wrote even more extensively about sake in 1620, giving a simple overview on how it was brewed and spending more ink on the ritualistic way it was enjoyed by the Japanese. Rodrigues says he was told so much sake was consumed in Japan that a third of the country's rice crop went to making the drink.

The Portuguese, however, were not the first foreigners to describe Japanese drinking traditions. That distinction goes to the Chinese, whose first mention of the Japanese fondness for alcohol appeared in the *Wei zhi* (The Wei chronicles), compiled in the late 3rd century. This is the earliest account of the Japanese, describing a people who walked barefoot, ate with their fingers, and adorned their bodies with tattoos—a little different from today's Japanese. (This was before the Chinese introduced chopsticks to

In this woodblock print from 1877, the police superintendent finishes off the last of a sake cask. The American Navy ended Japan's self-imposed isolation in 1854. By this time, Western-style clothing had long been adapted in Japan.

Japan, along with the concept of punitive tattooing, among other things.) Two aspects of Japanese life remain unchanged from that day to this: according to the *Wei zhi*, there was little crime in the country, and the people loved drinking. The Chinese text also mentions that alcohol played a part in the ancient Japanese funeral rituals.

The *Wei zhi* uses the kanji character 酒, which now means "sake" in Japanese, to describe the nation's liquor. What the Japanese were making at that time was completely different from today's sake, but still, this is the first example of that kanji character being used in relation to Japanese booze. Since Japan didn't have a writing system before Chinese was introduced, it's only logical that the Chinese character for alcohol would be readily adopted and used. However, it's still unknown whether this first description of Japanese liquor referred to a brew of rice or to something that was made from other grains, such as millet, or even a simple wine made from wild berries. Sadly, the early chronicles didn't provide tasting notes.

## The First Sake on Foreign Shores

When was the first sake shipped outside Japan to other countries? That's a difficult question to answer. It's fairly safe to assume that Japan's neighbors were drinking sake hundreds of years before the drink made it to the West. The first sake made outside Japan was probably brewed in Korea. During the Edo period (1603–1868), several thousand Japanese (actual estimates are as high as 4,500 people!) lived in a consulate compound in Busan, in the south of the Korean peninsula, where they ate Japanese-style meals. According to Hajime Yoshida, a researcher at Shuchiin University in Kyoto, these envoys were not great fans of the local Korean booze, so they must have been drinking imported sake or brewing their own from local rice. Later records do state that a Japanese man named Araki began

brewing unrefined sake in Busan in 1876; and that another Japanese man, named Okubo, began making refined sake a year after that. Records also show that a Japanese sake brewery was established there in 1884.

In the 16th and 17th centuries, Portuguese missionaries and explorers might have brought some sake home to Europe. The Dutch did export bottles of sake—as well as soy sauce!—back to the Netherlands. By the end of the Sengoku period (1467–1568), merchants, samurai and Japanese Christians had left their homeland for better opportunities elsewhere in Southeast Asia. Starting around 1600, Japanese sailing vessels known as *shuinsen*, or "red-seal ships," brought Japanese food and sake to the various *nihonmachi* (literally "Japan town") settlements. In 1636, however, the Tokugawa government issued a policy of national isolation called *sakoku*, meaning "locked country," which outlawed foreign travel under penalty of death. The vast majority of Japanese who had been living abroad returned home, but some stayed overseas, even getting work as samurai mercenaries on distant Southeast Asian shores. Sake found its way onto European ships traveling Asian seas, such as those controlled by the Dutch East India Company, to be sold to exiled Japanese who were wanting a boozy taste of home.

In 2006, the Japan Sake and Shochu Makers' Association officially identified the 1873 Vienna International Exposition as the first time sake was exported internationally. Japan brought sake to this exposition, and would continue to bring it to the world's fairs that followed in its wake. (Interestingly, in the Philadelphia 1876 Centennial Exhibition catalog, "sake" is listed under "Animal and Vegetable Products.") Just one year after the 1873 Vienna International Exposition, Nada Brewery Kiku Masamune was exporting its sake to the United Kingdom. Japan's local brew had gone international.

# DASSAI GOES WEST

"This has never been done before," says Kazuhiro Sakurai, president and CEO of Asahi Shuzo, maker of Dassai sake. It's early 2018, and Sakurai is sitting at table off to the side of the brewery's data lab as technicians run samples through lab equipment and write down figures on innumerable wall charts. Sakurai isn't talking about a brand-new brewing technique; he's discussing a new brewing location. Asahi Shuzo is planning to establish a new *kura* in America.

"When you think of the sake makers who have set up breweries in the United States, the location that probably comes to mind is California," says Sakurai. "Those were mass-market producers making *futsu-shu*, table sake." Asahi Shuzo's plan is radically different: the new brewery will be in Hyde Park, New York, and it will make *daiginjo* exclusively under a new brand name, "Dassai Blue."

This is fitting, because that's all Asahi Shuzo now makes and ships throughout Japan. The Dassai brand, launched in 1990, is now so popular that Asahi Shuzo took out a newspaper ad asking people not to mark up the price for resale, because the brewery works hard to make the best sake it can at fair prices. As for all that data on the wall charts, Asahi Shuzo uses it to pinpoint the best way to make sake. The result isn't clinical, however, but elegant; human hands are involved throughout the process.

The main brewery building, with its modern metal-and-glass exterior, looks like something you'd see in central Tokyo. All the brewery workers are young. The brewing facilities are state of the art, with airlocks that seal them off from outside contamination. Even the office staff are young and fashionable. Sakurai himself is decked out in a blue three-piece suit with his last name stitched into his white cuffs. It's all in stark contrast to this rural part of Yamaguchi Prefecture. The road up to the brewery snakes through the mountains, occasionally passing old farmhouses and offering spectacular views.

When Sakurai's father originally launched Dassai in 1990, he knew that he had to look outside its tiny hometown. Considering the declining local population, not doing so could be catastrophic. "We had no choice but to sell outside this local

TOP The Paris location offers *daiginjo* sake as well as pastries and other eats. ABOVE Asahi Shuzo president and CEO Kazuhiro Sakurai tests different glasses before the opening of Dassaï Joël Robuchon in April 2018. A sake's flavor can be impacted by the vessel in which it is served.

area," the younger Sakurai says. "We had to look outward." Tokyo, Texas, Taiwan or Paris, Sakurai says there's no difference. "For us, it's all the same market. There are different laws and regulations, but we don't differentiate."

If Asahi Shuzo is already making world-class sake in Japan, why set up a brewery in the United States? "Sake still has a ways to go in the drinks market outside Japan," Sakurai says, picking up a piece of paper and drawing a pyramid. In Japanese, at the top, he writes "expensive imported sake." Next to that he adds "duties" and "taxes." At the bottom, he writes "inexpensive locally-produced sake." There is nothing in the middle of the pyramid—it's blank. "If the American wine market was like this, with only table wine and super-premium wines like Opus One, you'd say something was wrong with it." For sake to grow in a healthy and sustainable way outside Japan, it needs excellent sake that is priced fairly to occupy that middle segment. "And since nobody is doing that, we thought it was up to us to meet that need."

Sakurai puts down his pen. "Because of the way things are now, outside of Japan, sake is a drink for rabid fans." He uses the Japanese word *maniakku* (maniacs). These are people who have either been to Japan or have a deep interest in Japanese food and culture. "We need to move beyond that," he says. "We want to offer a drink to people who may have zero interest in Japan, but simply like the way it tastes," he says, explaining why the brewery collaborated with Joël Robuchon for a Paris restaurant

serving delicious food and sake. "This is how the drinking culture will change."

Instrumental to that change is taking the foreign drink and making it local. New York was selected for three reasons. One, Sakurai points out, is that many trends emanate from there. Two, it's easy to ship sake to Canada and Europe from there. And three, New York's Hyde Park is the home of the Culinary Institute of America, and the institute wanted to collaborate with Asahi Shuzo, so they could teach one another.

As the new brewery finds its footing, the *kurabito* are from Japan. But the goal is to bring on US workers to make the sake. "It's difficult to make the same sake that we make here," Sakurai says. "The weather and the climate are different, and the water is different. But that's okay—what is the same is the idea of always improving and making better sake." Even if the New York brewery could make a perfect copy of the made-in-Japan Dassai, that would defeat its raison d'être. "There is already a Japanese Dassai," he says. "The made-in-America sake won't be identical, but similar." For fans of Dassai, those subtle differences could be appealing.

Real whisky wasn't made in Japan

Kazuhiro Sakurai and Asahi Shuzo chairman Hiroshi Sakurai with Joël Robuchon. The famed French chef, who passed away in August 2018, was a fan of Dassai sake.

until 1929. But less than 100 years later, some of the most lauded and desirable whisky on earth was being made there. Could the same thing happen with American sake? "I do think an American sake brewery could surpass what we make in Japan," Sakurai says. "Think about it this way: 50, 60 years ago, who drank California wines?" American sake might not take as long to be recognized as California wine or Japanese whisky. "Because of the interconnected world we live in, things could move even faster."

## America's First Sake Brewery

Sake brewed in places like Brooklyn or Texas might seem like a novelty, but it's not. In the late 19th century, Japanese chemist Jokichi Takamine planned a sake brewery in Chicago. In 1892, the *Pittsburgh Dispatch* reported that half of the necessary $250,000 in capital had been raised for the brewery, which the paper incorrectly said was to be called the "Takamine Shurm [sic] Jozo Kaisha." In Japanese, the company's name was actually "Takamine Shurui Jozo Kaisha" or "Takamine Alcoholic Drinks Brewing Company." The brewery never panned out.

Instead, the honor of being America's first official sake brewery goes to the Japan Brewing Company, which was established in 1902 in Berkeley, California, to make sake exclusively. The *Oakland Tribune* reported in February 1906 that the brewery was shutting down because it couldn't afford its $200 annual license, and a year later the brewery was sued for allegedly failing to pay for equipment. But was this really the first sake brewery on US soil?

On April 2, 1895, the *Hawaiian Gazette* reported, "Japanese are said to be manufacturing saki [sic] on Hawaii." There are no further details, and this could be saloon scuttlebutt. The US didn't formally annex Hawaii until 1898, so if there were any breweries—illicit or not—those would have been the first. That year, the *Washington Star* ran a story in which an anonymous navy officer warned people of the dangers of drinking too much sake. "Among other joys that we acquire in taking over Hawaii is saki [sic]," he said. "Saki is not indigenous to Hawaii. It got there from Japan. But it is there to stay. It is now an Hawaiian institution."

## The Legendary Sake of Hawaii

A group of 148 Japanese immigrants arrived in Hawaii in 1868. They were not the first Japanese recorded on Hawaiian shores; in 1806, some Japanese sailors had been blown far off course and landed there, starving and with no supplies. The 1868 group was the first official group of immigrants, however. They were known as the *gannenmono* ("first-year folks"), because they arrived in the first year of the Meiji era. The following year, more than 50 of them returned to Japan because the Japanese government banned emigration to Hawaii. This ban remained in effect until 1885, and then more Japanese arrived to work on the sugar plantations.

During the late 19th century, Hawaii started experiencing a sake boom, and the press was running stories about the drink's deleterious effects. On December 27, 1894, the *Honolulu Advertiser* ran a piece titled, "The Effect of Japanese Saki [sic] in This City." The editorial warned that the appeal of sake was its pleasant taste and low price. "The Hawaiians think it fine to get drunk at so cheap a cost," the article stated, adding that locals were stumbling out of bars after getting hammered on sake, even before the number of Japanese immigrants increased. That same month, however, another local paper proclaimed, "Saki [sic] is the drink of the future." In 1894, over 83,000 gallons of the stuff were imported, a massive leap from the 3,400 gallons of the previous year. The reason for this spike was simple: sake had become cheap. Initially, it had been taxed like distilled liquor, putting it in a higher tax bracket. That was overturned in 1894 after an importer filed to have it levied like still wine. The cheaper duty gave more bang for one's buck, and a whole generation of Hawaiian drinkers instantly developed a taste for sake.

With sake consumption skyrocketing, California wine producers complained that sake was cutting into their sales. To compete with the cheaper sake, the price of wine was lowered by more than 40 percent per gallon. In 1898, the *Los Angeles Herald* reported that new duties were being slapped on sake, much to the dismay of Hawaii's Japanese population. A legal battle ensued, with one importer even arguing that

RIGHT A Honolulu Japanese store around the beginning of the 20th century. BELOW The Honolulu Sake Brewery's first building in 1908, the year it was established.

RIGHT An advertisement for the Honolulu Sake Brewery's Polo Champion sparkling sake and its standard Takara Masamune stuff to commemorate Hawaii becoming a U.S. State in 1959. Note that even in the 1950s, the brewery was suggesting that its carbonated sake be served ice cold.

195

A parade to celebrate the Honolulu Sake Brewery's first release Takarajima (Teasure Island) and pray for success. A horse-drawn carriage pulls a cart that's been converted into a boat with the people aboard dressed like the Seven Lucky Gods.

sake should be taxed like beer (this would have put it at an even cheaper rate of 20 cents per gallon, compared to 50 cents per gallon for wine). In 1908, that case went all the way to the Supreme Court, with sake samples brought in exhibits. The justices declined to try the brew, but the *Buffalo Evening News* wrote, "The judges should have taken a recess for investigation." Two years later, the Supreme Court upheld the decision that sake should be taxed like still wine. (Fittingly, the Court's opinion was given by one Justice Brewer.)

So there was a market opportunity for making sake in Hawaii. Businessman Tajiro Sumida applied for a whole liquor license in the spring of 1907; a year later, he would establish one of the most important sake breweries of the 20th century, the Honolulu Japanese Sake Brewing Company, later known as simply the Honolulu Sake Brewery. The brewery also produced soy sauce and miso, as well as soft drinks. But what

made sake production possible in tropical Honolulu was that the company also was in the ice business. Its refrigerated warehouses and cold storage turned out to be essential for brewing sake in a tropical climate. The brewery was kept at 43°F (6°C) and sake was made year-round—both global firsts. This was decades before Kyoto brewer Gekkeikan would establish Japan's first refrigerated brewery in 1927 and begin brewing year-round in 1961. Cold storage had taken off in the United States during the late 1800s and was used for meats, fruit, dairy products and, increasingly, beer. At that time, Japan didn't have a widespread history of ice-cold drinks, because cold beverages didn't take off in Japan until after World War II, thanks to the influence of American GIs. Hawaii's beer breweries had cold-storage facilities by the early 1900s, so when Sumida wanted to brew sake in Honolulu, the necessary temperature-controlled infrastructure was already in place.

The Honolulu Japanese Sake Brewing Company went into production in late December 1908. By the following January, the test batches were turning out so well that *The Honolulu Advertiser* called them a "great success," adding that other Hawaiian sake breweries were "more or less failures." The brewery moved quickly to ramp up commercial production. Another Hawaiian sake maker, the Hilo Sake Brewery, was established and slated to begin production in February 1, 1909. But it wasn't until September 1913 that the Hilo Sake Brewery opened a "new modern plant" with a large cold storage plant that reportedly was like those used in beer production. The Honolulu Japanese Sake Brewing Company was besieged

with orders for Takarajima (Treasure Island)–branded sake, forcing the brewery to increase its capacity. The brewery was expanding to twice its original size, planning a new concrete cold-storage brewery with 5-inch cork and asphaltum insulation and state-of-the-art cooling equipment to ensure low temperatures. Hawaii's four major breweries—Hawaii Seishu, Hilo Sake Brewery, Honolulu Brewing & Malting and Honolulu Japanese Sake Brewing Company—were using 164 tons of rice each month to make sake (most of the grain was imported, but some of it was Hawaiian rice).

Then the unthinkable happened—Hawaii went dry.

President Woodrow Wilson signed an Executive Order in March 1918, banning alcohol from Oahu starting the following month. Later that same year, alcohol was banned on all the

A company Shinto ceremony blessing the first sake brewed after the repeal of Prohibition in 1933.

At the Honolulu brewery, a refrigeration system was installed along the walls. Mats were wrapped around fermentation tanks to help brewers control temperatures. The brewers can be seen checking the condition of the main mash.

islands. The stated reason for the ban was that foodstuffs shouldn't be used to make alcohol during World War I; in fact, however, this looked very much like a trial balloon for a nationwide alcohol ban. Sure enough, in 1920, Prohibition hit. The Hawaiian breweries that didn't close were either selling ice or focusing on soy sauce, miso or soft drinks. Production at the Honolulu Sake Brewery resumed after Prohibition ended, but the onset of World War II once again forced the brewery to temporarily close due to food rations. Founder Tajiro Sumida had left Hawaii during Prohibition to establish branch offices in Japan and set up coffee plantations in Saipan and Taiwan, leaving his brother Daizo and later his son to run the family's successful business in Hawaii. On August 6, 1945, the United States dropped a nuclear bomb on Hiroshima. *The Honolulu Star-Bulletin* reported that Tajiro Sumida and his family had earlier fled their home between Kobe and Osaka, areas the Americans firebombed, to return to Hiroshima. They were living three miles from the city center when the bomb hit. Sumida and his family

survived, but the businessman passed away five years later at age 68.

In the decades following World War II, the Honolulu Sake Brewery went through a golden age, but then its sake business started to slip. The *Honolulu Star-Bulletin* reported that by the mid-1980s, soy sauce was making up around 40 percent of its sales. In April 1986, Japan's Takara Shuzo purchased the Hawaiian brewery for $2.5 million. The two companies had a history going back to 1976, when Takara tried to sell cooking sake in Hawaii. The Honolulu Sake Brewery had balked, saying doing so would infringe on its own decades-old Takara sake brand, and Takara Shuzo had been unable to sell its product in the islands—though it was, and still is, a sake giant in the continental US. Picking up the Honolulu Sake Brewery was a major consolidation, and the

Misayo and Takao Nihei in their later years. Misayo passed away at the age of 88 in October 2018, a few months after being interviewed for this book. She was born in Kyoto and worked as lab assistant to her sake-making husband.

new owners invested $600,000 into renovating it, adding the latest brewing technology, such as a computer-controlled press. But making sake in Hawaii ended up being costly, and it was easier for Takara Shuzo to distribute what it brewed at its California location across the country and to the middle of the Pacific. Production at the Honolulu Sake Brewery ended in 1992. According to Chris Pearce, the Honolulu-based president of World Sake Imports, nothing remains of the brewery. Today, its former location is a residential neighborhood.

## The Father of American Sake

After World War II, the Honolulu Sake Brewery started again, but its fermented batches kept going to rot. The situation became dire, and in 1954, a brilliant young chemist with expertise in sake fermentation, Takao Nihei, was flown in from Japan. Nihei would not only go on to become one of the most important brewers of the 20th century, but would also be dubbed the father of American sake.

Takao Nihei first arrived at the Honolulu Sake Brewery in spring 1954 on a tourist visa. Locals called it the *yama no sakaya* (mountain sake brewery). It wasn't located in the mountains, but because the brewery sat atop a hill overlooking the houses below, the nickname stuck. It must have been quite a sight for Nihei, who would have been accustomed to breweries run by craftsmen producing high-quality sake. The Honolulu brewery had seen better days (and better sake). His Japanese colleagues described its brew as undrinkable.

Over the next two years, Nihei worked to help the brewery get back on its feet, stabilizing the

fermentation process—or so he thought. In summer 1957, after Nihei had returned to Japan, batches started going to rot again and he was called back for a two-month spell. The following year, the brewery hired Nihei full-time, securing him and his family permanent visas, and he returned to Hawaii. "We knew so many people from the two years prior we lived in Honolulu, so we didn't have any trouble settling in," his wife, Misayo, told me. "Everyone around us was so kind."

At the brewery, Nihei contended with problems that his counterparts in Japan did not have. For decades, the Honolulu Sake Brewery had been adapting its processes to brew in a tropical climate, because heat and humidity breed bacteria that can ruin batches. Temperature control and refrigerated rooms had helped overcome these intrinsic difficulties. Since 1947, the brewery had installed stainless-steel tanks to combat bacteria, before they became mainstays in Japanese breweries. "The brewery looked immaculate, with all those stainless steel tanks lined up," recalled Misayo.

Before World War II, the brewery imported Japanese rice, but in the postwar years it began using California rice. The rice was less sticky, making it easier to work with during steaming

199

# THE HISTORY OF SAKE COCKTAILS

**The saketini was not the first sake cocktail. Sake cocktails are mentioned in both English and Japanese publications from the 1930s. In a 1936 newspaper review of New York City Japanese restaurants, a syndicated columnist wrote the following about Miyako, a 58th Street establishment: "Miyako also offers a sake cocktail—a shockingly unorthodox concoction calculated to make a shogun shudder in his tomb."**

While there were sake cocktails in Japan around this time (and probably before), sake cocktails have been more of a Western, especially American, thing. Japanese cocktail bars have long taken their cue from American and European bars, and even today they are stocked with *yoshu*, or "Western alcohol," to serve straight or mixed.

Sake doesn't quite fit into the Japanese notion of traditional cocktails. Of course, it's possible to get sake cocktails in Japan, but they're not as prevalent as classics like Manhattans, highballs or gin and tonics. But sake cocktails, which are called *nihonshu kakuteru* or the more old-fashioned-sounding *seishu kakuteru*, were making enough of a stir that the sake industry publication *Journal of the Society of Brewing* ran a three-page opinion piece on sake cocktails in 1958.

During the 1950s, sake started gaining a following in the United States, especially in trendsetting California. American bartenders and punters were making sake mixed drinks like the "River Kwai" (no doubt named after the film), which a 1960 newspaper article described as "a new cocktail consisting of Japanese sake poured over crushed ice with a dash of Worcestershire sauce." The one I made tasted every bit as nasty as this sounds. Fortunately, much better sake cocktails followed that decade.

On September 25, 1960, the *Los Angeles Times* announced construction had started on "the first authentic Japanese department store in the United States." The Seibu Store opened on March 14, 1962 at the corner of Wilshire Boulevard and Fairfax Avenue. The store sold Japan-imported goods exclusively. There were restau-

**Tokyo's Sake Hall Hibiya Bar is one of the few sake cocktail specialty bars in Japan, making delicious saketinis like this.**

rants, as well as a rooftop cocktail lounge called the Happi Room with a Japanese garden, ponds, small footbridges and stone lanterns and views of the city. The drinks menu, which was written on Japanese fans, included the East-West Agreement, a sake and bourbon cocktail, and the saketini. The *Times* added that the saketinis were made of sake and gin—not vodka, apparently. Local radio broadcaster Fred Beck sampled some of the Seibu saketinis, and reported, "The only noticeable difference between these and martinis was that in some queer way they caused the elevators to descend at a 90-degree angle instead of vertically."

Seibu, still one of Japan's largest department-store chains, was aiming to strengthen US-Japan relations with its LA Seibu store. Restaurants staffed with kimono-clad women serving Japanese and American food as well as sake-infused cocktails were part of that larger diplomatic push. It didn't work, however, and the Seibu Store was a failure, closing down after only two years. The building still stands, and currently houses the Peterson Automotive Museum.

The saketini lived on too, found in other Japanese restaurants across the country, including Yamato in Century City, which ran ads stating "Join Us For Saketini Time," and Azuma Sukiyaki House in Chicago, which served saketinis and Sakehattans (the sake version of the Manhattan). American newspapers ran stories about sake cocktails, and provided recipes for the saketini (1 part sake, 3 parts dry gin, stirred with ice, strained and served with

an olive), the Sakehattan (1 part sake, 2 parts rye whiskey, stirred with ice, strained into a cocktail glass and served with a cherry) or one called "The Geisha" (1 part sake, 2 parts bourbon, one tablespoon of sugar, juice from a halved lemon, ice, shaken and strained). In 1970, international news agency United Press International reported from Tokyo that the country's sake brewers were trying to get bar patrons to drink sake "martini style."

The Sakenic, a sake tonic, is Sake Hall Hibiya Bar's most popular cocktail. Made with sake, soda, tonic water, and an orange twist, it does not contain any distilled liquor. "For cocktails made from typical distilled liquors, the most important points are harmony and intimacy, using several different ingredients to achieve a balance," says the bar's planning director Toshiharu Yamamoto. This bar does that very well.

and *koji* making. It was also high in potassium, a yeast nutrient that promotes robust fermentation. The drawback was the distinctive smell it caused. A breakthrough came in 1959. Nihei noticed the foam in the *moromi* mash did not rise as high as normal. Yet the fermentation was robust, the aroma was pleasant and the acidity was low. The resulting sake was good. Nihei had discovered a low-foaming mutant yeast strain that, with some trepidation, he used again. The next batch was also delicious, without any bitterness or astringency and suited to California rice. Nihei had found his yeast.

There were other challenges, such as American labor laws that made it impossible to brew sake the traditional Japanese way. In Japanese breweries, the concept of overtime did not exist. Sake making was—and in many places continues to be—a 24-hour gig. Abiding by the American 40-hour work week would force the Honolulu brewery to pay pricey overtime and nighttime wages that were unthinkable in Japan. Nihei had to reframe the entire sake-making process into eight-hour shifts to suit American regulations. In 1960, he did just that. But he didn't simply have workers clock in for eight-hour days. Instead, he streamlined the process so any worker could do any job. Instead of making koji by hand, he used simple equipment of the type used to make koji for soy sauce. This way, the koji didn't need constant watching overnight. Most importantly, Nihei felt the koji the brewery produced was good and suited the California rice. The following year, in 1960, the Nihei's success in shortening the workday to eight hours inspired a sake maker in Yamaguchi to follow suit—the first Japanese brewery to do so.

Nihei was forced to approach sake making differently. He was making sake, but he was not making sake in Japan. There were too many daily reminders to shatter that illusion. "I think he wanted to make sake that suited Hawaiian food," said Misayo about her husband's sake, which she described as having a slightly dry taste. Of course, it suited both Japanese and Western food, but making sake in Hawaii with California rice, as well as eating both Japanese and American food, naturally led Nihei to see larger possibilities for sake.

Even though Nihei was never naturalized as an American citizen, he was making sake for Americans. He couldn't follow the old rules; had to make new ones in order to brew his beloved sake. He was a pioneer, putting down roots in a new land and bringing culture from his home country. The result wasn't Japanese sake—it was American. In 1978, Nihei wrote that he believed that sake could blossom into an international drink; he saw Hawaii at the vanguard of this movement. "I ask you for your support," he added. He has our admiration and thanks.

## The Nobel Prize Sake

"Our sake Fukuju was first served at the Nobel Prize Banquet in 2008," says Hironobu Kubota, the 40-something-year-old vice president of Kobe Shushinkan. There were four Japanese Nobel laureates in that year, and the Nobel Foundation decided to serve Fukuju. It continued the tradition in the years that followed.

Downstairs in an alcove where the brewery tour begins, is a glass case displaying Fukuju bottles autographed by Nobel laureates. The adjacent case holds glasses used at the ceremony. I peer closer through the glass case to make out the signatures of physicist Shuji Nakamura and economist Alvin E. Roth.

"Other sake brewers often say to us, 'You guys must be really good at self-promotion to get your sake served at the Nobel Prize Banquet,'" says Kubota. "But that's now how it happened." Instead, the Nobel Foundation had asked a local sake importer in Sweden for recommendations. He offered a couple to try, and the foundation liked Fukuju best. Fukuju Blue Label won out. "So it wasn't about PR, but knowing the right

# AMERICAN SAKE RICE

**Rice has a long history in the United States. Its first documentation as a commercial crop dates back to trial plantings in Virginia in 1609. As of 2019, Arkansas is the largest rice grower in the United States, comprising over 40 percent of all domestic production. The Arkansas prairies have proven fertile ground for rice and have helped the state surpass other rice-growing states like California and Texas. Traditionally a common variety used for American sake is Calrose, but there is an increasing demand for homegrown Yamada Nishiki.**

The first Calrose variety was released in 1948. A japonica cultivar, "Cal" refers to California while "rose" refers to medium grain rice like Louisiana's Blue Rose. It is a relative of Yamada Nishiki, but better suited for eating than its famous sake-rice relative. In the US, Calrose dominates Japanese and Korean cuisine because the rice remains soft even after it cools, making it ideal for localized versions of both countries' dishes. Calrose is the default grain for American sake brewers due to its quality and easy availability. But unlike Japanese sake rice, such as Yamada Nishiki or Gohyakumangoku, it does not have a *shinpaku* (white starchy core), making it more difficult to brew crisp and fruity ginjo and daiginjo. Also, Calrose requires a soaking time of eight hours or more, compared to the 10 to 20 minutes for Japan-grown Yamada Nishiki with a minimum 50 percent rice polishing ratio.

Yamada Nishiki, the king of sake rice, is grown in California and Arkansas. However, US-grown Yamada Nishiki isn't the same as its Japanese

counterpart, especially when compared to premium Hyogo-grown Yamada Nishiki. (Note that there is even a wide variety of Yamada Nishiki grown in Japan. For example, Yamada Nishiki grown in the Kanto region around Tokyo is different from the top-notch Hyogo variety, featuring a much smaller shinpaku.) Different or not, it's an appealing grain for American brewers. Chris Isbell of Isbell Farms in Lonoke County, Arkansas has been a pioneer in growing Japanese rice varieties. In 1991, he started growing Koshihikari, Japan's favorite table rice. Japanese TV crews arrived on Isbell's doorstep, wanting to know just how this American farmer had grown the beloved grain. Isbell's Koshihikari was even exported to Japan. "We are always looking for more profitable markets and sake rice seemed to be perfect for us," says Isbell, a second-generation rice farmer long interested in experimenting with a range of rice varieties. Isbell Farms' staple is long-grain rice, growing around 3,000 acres each year. In comparison, Isbell grows around 60 to 100 acres of sake rice with about 350,000 pounds annually. As of 2019, two large US brewers and a dozen or so smaller ones are buying the Arkansas Yamada Nishiki. Sales are up at around 2 percent annually. "We expect that to jump in the coming years."

Isbell Farms started growing Yamada Nishiki in 2007 for testing purposes for Takara Sake USA, making it the first, or at least one of the first, American farms to grow the legendary sake rice. In Lonoke Country, the average day and night temperature difference is only around 10 to 15 degrees Fahrenheit, but that divide widens during late summer and early fall, making good conditions for Yamada Nishiki to grow until its October harvest. "So far our shinpaku has remained high and stable," says Isbell. "You could call it American Yamada Nishiki, but it compares very favorably with Japanese Yamada Nishiki, I believe." Besides the king of sake rice, Isbell Farms has also grown a variety of other legendary brewing grains, including Wataribune, Omachi and Gohyakumangoku. "We'd grow these varieties upon request," says Isbell. "But so far, everyone wants the Yamada Nishiki."

**A close-up look at the Yamada Nishiki grown by Isbell Farms in Arkansas.**

LEFT Casks at the Nadagiku Sake Brewery in Himeji, Japan. Mikinosuke Kawaishi, the younger brother of the brewery's founder, helped spread the sport of judo in France, which Nagagiku honors with Judo-branded junmai daiginjo sake. BELOW A row of Fukuju sakes at Kobe Shushinkan. The distinctive blue bottle has been served at the Nobel Prize Banquet. FACING PAGE A brewer does *kai-ire* pole mashing at the Sakecul brewery in Culiacán, Mexico.

people and being lucky enough to be chosen."

There isn't a more fitting sake to be served at the Nobel Prize Banquet. For one thing, it's a smooth, fruity junmai ginjo that pairs well with a range of European food. Furthermore, in Japanese, Fukuju (福寿) contains two highly auspicious kanji: "Fuku" (福) meaning "good fortune" and "ju" (寿, which is also read as "kotobukiya" on its own), meaning "congratulations." Together, they are translated as "long life and happiness." And besides the quality and the name, the other thing that makes this sake a perfect fit for the Nobel Prize Banquet is its blue bottle. What better sake to serve in Stockholm's Blue Hall, where the dinner is held?

This explains why Fukuju Blue Label has been served at nine Nobel banquets since 2008. During the 2014 ceremony, Japanese researchers were awarded the Nobel Prize for developing the blue LED, drawing unintended connections with Fukuju's blue bottle. "In 2017, there were no Nobel Prize laureates from Japan, but they still served Fukuju," says Kubota. The decision to continue serving Fukuju even in the absence of Japanese prizewinners is a welcome sign for the future of Japanese sake. It shows that sake doesn't need a direct connection to Japan for it to be enjoyed. Fukuju Blue Label is delicious on its own and doesn't need an excuse to be served.

"My dream is that one day sake will be on restaurant menus just like wine or beer," Kubota says, pausing to look at the plum blossoms outside. "And that will be completely normal. I want that time to come." At an important banquet in Stockholm, it already has.

## The Worldwide Sake Boom

The world is embracing sake like never before. The *Nikkei* newspaper reported that in 2018 Japan's sake exports doubled since 2013, hitting a record high of $200 million. Globally, people aren't only drinking more sake, they are also making more sake. There are craft breweries all over the world, producing very good sake, whether that's in France, New Zealand or Vietnam. Japan is also starting to take foreign sake more seriously. Each year, new breweries continue to open outside Japan. In the United States alone, the number of breweries has jumped from five in the year to 2000 to over twenty in 2019. "In five years, there will likely be 100 brewers in the US," says Yasutaka Daimon, president of the Daimon brewery in Osaka.

This isn't the first sake boom. There have been a series of mini-booms over the years. In the 1950s, Hollywood released a handful of movies set in Japan, such as *House of Bamboo* and *Sayonara*, which captured the imagination of Americans, with trendsetters like *Vogue* magazine gushing about hot sake. During the 1980s, interest in sake was sparked again, coinciding with the rise of sushi, exported Walkmans and Toyotas. Giants like Takara

Shuzo and Hakutsuru set up breweries in California that same decade, joining Ozeki who had arrived first in 1979. Their sake was well made and filled a niche market. But now, a new generation of brewers is emerging, keen to put their own spin on the traditional Japanese beverage and bring it to a wider drinking public.

## Craft Sake Goes Global

When the Japanese sake-brewing giants established operations in the US, they churned out mass-produced sake. Small batch wasn't part of the business model. "Craft sake" typically refers to sake that isn't mass-produced and is usually reserved for small-batch sake. It does not necessarily mean 100 percent hand-made, however, because even in Japan, many small so-called craft breweries have also instituted automated steps in their brewing process for various reasons: the breweries might be short-staffed or, as is more often the case, they want to achieve certain, highly pure flavors that aren't possible by hand.

LEFT Brooklyn Kura founders Brian Polan and Brandon Doughan.
BELOW LEFT A Brooklyn brewed junmai paired with a sandwich and pickle.
BELOW RIGHT The 2,500-square-foot Brooklyn Kura is located in the borough's Sunset Park. It's part of the new generation of American sake makers.

It wasn't until the late 1990s that craft sake started being made in the continental United States. Enter Oregon-based brewery SakéOne. "Since we were in fact the first American craft sake brewery, the term 'craft sake' could essentially be defined by what we produced in our early years of sake brewing—starting in 1997—and how that has evolved to what we produce today," explains SakéOne president Steve Vuylsteke. The Pacific Northwest is an ideal place to make sake, with humidity that's lower than in Japan, making it easier to prevent spoilage. There's access to excellent soft water from Oregon's Coast Mountain range that the

brewery's founders thought was similar in character to the soft snowy water of Aomori Prefecture in northern Japan. However, unlike in Japan, where groundwater can be used, American brewers have to use water from the local water supply. SakéOne has a sophisticated UV filtration system to remove chlorine, fluorine and other organic matter. "I think craft has more to do with small batch size and an artisanal approach to production, such as hands-on rice milling, koji rice preparation and batch building." While Vuylsteke likes the term "craft sake," he thinks it's losing some of its luster these days as large beverage companies are slapping it on a range of releases in hopes of appearing more "authentic." In the case of foreign sake, the term is the best way to distinguish the aims of the new crop of smaller brewers.

"We're calling ourselves an American craft sake brewery," says Brandon Doughan, who is the head brewer at Brooklyn Kura, which opened in early 2018. "I want to learn as much as I can from brewers in Japan, but at the end of the day, we're not in Japan." The brewery uses American rice from California and Arkansas and soft Brooklyn water from the Catskills. "So we're going to be different just based on those reasons." Doughan was previously a research scientist developing drugs to fight cancer and heart disease before a chance meeting in 2013 with his future business partner, Brian Polan, at a friend's wedding in Japan. For Doughan, who had been home brewing beer for decades, sake's delicate flavors were a revelation. Sake, though,

can be a daunting drink for newbies. "For people outside Japan who don't understand the language and can't read sake labels, getting into sake can be difficult," says Doughan. "If you want to get into sake, that is a big initial hurdle." That's why Brooklyn Kura and other international breweries use the local lingo where possible. However, it doesn't make sense to translate established terms describing sake styles, such as junmai or ginjo. "We don't have any Japanese writing on our bottles, but we use Japanese words for the key terms," he explains, adding, "You're not going to make a new word for 'merlot.'"

At Brooklyn Kura, the taproom looks like something you'd see at a beer brewery and not a traditional sake one. The sake is served in wineglasses, which spreads the message—

The Dojima Sake Brewery in Fordham, England. The character on the side of the building reads "sake."

Dojima Sake Brewery production manager Tony Mitchell previously worked at the Wakatakeya Sake Brewery in Fukuoka Prefecture.

Brooklyn Kura, while others are Japanese ventures. For example, Wakaze, a Tokyo-based brewing start-up, received $1.4 million in funding to set up a small sake brewery outside Paris. Asahi Shuzo, of Dassai fame, established a brewery in Hyde Park, New York. In 2018 Kotobuki Shuzo from Osaka set up a craft sake maker called the Dojima Brewery in Fordham, England. Sake brewer Tony Mitchell previously worked and lived at his wife's family brewery in Japan, for three and a half months—something he calls a "life changing, semi-religious experience." The Dojima Brewery uses imported Yamada Nishiki and Akita Sake Komachi rice, as the UK doesn't have any suitable brewing rice of which Mitchell is aware. The local water well water is two to three times harder than Japan's legendary sake-brewing water, *miyamizu*, and according to Mitchell, the water's hardness is brought down "quite a bit." Yet, all of this is happening in England and over time, the local character will manifest itself in the sake. Dojima's stuff isn't cheap, at an extraordinary £1,000 a bottle "Our founders' mission is to raise the worldwide profile of sake," says Mitchell. "They want to see it compete shoulder to shoulder in Michelin star restaurants with fine wine."

## The Difficulty of Making Sake Abroad

Sake production is suited for Japan—particularly regions with cold winters. Taiwan, Brazil and Mexico all make good sake, but as in Hawaii (see page 194), the local climates pose challenges.

After Taiwan came under Japanese imperial rule in 1895, the island was populated with Japanese migrants, thirsty for a taste of home. By 1907, some Japanese had sake-brewing licenses, but the humid weather, which causes

especially to restaurants—that you don't need special drinking vessels to offer sake to customers. Foreign brewers are starting to experiment—adding dry hops, using different yeasts, or aging sakes in bourbon casks. Some work. Some don't. But there is a willingness to try things out, and a dedication to sake making. "I want to make sure we're producing a top quality junmai," says Doughan. In Brooklyn, they are.

Some international craft breweries are entirely owned by locals, such as the aforementioned batches to rot, made brewing proper sake difficult. Making *shubo* yeast starter was particularly difficult, so the *mizumoto* technique, originally developed for brewing in summer, was successfully adopted. In 1913, one of the most advanced breweries in the world, Nihon Houjousha, was established in Taipei by Tetsuji Fujimoto. The goal was to make a pure-rice sake without the preservatives needed to make the trip from Japan. The brewery had reinforced, double-brick walls and inside was kept to a chilly 41 to 42°F with an advanced cooling system. The year-round brewery even used rice imported from Okayama for its Butterfly Orchid–branded sake. An elaborate setup like this costs money and without the sales to support the operation, the brewery shuttered a few years after opening. Other breweries did open and find more success, but in 1922 the government nationalized sake production and finally ceased sake making in 1973. It was revived in 1997 by the then state-owned Taiwan Tobacco and Liquor Corporation. In 2007, Wufeng District Farmers Association established a brewery in Taichung, sending staff to Niigata to study sake making. So far, the results have been impressive. Made from local fragrant rice, Wufeng's sake has won several international awards. Brewery director Huang Ching-chien told *Taiwan News* in 2009, "The sake produced at the Wufeng Brewery is the only Taiwanese sake which corresponds to the demands of Japanese sake standards. The drink can make its makers proud; you can taste the joy put into the production process by its brewers."

Brazil has been making sake since the early 20th century, overcoming a less-than-ideal climate. A wave of Japanese immigrants started arriving in the early 20th century and it was inevitable that a domestic brewing industry would arise. The country's most famous brand, Azuma Kirin, was created at the Campinas

ABOVE The entrance to the Taiwan Tobacco & Liquor Corporation brewing facility in Taoyuan, Taiwan. Its sake brand Yuchan is widely available in supermarkets and convenience stores nationwide.
LEFT Japanese gastropub Izakaya Issa in São Paulo, Brazil. In the past few decades, Japanese food and sake have reached a wider audience in Brazil.

Agricultural Industry Ltd. sake brewery in São Paulo in 1934. Hisaya Iwasaki, son of Mitsubishi founder Yataro Iwasaki, founded the brewery and in 2015, Kirin Holdings took control of it. Still, the Azuma Kirin brand lives on.

Civilian leaders and members of the US military perform a *kagami-biraki* ("opening the lid" of the sake barrel) ceremony, which is said to be auspicious and unlock harmony.

Like Brazil, Mexico had to overcome adverse temperatures to make excellent international sake. Conceived in 2014, Sakecul in Culiacán is the country's first brewery, staffed by toji Jesús Ernesto Reyes Valenzuela and four young brewers, some with biochemical backgrounds. Sakecul's Nami-branded junmai is made with soft local water and imported Yamada Nishiki. The result is a delicious ricey junmai that pairs well with fresh local seafood or spicy dishes. Not only is brewing in such a hot climate tricky, Sakecul says it had to educate locals, many of whom initially thought sake was a high-proof, distilled drink like tequila!

Overseas, basic infrastructure can be lacking. Getting equipment is expensive and hard. Brewers don't have the same wealth of options in procuring rice. SakéOne in Oregon is a rarity among smaller craft producers as it has rice mills and does its polishing onsite. In Japan, the tax office has helped create a support system to ensure brewers know how to make good sake and can get the raw materials they need. The Japanese government wants good sake to be made so it can tax the brews. Without this support, foreign brewers must be incredibly driven to succeed. So when French brewery Les Larmes du Levant in Pélussin makes its savory and ricey brews, it has to jump through many more hoops than French wine makers or the sake makers back in Japan. But despite these hurdles, the quality of foreign-produced sake continues rises year after year—and will no doubt continue to do so.

# THE BREWERY WHERE
# EAST MEETS WEST

**"The sake goddess led us to meet," says Yasutaka Daimon, president of the Daimon brewery, gesturing to his American business partner Marcus Consolini. "I'm very happy about that." Consolini is the first foreign owner of a sake brewery in modern times. "Daimon-san is the sixth generation *kuramoto* and I'm the seventh," he explains. The brewery is located in Katano, Osaka Prefecture, on the border of Nara and Kyoto.**

Daimon-san is spritely and charismatic. He speaks fluent English, which is somewhat rare for has those of his generation. Now in his early 70s, Daimon-san went on an international odyssey in 1969, seeing the world, visiting 65 countries and picking up English (and some French) before returning to the brewery in 1975. "In my era, the brewery and the sake business were secure," says Daimon. "When I came back to the brewery, I could see the rest of my life. But for my son, it wasn't clear. It's not just in this brewery, but throughout the industry, no one can predict the future." Worried about security, Daimon advised his sons to choose other career paths.

While Daimon-san co-founded the Japan Sake Export Association and worked hard to not only make the industry but his own brewery more international, instability at Daimon Brewery forced him to take over as toji in 2003. With the future looking grim, land developers circled, hoping to bulldoze the brewery and divvy up the space for residences. The brewery and its lovely garden with the traditional Japanese home where Daimon grew up would be lost forever. Thankfully, the brewery was saved, but the new owners

didn't understand the world of sake. The result was a disaster. The brewery was put up on the market once again. The future was a question mark.

That's when fate intervened. Consolini, who had been working throughout Asia-Pacific for the past 25 years in the financial sector, dropped by the brewery one day, hoping to see the Daimon residence for renovation ideas.

Daimon greeted the New Yorker warmly and explained the financial pickle the brewery was in. Consolini was intrigued and decided to make an offer to buy the brewery. In 2017, Consolini became the CEO, hardly a typical arrangement in the traditional world of sake. Consolini not only respected the brewery's nuanced, umami-rich house style, but the family that had run the brewery since its founding in 1826. "In other acquisitions in this industry, the previous owners step away," explains Daimon. "But I think it was wise that the investors not only acquired this brewery, but involved the family as well with a stake and a say."

"This project is not just a business anymore," says Consolini. "I've sat next to Daimon-san everyday for

The partnership between Yasutaka Daimon and Marcus Consolini has not only saved the Daimon Brewery, but also the traditional house where Daimon grew up and the garden he played in as a boy.

the past few years, seven days a week. My three year-old daughter literally believes that he is her grandpa." Consolini was keen to make sure that Daimon's sons are involved in the brewery and both coming onboard speaks volumes about the brewery's future. Says Consolini, "In the first year of this brewery's rebirth, we became the largest exporter of Osaka sake. I think Daimon Shuzo will become even more craft oriented, more purist and more traditional," says Consolini. The brewery runs an internship program, with interns living and working at the brewery for a week—with everything explained in English. "I think Daimon Shuzo will become an international center of training," says Consolini. "Daimon Shuzo will train the world."

# REVIEWS AND TASTING NOTES FOR OVER 100 SAKES

**by Takashi Eguchi**

These tasting notes include over 100 diverse, high-quality sakes, from inexpensive to premium. Most are available outside Japan, whether through online retailers, specialty shops, or bars and restaurants that specialize in sake. The goal is to show the range of flavors and nuances that sake encompasses. I tasted the sakes in bars, restaurants, and at home. All of them were paid for out of pocket. No tastings were done at the request of any sake brewery.

## About the Tasting Notes

My notes cover flavor, background on the sake or brewery, and food pairings. To describe a beverage, especially sake, I believe these are essential. I also include sake type, the rice and its polishing ratio (if specified) and brewery name and location. The type of yeast isn't typically listed on a sake bottle label, but is mentioned in the tasting note when deemed appropriate.

Sake has a wide range of aromas and flavors. Unlike wine or whisky, many sakes are not fragrant when nosed; their flavors are retronasal, appearing once you've taken a sip. Bitterness and astringency are common, and for brewers, are considered necessary for a pleasant finish. They also add complexity, but balance is important.

Flavors also change at different temperatures; these sakes were tasted either chilled, at room temperature, or warmed to varying degrees. Warming sake can make for a new experience. In these notes, I recommend temperatures I think work best. However, use them as a rule of thumb as you discover which serving styles you prefer. Recently, there has been a focus on chilled sake, hindering what makes sake so great and different from other beverages.

The sakes were tasted in a variety of vessels, including traditional *choko* and *guinomi*, and modern wineglasses. Where appropriate, the recommended drinking vessel is also noted.

## The Philosophy of Pairing

Though sake pairs very well with a wide range of food, this is not the way it has traditionally been considered. Sake was drunk with *otsumami*, umami-concentrated salty snacks or light eats that enhance the taste of sake. When served with Japanese meals, sake was typically selected to discreetly support the food and not disturb the flavors. Now, with the influence of wine culture, sake pairing is more dynamic. Either approach is valid; the main point is to enhance the food.

The basic principles of food pairing are to

harmonize and compliment. Flavors, aromas or textures that are similar are harmonious, whereas complimentary ones add to the experience. Imagine vinegar or lemon juice on deep-fried food. Sake with refreshing acidity can perform a similar function. Sometimes certain dishes seem like they might be a good match for a sake, but turn out not to be. This makes pairing an act of discovery, which is part of the enjoyment. Don't be afraid to try unexpected matches. You might be pleasantly surprised.

Every sake doesn't go with every Japanese dish. Often, you can defer to the restaurant for an in-house recommendation. In these notes, I have tried to pick international rather than Japanese dishes to show the versatility of sake.

## Scoring

Sake is an agricultural product, not an industrial one, even when it is mass-produced. That's why scoring sake is so difficult. But at the same time, scores can help give an idea of the quality. This book uses a five-point scale, with one star being poor, two stars being okay, three stars being good, four stars being great, and five stars being excellent. Even the best sakes aren't perfect; also, scores express personal preference. There are no sakes below three stars in this book; I do recommend every single sake listed. Think of each star as the degree to which the sake is recommended. My scores are based on the sake's flavors in terms of originality and balance. Even if there are off-flavors, if they are well balanced, the sake can be good. The brewer's philosophy, regional characteristics and history are also important in appreciating a sake. Thus, I'm not simply evaluating the chemical composition of the drink, but the larger story it encompasses.

Sake is typically grouped into categories such as *futshu-shu*, *honjozo*, and so on. However, these categories do not always reflect the flavors. Sake is also often categorized by region, but not every sake embodies the place it's brewed. This makes grouping sake difficult. I have divided these notes into three sections: light bodied, medium bodied and full bodied. The sakes are then sorted within each category by alphabetic ordering of the brewery name.

As a professional sommelier, I believe my approach to scoring the sakes in this book is rational and reliable. But everyone has their own preferences, and taste perception varies from person to person. I hope you find my recommendations helpful and that you thoroughly enjoy the process of discovering the sakes that you love most!

Sake is an excellent companion to food. Taste, aroma, texture, and temperature of both sake and food are key in pairing. But they are not only things to keep in mind. The region where sake is made and the people who brew it should be kept in mind, too. Pictured is a Jikon Junmai Daiginjo. See page 218 for the tasting note.

## LIGHT BODIED

### Aramasa No. 6 S-type Nama

Aramasa (Akita, Akita Prefecture)

★★★⯪☆

**Distinct acidity and refreshing aromas**

With its own No. 6 yeast, kimoto starter and no additives, this unpasteurized version of Aramasa's standard expression is brimming with character. Unlike ordinary sakes, it has a subtle rice nuance, which makes it easy to drink even for non-sake diehards. Straight out of the fridge, the first impression is elegant apple and citrus juice. The mouthfeel is sharp and refreshing with a touch of fizz and acidity followed by apple, Asian pear, green citrus and whey. Rejuvenating stuff, but with loads of flavor. The alcohol is hardly noticeable. It finishes softly as if it's floating away, leaving some unwanted bitterness and sweetness. As it warms to room temperature, this kimoto quickly begins to lose balance. It's best served chilled.

**Recommended pairings:** This refreshing and acidic sake pairs well with sautéed pork, baked cheddar cheese, apples or pears. Its carefully calculated flavors can also be enjoyed solo. **Type:** Junmai, kimoto, nama. **Rice variety:** Not specified (55% polishing ratio).

### Dassai Beyond

Asahi Shuzo (Iwakuni, Yamaguchi Prefecture)

★★★★☆

**Super-premium sake**

If Dassai 23 is premium sake (and it is), then Dassai Beyond is super-premium sake. It's expensive, but Asahi Shuzo has thrown its whole weight behind it. This is an exceedingly carefully made handcrafted sake. Dassai Beyond is not a daily drink, but one for very special occasions.

Chilled to around 54°F (12°C), this is one delicious sake. More importantly, it oozes Dassai's signature nuanced flavors. The granulated-sugar sweetness dissolves like cotton candy on the palate; the acidity is reminiscent of an Asian pear. There are aromas of melon, apricot and rice. Apricot returns in a long finish and lingers on the palate. At room temperature, however, there is some astringency; chilled there was none. This shows just how specific and focused Dassai Beyond is. Serve chilled.

**Recommended pairings:** Dassai Beyond is best savored on its own. **Type:** Junmai daiginjo. **Rice variety:** Yamada Nishiki (polishing ratio not specified).

### Kubota Senju

Asahi-Shuzo Sake Brewing (Nagaoka, Niigata Prefecture)

★★★⯪☆

**Dry and light bodied**

The Asahi-Shuzo brewery sums up this sake with an old saying: "True taste is not thick and strong; rather, it's moderate and simple, just like an amazing person who looks ordinary." Chilled, this sake is dry, light and smooth, but its modest, mellow and balanced notes lend weight. There are subtle fruity bouquets of just-sliced apple, fresh cream and rosemary along with simple and elegant sweetness. The finish is quick: acidity soon vanishes and the peppery, milky and umami nuances linger. At 113°F (45°C), the rice notes are teased out, with a lovely soft finish, as if the sake evaporates right off the tongue. The scent of rice remains. Good ginjo always works well warmed.

**Recommended pairings:** This sake made me hungry! Yes, this brew increases one's appetite. Chilled, try with cheese, seafood tempura and Thai cuisine. **Type:** Ginjo. **Rice variety:** Gohyakumangoku (polishing ratio: koji-mai 50%, kake-mai 55%).

## LIGHT BODIED

### Number Fourteen Junmai Ginjo

Brooklyn Kura (Brooklyn, New York, United States)

★★★★☆

**Cheerful, elegant and cosmopolitan**

The copious excitement around the Brooklyn Kura (see page 207) is not just hype. This sake is the real deal. Using excellent New York water, Brooklyn Kura has made a delicious, well-balanced and sophisticated brew. Nosing the glass reveals a lovely bouquet: apple, pear, chantilly cream and white clover. On arrival, the sake is mellow, sweet and round with apple, orange, peach and cream cheese notes. It finishes with acidity and lingering orange peel sprinkled with cacao. Warming the sake to 50°F (122°C) brings out new flavors: lavender, ice-cream wafers and marshmallows. Try it warmed, but this sake is best served chilled.

**Recommended pairing:** Burgers, BBQ, meatball spaghetti and steak. To be honest, it's hard to think of food this Brooklyn sake doesn't suit. **Type**: Junmai ginjo. **Rice variety:** Yamada Nishiki (koji-mai, 60% polishing ratio), Calrose (kake-mai, 50% polishing ratio).

### Fukumasamune Black

Fukumitsuya Sake Brewery (Kanazawa, Ishikawa Prefecture)

★★★★☆

**Reasonably priced, but well executed**

Fukumasamune Black is a wonderful well-priced junmai that shows how much effort the brewery puts into its regular lineup. Soft and delicate, it has an abundantly elegant flavor. At room temperature, Fukumasamune Black is especially soft. On the palate, there is a one-two-three punch of sweetness, acidity and bitterness. For a daily sake, this is a regal drink, with a texture like carefully folded silk. Aromas of evaporated milk and grapefruit come up through the nose. The finish is peppery and short. Warmed to 113°F (45°C), this brew becomes far more balanced, with sweetness and nectar notes more readily apparent. The finish is long and milky and the alcohol's sharpness is toned down. This is a flexible sake that works well at a variety of different temperatures. Feel free to experiment.

**Recommended pairings:** Steamed fish or grilled lemon chicken. **Type:** Junmai. **Rice variety:** Not specified (70% polishing ratio).

### Fu

Fukunishiki Sake Brewing (Kasai, Hyogo Prefecture)

★★★★☆

**A low-alcohol brew**

The Fukunishiki Brewery's Fu sake is a low-alcohol brew that clocks in at 8 percent alcohol by volume. It was initially exported as an aperitif, which makes sense, as it leaves a strong impression of fruit juice. Plus, it turns out that Fu can also be enjoyed with food, especially spicy dishes.

This is a fruity sake, with aromas of Asian pear, apple and citrus juice. The sweet-and-sour flavors make this sake remarkably refreshing. On the palate, Fu is thick and smooth, and very sweet. The finish is crisp with apple juice nuances. Drink chilled.

**Recommended pairings:** Beef and pork pair well, as the sake's fruity acidity cuts down the fatty meal. Its intense sweetness also makes it a good companion for spicy foods. **Type:** Junmai. **Rice variety:** Kinuhikari (70% polishing ratio).

### Hakkaisan Junmai Ginjo Yukimuro Chozo 3-Year

Hakkaisan Brewery (Uonuma, Niigata Prefecture)

★★★★☆

**Aged for three years in the snow**

In Niigata, there is a tradition of preserving food and drink in the snow by digging a hole to make a snow-insulated cellar called a *yukimuro*. Hakkaisan, one of the biggest Niigata breweries, ages this sake for three years in an enormous yukimuro structure with 1,000 tons of snow, cooled to 37°F (3°C). The low temperatures create a round, smooth sake with almost no distinct matured flavor despite the aging; this sake still tastes very fresh. It's a soft junmai ginjo with acidity and delicate aromas of green citrus and apricot. Gentle sweetness gives way to intense bitterness, while light acidity dances on the tongue. The finish is crisp and indicative of Niigata's signature tanrei style. Afternotes of citrus juice, apricot and rice linger. Serve at 50°F (10°C) in a wineglass.

**Recommended pairings:** Grilled fish and raw oysters. **Type:** Junmai ginjo, koshu. **Rice variety:** Yamada Nishiki (koji-mai), Yukinosei and Gohyakumangoku (kake-mai) (50% polishing ratio).

### Hakutsuru Dry Hisho

Hakutsuru Sake Brewing (Higashi Nada, Kobe, Hyogo Prefecture)

★★★★☆

**Highly skilled brewing technique**

Hakutsuru is one of Japan's biggest sake-brewing companies, exporting to 50 countries. In some countries, such as Brazil where I tasted this sake, the brand is synonymous with sake. While the brewery makes some incredible small-batch ginjo and daiginjo, it also makes terrific honjozo alcohol-added sake. Many consider honjozo lower-grade stuff because it's generally made from table rice and fortified with brewer's alcohol. But there are many high-quality honjozo sakes. Case in point: Hakutsuru Dry Hisho. Nosing the glass brings milky green-grass scents. A sip reveals a smooth and soft sake, with retronasal aromas of green citrus and yogurt. The finish is sharp and well executed, with rice flavors lingering briefly. This honjozo works well in a wineglass. Serve chilled or at room temperature.

**Recommended pairings:** Holds its own well against steak, but it can also pair with more delicate fish flavors. **Type:** Honjozo. **Rice variety:** Not specified (koji-mai 65% polishing ratio; kake-mai 70%).

### Bijofu Tokubetsu Junmai

Hamakawa Shoten (Tano, Kochi Prefecture)

★★★☆☆

**Light and delicate aromas of rice and citrus**

The Hamakawa Shoten brewery uses exceedingly soft water. The result is gentle sakes like this.

Chilled, the arrival is strong, with a soft texture. But it is also sharp and refreshing with modest fruity aromas of apricot, winter melon and fine rice flour. There is a slight bitterness reminiscent of green citrus. The finish is long with tongue-tingling acidity. Warming will make the sake's milky nuances more apparent. The mouthfeel also becomes smoother and lighter. Drink this tokubetsu junmai at 140°F (60°C), or chilled.

**Recommended pairings:** Mozzarella cheese, honey-grilled pork chops and other fatty, savory-sweet foods complement this sake's refreshing acidity. **Type:** Tokubetsu junmai. **Rice variety:** Not specified (60% polishing ratio).

## LIGHT BODIED

### Umakara Mansaku

Hinomaru Jozo (Yokote, Akita Prefecture)

★★★★☆

**High-minded flavor with quick and gentle finish**

*Umakara* stands for "umami and dry." Dry sake tends to have less richness in flavor. However, that isn't the case for this brew.

The first impression is of a vivid, spreading rich flavor, which soon disappears. After a short pause, there's suddenly a lush, flowing aftertaste. Melon aromas, overtones of fine rice flour, good acidity and pleasant bitterness mingle with umami and the sharpness of alcohol. At 136°F (58°C), this sake is light and smooth with sweet notes of rice followed by savory umami. The finish is clean. Umakara Mansaku is an unpretentious sake that makes quite an impact. Best served chilled.

**Recommended pairings:** This highly versatile sake works well with umami-rich meals. Stewed fish and meat, in particular, bring out the rice aromas. Marinated dishes juxtapose nicely with this sake's refreshing spirit. **Type:** Tokubetsu junmai. **Rice variety:** Aki no Sei (55% polishing ratio).

### Kikutsukasa Bodaimoto Junmai

Kikutsukasa Jozo (Ikoma, Nara Prefecture)

★★★★☆

**Dry but savory; atypical**

In the 1990s when a group of Nara breweries revived bodaimoto, they initially aimed to make full-bodied, umami-rich sake. But after about 10 years, the breweries went their own way, devising their own takes on bodaimoto. So, Kikutsukasa is dry and light with pungent acidity and intense umami at room temperature. Floral and herbal notes are followed by milky aromas of rice, as well as flavors of soy sauce, ice-cream wafers and milk chocolate. In addition, there is a hint of smoke. The distinctive afternotes are tangy bitterness and astringency, both of which are rather unpleasant. However, there are agreeable lingering notes, such as cooked rice, hay, cacao and milk chocolate.

**Recommended pairings:** Smoked cheese, cream cheese and teriyaki. **Type:** Junmai, bodaimoto. **Rice variety:** Not specified.

### Jikon Junmai Daiginjo

Kiyasho Brewery (Nabari, Mie Prefecture)

★★★★☆

**Completely in the moment**

*Jikon* means "to live out today without being trapped in the past or the future." It's a word made famous by Dogen, a 13th-century Zen Buddhist monk. Brewed with locally grown Yamada Nishiki, this sake leaves a straightfoward impression without any unwanted flavors whatsoever. Tasted from a wineglass at 50°F (10°C), intense fruity apple aromas are followed by a modest and sweet rice scent. The texture is refined and mellow, and the sake finishes quietly, as if absorbed into the tongue. Subtle umami and sweetness linger. Warmed up to 68°F (20°C), it's still well balanced; a bouquet of lychee and rice flour appears. Drink chilled or at room temperature.

**Recommended pairings:** Daikon radish with mild vinegar, dill pickles, fresh shellfish. You can always enjoy it alone. **Type:** Junmai daiginjo. **Rice variety:** Yamada Nishiki (40% polishing ratio).

### Honjozo Kita no Nishiki Houmon

Kobayashi Shuzo (Kuriyama, Hokkaido Prefecture)

★★★★☆

**Strong, yet floral, with a frontier spirit.**

The strong alcohol notes in this lightly unbalanced and top-heavy sake are immediately evident. In any other brew, that might be a criticism, but this Hokkaido sake evokes the hearty frontier of Japan's northernmost island. In the glass, it smells of anise and flowers. The texture is round and soft, but is soon overtaken by strong alcohol notes, making you realize that, yes, you're drinking booze. There is a powdered-sugar sweetness and a citrus-like acidity, followed by a nuance of diluted milk with strawberry. Aromas of candy, cooked rice and a hint of honey follow. The afternotes are short, with apricot and the strong bitterness of alcohol. Serve warmed to around 104°F (40°C) to enjoy a sweet rice bouquet and a mellow umami finish reminiscent of vegetable broth.

**Recommended pairings:** Performs surprisingly well with a variety of food. **Type:** Honjozo. **Rice variety:** Kirara 397 (70% polishing ratio).

### Kouro Ginjo

Kumamoto Prefecture Sake Research Center

★★★★☆

**Old-school style**

This brewery (or, better yet, research center) was established in 1909 to improve the quality of Kumamoto sake, and isolated a high-quality ginjo yeast that is still distributed nationwide.

Chilled to 54°F (12°C), this is very much an old school ginjo. The fruity elements are simple and modest. There are nuances of apple, apricot and subtle Japanese citrus. It also contains fine rice and a gentle sweetness. The texture is light and smooth. The sweetness isn't cloying or annoying. It's simple, but defined. Apple, apricot and rice linger with peppery spices. Warmed to 108°F (42°C), it's silky, milky and tongue-tingling. There is a good ricey characteristic when warmed, but it's best chilled or at room temperature.

**Recommended pairings:** This sake pairs well with modestly seasoned dishes, as well as sashimi and white fish. Try it with shortbread. It is also good on its own. **Type:** Ginjo. **Rice variety:** Unspecified (Koji-mai: 45%, Kake-mai 55% polishing ratio).

### Kunimare Junmai Ginpu

Kunimare Sake Brewery (Asahika-wa, Hokkaido Prefecture)

★★★½☆

**A dry sake with a strong kick**

Right off the bat, this sake seems light and dry, with noticeable alcohol notes. It's emblematic of Hokkaido-style brews, which are known for leaving a strong impression of alcohol as if they were distilled spirits, even though they are no stronger than your typical sake. But here, underneath that alcohol, there is a gentleness and a soft and subtle sweetness like flower nectar. The acidity is thin and dry. Rosemary and mint notes are joined by the scent of cooked rice. Aromas of harsh wild grasses and unripe strawberries contrast with lush flower nectar. Going further into this brew, there are more vegetal notes and even more flower nectar. Serve at room temperature.

**Recommended pairings:** Tempura, calamari and shellfish. Since this sake is short on acidity, it is excellent with vinaigrette-dressed salad. **Type:** Junmai **Rice variety:** Ginpu (65% polishing ratio).

## LIGHT BODIED

### Tsuki no Katsura Asahi-mai Junmai

Masuda Tokubee Shoten (Fushimi, Kyoto Prefecture)

★★★★☆

**A sake made from heirloom rice**

In the early 20th century, a farmer named Shinjiro Yamato discovered Asahi-mai (Asahi rice) in Kyoto, and the grain went on to find success as a table rice. By the 1930s, one third of the rice fields in western Japan were planted with Asahi-mai. But by the end of the century, it had fallen out of favor. In 2001, a local farmer started growing it near the Masuda Tokubee Shoten brewery, which began using it to make this Fushimi sake. The result is mellow and chewy. The signature chestnut sweetness of koji is strong, with a tangy acidity that rises up and spreads throughout the mouth. Aromas of apricot, honey and azaleas fill the senses. Acidity comes back in the finish with notes of grape skins. Warming it up brings out cottage cheese, lime and orange-peel aromas. The finish is sharp and acidic, with milk and rice nuances. Serve chilled or warmed to 113°F (45°C).

**Recommended pairings:** Sweet and sour pork or teriyaki. **Type:** Junmai. **Rice variety:** Asahi No. 4 (60% polishing ratio).

### Miyoshikiku Origarami Tokubetsu Junmai Muroka Nama Genshu

Miyoshikiku Shuzo (Ikeda, Tokushima Prefecture)

★★★★☆

**Welcome to the citrus kingdom**

Shikoku is Japan's citrus kingdom, so it's no wonder that this unfiltered Shikoku sake has citrus notes. This cloudy brew tastes different, even unorthodox. It is refreshing, with mellow acidity and notes of powdered sugar, cream cheese and whey. There are also nuances of mandarin orange and lime peel. The finish is pleasantly bitter, with lingering yogurt and candied citrus aromas. This brew is made with a locally grown grain known as Awa Yamada Nishiki. "Awa" is the traditional name for this area, which is known for growing high-quality Yamada Nishiki thanks to its soil, climate and skilled farmers.

**Recommended pairings:** Salad with vinaigrette dressing or any vegetables with a sour flavor. New York–style cheesecake harmonizes with the cream cheese notes in the sake, and the citrus nuances provide an accent for the dessert. **Type:** Tokubetsu junmai. **Rice variety:** Awa Yamada Nishiki (60% polishing ratio).

### Zenkuro Sake

New Zealand Sake Brewers (Queenstown, New Zealand)

★★★★☆

**A taste of New Zealand**

Toji David Joll first visited Japan as an exchange student in high school. He came back to continue his university education in Tokyo. His love of Japan led to him to a lifetime of learning about nihonshu and the decision to establish New Zealand's first sake brewery. Located in Queenstown, the brewery has access to good soft water. In answer to the current craze for organic wine in New Zealand, the brewery offers unfiltered namazake, and has been introducing recipes using sake *kasu* (sake lees) to local chefs. Zenkuro (which translates as "all black," geddit?) is matured for a year, giving the sake a lightly aged hue. The aged aromas and flavors are both elegant and discreet. This is a honeyed sake with lily nuances. On the palate, it's dry with slight acidity. The finish is crisp, with a floral yet peppery bitter afternote.

**Recommended pairings:** Steak or even lamb. **Type:** Junmai. **Rice variety:** Sasa Nishiki (koji-mai), Calrose and Gohyakumangoku (kake-mai) (60% polishing ratio).

### Honjozo Muroka Nama Genshu

Noguchi Naohiko Sake Institute (Komatsu, Ishikawa Prefecture)

★★★★⯪

**Elegant and tasteful**

Toji Naohiko Noguchi (see page 68) is one of the great honjozo brewers. At the Naohiko Noguchi Sake Institute, he gets to shows off his skills. Adding alcohol to sake unfairly gets a bad rap, because honjozo requires a high level of brewing technique, which is on clear display with this sake.

Chilled to 59°F (15°C) in a wineglass, the mouthfeel is soft. Sweet, graceful fruity notes of apple and Asian pear are complimented with refreshing acidity. A peppery nuance adds sharpness. Delicate bitterness follows, and the rich, fruity flavor and silky scents of rice gradually expand. The finish is crisp with lingering mandarin juice. Warmed gently to around 113°F (45°C), the texture becomes tremendously soft, and the silky notes of rice unfold. Best served chilled, but not over-chilled, so take it out of the fridge, and wait a moment before drinking. It's also good slightly warmed.

**Recommended pairing:** Pickled vegetables, sashimi, shellfish and Gouda or Comté cheese. **Type:** Honjozo. **Rice variety:** Gohyakumangoku, plus undisclosed rice (60% polishing ratio).

### One Cup Ozeki

Ozeki (Nishinomiya, Hyogo Prefecture)

★★★⯪☆

**A ready-to-drink icon**

When One Cup Ozeki was first released, there was nothing quite like it. Sake in a cup! What a great idea. Unsurprisingly, it spawned countless copycats and established a now well-defined genre known as cup sake.

At room temperature, One Cup Ozeki is soft, with sweet milky aromas and rice flavors. The acidity is surprisingly strong. Aromas of apricot are joined by ripe banana and subtle green citrus. In the finish, there is lime peel followed by melon and more apricot. The sharpness of the alcohol is muted when served at higher temps. One Cup Ozeki improves when warmed to 104°F (40°C) or higher: it's smoother and more savory with a milky sweetness that coats the palate.

**Recommended pairings:** Cheese complements the One Cup's lactic-acid notes. Try it with a savory quiche. **Type:** Futsu-shu. **Rice variety:** Not specified (polishing ratio not specified).

### Sasshu Masamune Junmai Ginjo

Satsuma Kinzangura (Ichiki Kushikino, Kagoshima Prefecture).

★★★★☆

**Elegant with light, dry citrus impressions**

The Satsuma Kinzangura started brewing sake in 2014, making it Kagoshima's lone sake brewery. Long known as a shochu distillery, it actually started brewing to gain greater knowledge of alcohol production to enhance its shochu.

Chilled to 54°F (12°C), this junmai ginjo has floral notes such as lily and the aroma of cream cheese. Taking a sip, a slightly peppery texture and bitterness appear, followed by a simple sweetness and glittery acidity. Greenish citrus and mandarin rise up, giving way to rice nuances. This is a well-balanced, dry and light sake that is elegant and defined. Warmed to 108°F (42°C), the sweetness is more noticeable and this brew becomes reminiscent of flower nectar. In the background, there are melon aromas and modest sweet rice notes. It's best chilled or slightly warmed

**Recommended pairings:** Cod or grilled chicken. **Type:** Junmai ginjo. **Rice variety:** Gin no sato (60% polishing ratio).

## LIGHT BODIED

### Sequoia Coastal Ginjo

Sequoia Sake Company (San Francisco, California, United States)

★★★★☆

**A peaceful sake from California**

Located in San Francisco, the Sequoia Sake Company offers weekly tours, hoping to educate locals on everything from koji to sake fermentation. It also works with local chefs to help ensure that sakes are properly paired with food.

This is an excellent ginjo made with American rice and water from Yosemite. Upon first sip, the strong sweetness and acidity are immediately apparent. The sweetness is not cloying, and the acidity is sharp and well defined. Both dissolve on the palate in a way I've never quite experienced in a sake. Nuances of orange, lemon and honey round out the flavor profile. It's all very tranquil, like a cozy bar late in the evening.

**Recommended pairings:** Roast beef and grilled chicken with salt and pepper. **Type:** Junmai ginjo. **Rice variety:** Not specified.

### Suginishiki Bodaimoto Junmai

Sugii Shuzo (Fujieda, Shizuoka Prefecture)

★★★★☆

**Like a grassy field in autumn**

According to Kinnosuke Sugii, the toji and owner of the brewery, this bodaimoto was designed to easily pair with food. How did he do it? Amazingly, even though he uses ambient yeasts that don't thoroughly break down the sugars in the mash, he is still able to create a very dry brew.

This junmai has a beautiful golden-yellow hue and rice aromas that evoke the September and October harvests. Nosing the sake at room temperature evokes the scent of cooked rice. This is not a heavy sake, but it's highly acidic. The sweetness is subtle and honeyed. Cooked rice returns in the long, dry, grassy finish. It's good at room temperature, but better warmed to 113°F (45°C).

**Recommended pairings:** Dim sum, seafood gumbo, garlic and chilli shrimp. **Type:** Junmai, bodaimoto. **Rice variety:** Homarefuji (70% polishing ratio).

### Honjozo Reimei Josen

Taikoku Shuzo (Uruma, Okinawa Prefecture).

★★★★☆

**Light and dry, the Okinawan sake**

As of writing, Taikoku Shuzo is the southernmost sake brewery in Japan and the only firm that brews sake in Okinawa. Established in 1968, responding to the then high sake demand, it went on to dominate about 70% of the local sake market by 1972. To cope with the less-than-ideal climate, Taikoku Shuzo has year-round refrigerated brewing facilities, which keep the brewing environment constant and stable across the year.

When chilled to 54°F (12°C) this sake has slight ricey notes followed by green citrus ones. It's light and dry—perfectly complementing Okinawa's warm weather. The peppery aftertaste is pleasant and followed by cottage cheese and citrus peel nuances. Warmed to 108°F (42°C), the texture softens and the pleasant ricey nuances are more noticeable. There are lingering milky afternotes of cream cheese and rice flour. Best slightly warmed.

**Recommended pairings:** Stewed pork, sashimi or fish tempura. **Type:** Honjozo. **Rice variety:** Unspecified.

### Yuchun Junmai Seishu

Taiwan Tobacco & Liquor Corporation (Taoyuan, Taiwan)

★★★⯪☆

**Modest, quiet flavors**

Yuchun is one of the most popular sake brands brewed by Taiwan Tobacco & Liquor Corp (TTL), the largest alcoholic-beverage producer in Taiwan. In 1922, TTL was formed as a government conglomerate of breweries to improve quality and collect local taxes.

At room temperature, the textures are watery, and the arrival is subdued. It has a sweetness like granulated sugar and the acidity of an orange. The aromas are reminiscent of cooked rice and orange peels. Flavors peter out toward the finish, and the aftertaste has some unpleasant astringency. Warming dramatically improves this sake, bringing forth delicate honey, clover and fresh grass aromas. Recommended warmed to 131°F (55°C).

**Recommended pairings:** Parmigiano Reggiano or fried fish. **Type:** Junmai. **Rice variety:** Penglaimi (polishing ratio not specified).

### Ise no Shiroki Koshiki Nidan Jikomi

Takahashi Shuzo (Yokkaichi, Mie Prefecture)

★★★★☆

**Sparkling cloudy sake brewed by an ancient method**

Takahashi Shuzo is famous for providing the ritual sake for the offering at the Ise Grand Shrine, one of Japan's most important Shinto Shrines. *Shiroki*, or "white sake," has been used in Shinto rituals since the 7th century. This nigori is brewed with an ancient two-step preparation for fermentation mash called *nidan jikomi*, giving us a chance to taste a modern interpretation of this unusual style. It's slightly sparkling and cloudy in appearance. There's a refreshing texture on the palate with delicate, stimulating bubbles, strong sweetness and acidity. Apple, Asian pear, citrus, rice and yogurt are present. The finish is sharp and refreshing, with slightly bitter notes and fruity apple aromas. Best chilled to 50°F (10°C).

**Recommended pairings:** Due to its refreshing flavor, it's ideal for an aperitif. It's also good with spicy dishes, such as Szechuan cuisine. **Type:** Junmai, nigori, sparkling. **Rice variety:** Haenuki (60% polishing ratio).

### Tamanohikari Junmai Ginjo Karakuchi

Tamanohikari Sake Brewing (Fushimi, Kyoto Prefecture)

★★★★☆

**The dry sake you must try**

If you were asked for a good *karakuchi* (dry) sake, the most obvious answer would be a Niigata brew. The less-obvious reply would to look elsewhere—to Kyoto's Fushimi district, even.

In years past, Fushimi sake was pigeonholed as "feminine," "light" and "gentle." These adjectives no longer define the district, with the area's breweries increasingly doing their own thing. The Tamanohikari brewery, best known for reviving junmai sake, makes excellent karakuchi stuff. If I were to recommend one karakuchi sake you must try, it would be this. Unexpected, sure, but that's half the fun.

Taking a sip, the texture is smooth, light and peppery. Subtle aromas reveal herbs, cooked rice, apricot, melon and a touch of brown sugar. The finish is crisp with savory umami and more pepper. Serve chilled or warmed to 113°F (45°C).

**Recommended pairings:** Hainanese chicken or chicken with ginger. **Type:** Junmai ginjo. **Rice variety:** Not specified (60% polishing ratio).

**LIGHT BODIED**

**MEDIUM BODIED**

### Chuwu Ginjo Silver Label

Wufeng Farmers' Association (Wufeng, Taichung, Taiwan).

★★★★☆

**Complex and fascinating**

One of the best breweries outside Japan, Wufeng Farmers' Association has created a complex and fascinating expression, with distinctive matured aromas reminiscent of the tropics: dried dates, hibiscus preserved in sugar, wet almond, tree bark, chestnut jam and yogurt. This sake is light on the palate, but the aromas and sweetness are intense. A medium finish brings mint chocolate notes.

At room temperature, Silver Label is overwhelming. Warmed to 122°F (50°C), everything becomes better balanced. The earthy aroma of fragrant Taiwanese rice balances the heavier aromas, such as the dried dates. The temperature knocks the intense sweetness down a peg and the nose is more floral.

**Recommended pairings:** Taiwanese food is the default. But it goes well with any highly flavorful food, particularly seafood or pork. **Type:** Honjozo, ginjo. **Rice variety:** Ichuan Hsiangmi (60% polishing ratio).

### Shichiken Tanrei Junmai

Yamanashi Meijo (Hokuto, Yamanashi Prefecture)

★★★★☆

**Dry, fresh and fruity**

Outside Japan, whisky has made the Hakushu region in Yamanashi famous. The Japanese government has designated the area's water as among the best in the country. While Suntory is making excellent single malts and grain whisky in Hakushu, breweries like Yamanashi Meijo are also fermenting excellent sake with the region's soft, pure water.

Shichiken Tanrei Junmai has a nice, slightly golden yellow hue. Straight out of the fridge, it's refreshing. The sweetness is pure, like powdered sugar. Rising acidity follows. Apple flavors give way to delicate rice. The finish is crisp with notes of, once again, freshly sliced apple. Slight astringency and bitterness come through in the aftertaste. Even though this isn't a ginjo, it sure smells like one. Best enjoyed cold.

**Recommended pairings:** The refreshing acidity and fruity aromas make deep-fried food a perfect match, especially fried chicken. **Type:** Junmai. **Rice variety:** Hitogokochi, Asahi no Yume (70% polishing ratio).

### Dassai 23

Asahi Shuzo (Iwakuni, Yamaguchi Prefecture)

★★★★☆

**Elegant, delicate and delicious**

In 2017 the Asahi Shuzo brewery took out a full-page newspaper ad to ask fans to stop paying above retail price for its Dassai sake. Unscrupulous sellers were charging a premium, and the brewery didn't want its fans to overpay. Out of all the Dassai sakes, Dassai 23 is the most emblematic. Nosing the glass reveals highly fragrant notes of sliced apple, Asian pear, grass, bamboo leaves, rice and a hint of milk chocolate. On sipping, Dassai's signature no-nonsense sweetness is readily apparent. The acidity is solid, while the mouthfeel is soft and mellow. It's refreshing. The finish has a flourish of acidity with short notes of apple. The standard line on Dassai is that it's best cold, but this is pretty good heated to 122°F (50°C); milkier notes emerge, punctuated with celery and umami. Still, serve chilled.

**Recommended pairing:** Italian food, especially tomato dishes. French cuisine is also good. **Type:** Junmai daiginjo **Rice variety:** Yamada Nishiki (23% polishing ratio).

### Azuma Kirin Saquê Nama

Kikkoman do Brasil (Campinas, São Paulo, Brazil)

★★★★☆

**Well balanced, high quality with Brazilian flair**

Founded in 1934, Azuma Kirin is Brazil's oldest and largest brewery. The sakes it makes are good enough to hold their own against imported Japanese brews. Its nama is the best domestic sake bar none. Made from Miroku rice grown in Uruguay, this sake is soft, but not cloyingly sweet, nor very acidic. There is a hint of melon, muscat, Rice Krispies Treats and honey. The crisp finish with a slight lactic peppery note is quite nice. Warming this nama causes it to blossom with bitter dark chocolate flavors, hiding any weakness it has at room temperature or chilled. This distinct bitterness is found in other sakes brewed in tropical regions—perhaps an expression of terroir. However, it still goes exceedingly well with traditional Japanese food.

**Recommended pairing:** You can't go wrong with fried foods. Even fish and chips are good. **Type:** Not specified. **Rice variety:** Miroku and unspecified (70% polishing ratio).

### Daishichi Junmai Kimoto

Daishichi Sake Brewery (Nihon-matsu, Fukushima Prefecture)

★★★★☆

**The Kimoto**

Few brewers are more dedicated to the kimoto method than Daishichi. It's what they do, and they do it very, very well. When other breweries had long given up on kimoto, Daishichi was keeping it alive. Thank goodness for that. (For more on Daishichi's kimoto, see pages 48–49.)

Nosing the cup doesn't turn up many noticeable scents. Here, the aromas are enjoyed after taking a sip. There are dominant notes of cooked rice. The mouthfeel is extraordinarily soft, while the flavors are milky, thanks to Daishichi's kimoto starter. There is strong acidity, adding complexity. Umami comes through in the finish, as do rice aromas. Recommended warm 113°F (45°C).

**Recommended pairings:** Try it with prosciutto; the saltiness brings out this kimoto's umami, and the fat pairs well with the brew's milky nuance. **Type:** Junmai, kimoto. **Rice variety:** Not specified.

### Dewazakura Oka Ginjo

Dewazakura Sake Brewery (Tendo, Yamagata Prefecture)

★★★★☆

**Ginjo-shu with history**

First released in 1980, the award-winning Oka sparked the decade's subsequent ginjo boom (for more see pages 18–19). At the time, there were few—if any—sakes like the Oka Ginjo. Since then, nearly every brewery across the country has created its own ginjo brew.

This is a well-balanced, fruity sake with vivid aromas reminiscent of apple, Asian pear, freshly cut grass and rice flour. Its smooth and transparent texture is followed by the pleasant sharpness of alcohol. Here, sweetness, acidity and bitterness coexist in harmony. Slight umami and astringency come through in the finish. Best served chilled.

**Recommended pairings:** Fish, tempura and sashimi are all winners. Try it with grilled rosemary chicken. **Type:** Ginjo. **Rice variety:** Not specified (50% polishing ratio).

225

## MEDIUM BODIED

### Gekkeikan Josen

Gekkeikan Sake (Fushimi, Kyoto Prefecture)

★★★★☆

**Light and easy to pair with food**

Gekkeikan, the titan of Kyoto's Fushimi brewing district, produces mainly futsu-shu made from table rice. This isn't expensive sake, but that doesn't mean it's not good—it is. Gekkeikan Josen is a light, easy-drinking sake that offers tremendous bang for your yen. It doesn't have much of a nose, but the aromas that stick out are brown rice, cottage cheese and a hint of citrus. There isn't much texture, either. It has a well-balanced delicate sweetness and acidity, followed by some intense bitterness and savory umami. More bitterness shows up in the sharp finish. For an unassuming sake without noticeable brewing pyrotechnics, there is a lot to admire. The workmanship quality is straightforward and yet the flavors are still complex and layered. It's all well executed and a good example of how delicious futsu-shu can be.

**Recommended pairings:** Goes with a wide range of food, but works best with flavorful dishes such as salted fish. **Type:** Futsu-shu. **Rice variety:** Not specified.

### Mutsu Hassen Isaribi Tokubetsu Junmai

Hachinohe Shuzo (Hachinohe, Aomori Prefecture)

★★★½☆

**A fine companion to seafood**

"Isaribi" literally means "fishing fire." In the Hachinohe region of Aomori Prefecture, fishermen have traditionally used fire to lure squid at night, especially during the summer and autumn months. (These days, spotlights are more common.) The name of this sake implies that it goes well with seafood.

On arrival, the texture is pleasant and soft, with some spicy bitterness. This gives way to a hint of rice, fruity melon notes, tangerine peel and milk. Warming to 140°F (60°C) brings out the rice nuance. The finish is long, with the aroma of ice-cream wafers. Since this junmai works well both warmed and at room temperature, matching the temperature of the food is recommended.

**Recommended pairings:** Tempura is especially good, as are white fish, squid and octopus. **Type:** Tokubetsu junmai. **Rice variety:** Hanafubuki (60% polishing ratio).

### Kuro Kabuto Yume Ikkon

Ikekame Shuzo (Kurume, Fukuoka Prefecture)

★★★★☆

**Cross-cultural flavors**

*Kuro koji* (black koji), used to make shochu, creates far more acidity than the *ki koji* (yellow koji) that's used in sake brewing. The Ikekame Shuzo brewery in Fukuoka has been a kuro koji pioneer in the world of sake, using the microorganism to create highly acidic brews. The result here is Kuro Kabuto, or "black helmet," because kuro-koji-kin apparently looks like a samurai's helmet under a microscope.

At room temperature, the texture is somewhat smooth, with some bumps along the way. While the acidity is high, with a citric intensity due to the kuro koji, this sake does have a candy-like sweetness. There are nuances of melon, banana, lychee and rice flour. Acidity comes back in the finish, with a tinge of astringency.

**Recommended pairings:** Like lemon, the strong acidity suits fried and fatty foods. Try it with fried chicken. **Type:** Junmai ginjo. **Rice variety:** Yamada Nishiki (koji-mai), Yume Ikkon (kake-mai) (55% polishing ratio).

### Ishizuchi Junmai Ginjo Green Label

Ishizuchi Shuzo (Saijo, Ehime Prefecture)

★★★★☆

**Clean lines with citrus aromas**

The Ishizuchi Shuzo brewery, on the island of Shikoku, uses water from Mt. Ishizuchi, the highest in western Japan. Shikoku is also famous for citrus fruits, especially mandarins.

Fittingly, those citrus aromas find their way into this sake when chilled. There are lovely apple notes too! Orange peel lingers in the finish. The sweetness and acidity give this sake a refreshing and crisp impression, resulting in a well-defined brew with clean lines. At room temperature, aromas of rice appear. Warmed to 122°F (50°C), this brew really comes to life. Light and smooth, the rice aromas are followed by a pleasant astringency and, again, orange peel notes. Recommended served chilled or warmed.

**Recommended pairing:** Goes well with cream cheese or chicken broth. Also good solo. **Type:** Junmai. **Rice variety:** Yamada Nishiki, Matsuyama Mitsui (koji-mai 50%, kake-mai 60% polishing ratio).

### Tenon Yamada Nishiki Yamahai Junmai

Itakura Syuzo (Izumo, Shimane Prefecture)

★★★★☆

**Sake offered to the gods**

Made with ambient yeasts, this sake is boisterous but easy on the palate. The texture is rich and thick, with well-balanced sweetness and intense acidity. Bouquets of strawberry and pear are followed by rice flour, ice-cream wafers, milk chocolate, hay, cottage cheese and yogurt. Warming makes the texture much softer, and grainy aromas open up—like being in the middle of a rice field during harvest. Recommended slightly warmed to 104°F (40°C). The brewery is located in Izumo, home to the Izumo Taisha Shrine, one of the most important Shinto religious sites. *Toji* Tatsuro Kojima offers all the sakes he brews to the deities, even those brewed for commercial release. The brewers' prayers are believed to influence the quality.

**Recommended pairings:** Light foods such as fish, Cobb salad or tofu dishes. **Type:** Junmai. **Rice variety:** Yamada Nishiki (70% polishing ratio).

### Nishinoseki Tezukuri Junmai

Kayashima Sake Brewing (Kunisaki, Oita Prefecture)

★★★½☆

**Well balanced when warmed**

Oita Prefecture is located in Japan's southern island of Kyushu, where shochu is king. But Oita also makes excellent sake and this junmai is a good example.

When chilled, this brew is sweet and mellow with hints of mandarin, mango, cream cheese and fresh cream. Its intense sweetness is underpinned by firm acidity. The flavors blossom at room temperature. The finish is crisp with afternotes of melon, apricot and lingering sweet rice. To fully appreciate this sake, warm it to 108°F (42°C). It starts mellow and modest, but then, the flavors expand in the mouth. The acidity is more prominent and the finish is sharp with slightly sweet aromas of rice.

**Recommended pairings:** This junmai goes well with highly acidic foods, such as pickled veggies or fish. It also goes well with young Comté cheese. **Type:** Junmai. **Rice variety:** Hattan Nishiki (koji-mai, 60% polishing ratio), Hinohikari (kake-mai, 60% polishing ratio).

## MEDIUM BODIED

### Kuromatsu Kenbishi

Kenbishi Sake Brewing (Higashi-nada, Kobe, Hyogo Prefecture)

★★★★★

**Well balanced with dignity**

Inexpensive and widely available in Japan, this brew is also sold abroad. Sakes made in Nada are often pigeonholed as beefy and brawny (and typically contrasted with the more "feminine" Kyoto sakes), but Kuromatsu is remarkably smooth and soft, gracefully balancing flavors with elegance and dignity.

When warmed to around 113°F (45°C), Kuromatsu softens, but good acidity remains. Faint, delicate aromas of steamed rice and evaporated milk are followed by this sake's signature savory umami, which, along with green citrus and a slight bitterness, lingers in the finish. Best served warm.

**Recommended pairings:** Roasted dried fish or grilled fatty pork, but also try it with warm tofu. **Type:** Honjozo. **Rice variety**: Not specified.

### Tomio Tanshu Yamada Nishiki

Kitagawa Honke (Fushimi, Kyoto Prefecture)

★★★★⯪

**An all-Kyoto sake**

Brewed with Fushimi's noted soft water, rice cultivated in Ayabe, Kyoto Prefecture, and Kyo no Koto sake yeast developed by Kyoto Municipal Institute of Industrial Technology and Culture (see page 108), this is a pure Kyoto sake.

Chilled to around 50°F (10°C), aromas of sliced apple, white peach and melon are followed by slight fragrances of crème chantilly and a hint of fresh dill. In a wineglass, the nose is intense but pleasant. Taking a sip, citrus acidity and bitterness bring a dry and sharp impression with a soft and gentle sweetness. The finish is crisp and ricey notes linger. Warmed to 108°F (42°C), everything becomes much softer. Here, the citrus aromas of orange and rice play a major role. It's easy to drink and a nice companion for food.

**Recommended pairings:** It marries well with fish carpaccio or Cobb salad when chilled and lightly seasoned roasted chicken when warmed. **Type:** Junmai ginjo. **Rice variety:** Yamada Nishiki (55% polishing ratio).

### Tomio Junmai Ginjo Gion Komachi

Kitagawa Honke (Fushimi, Kyoto Prefecture)

★★★★☆

**Emblematic of Fushimi**

These days, it seems like every brewery in Kyoto's venerated brewing district Fushimi is doing its own thing. Gone are the days when Fushimi's sake can easily be described as "feminine." However, Tomio is still making a brew that is a good example of the traditional style. This is exactly why this sake is called "Gion Komachi," which refers to a beautiful woman of Kyoto's entertainment district.

This is a very mellow sake. It's elegant and sweet with refreshing acidity. Nuances of strawberry, melon, rice and even the distinct chestnut flavor of koji are all present. The melon-flavored finish is crisp and gentle. It's best served warmed to 113°F (45°C). Apricot and cottage cheese become more pronounced, as do gentle rice flavors. The mellowness and strong koji notes are hallmarks of the traditional Fushimi style.

**Recommended pairings:** Anything fermented. Seriously. Anything. (Oh, it's also good with sashimi.) **Type:** Junmai ginjo. **Rice variety:** Not specified (58% polishing ratio).

### Kokuryu No. 88

Kokuryu Sake Brewing (Eiheiji, Fukui Prefecture)

★★★★☆

**Premium sake that goes with food**

This premium daiginjo is brewed with superior-quality Hyogo-grown Yamada Nishiki. The number eight is lucky in Japan because its kanji character (八) looks like it's spreading out and is therefore seen as properous. So, the number 88 would appear twice as auspicious. At Kokuryu, this sake was stored in the number 88 tank. How fortunate!

Nosing the sake at 59°F (15°C) in a standard wine tasting glass, there are sweet, fruity aromas of apple, pear and fine rice flour with a hint of fresh dill in the background. Clear nectar sweetness expands in the mouth, supported by an elegant acidity. The finish is gentle with bitterness, sweetness and a lingering hint of orange. Warmed to 108°F (42°C), the texture softens, and the sake becomes slightly richer. It's better suited for food at this temperature.

**Recommended pairings:** Roast beef and terrine. Sashimi and grilled salted fish are also good. **Type:** Junmai ginjo. **Rice variety:** Yamada Nishiki (35% polishing ratio).

### Sawaya Matsumoto Kocon

Matsumoto Shuzo (Fushimi, Kyoto Prefecture)

★★★★☆

**A Kyoto icon**

There are two breweries in Kyoto's Fushimi that are perhaps most iconic of all. Gekkeikan's rooftops cut a striking scene against the sky, but the prettiest of the Fushimi breweries has to be Matsumoto Shuzo. It's not just good-looking, either: Matsumoto makes some terrific sake.

On encountering this sake, the first impression is rosemary and sour citrus. The acidity is fresh, completed with the bitterness of grapefruit peel. Going deep into the flavor profile, there is sweetness and a scent of rice. The finish is sharp and acidic. Serve chilled.

**Recommended pairings:** Salty and savory food like anchovies complement this sake's fresh, citrusy flavor. **Type:** Unspecified. **Rice variety:** Yamada Nishiki (polishing ratio not specified).

### Matsu no Tsukasa: Junmai Daiginjo Azolla 35

Matsuse Sake Brewery (Ryuo, Shiga Prefecture)

★★★★☆

**Reflecting the region's character**

This organic junmai daiginjo uses Yamada Nishiki from local rice fields filled with the delicate fern known as azolla, which has a low resistance to agricultural chemicals. This means rice fields filled with azolla are about as organic as they come. The brew itself is made with a kimoto starter with ambient yeast. According to toji Keizo Ishida, it makes sense to do so for this organically grown rice.

Chilled to around 61°F (16°C), this sake has a mellow and soft texture but with sharp and intense acidity. On arrival, there are fruity peach notes as well as ricey nuances and grassy aromas. Long lingering umami, acidity and the pleasant astringency of vegetable soup follow. Warmed slightly to around 108°F (42°C), this sake becomes well balanced with hints of rice and citrus. Served slightly chilled or slightly warmed.

**Recommended pairings:** Grilled or sashimi halibut, flounder, prosciutto and stuffed green olives. **Type:** Junmai daiginjo, kimoto. **Rice variety:** Yamada Nishiki (35% polishing ratio).

## MEDIUM BODIED

### Hayaseura Shinshu Fune-shibori Junmai

Miyake Hikoemon Shoten (Mihama, Fukui Prefecture)

★★★★☆

**Ideal for home aging**

To be honest, home aging is a crapshoot. However, the Miyake Hikoemon Shoten brewery has created a junmai with enough backbone to age nicely. It's ideal for trying out home maturation. Freshly pressed in a *sakabune* (see page 57), this is a beautiful sake with a lovely golden-yellow appearance. It's mellow with milky notes, followed by apple and pear. The acidity is exquisite. In the finish, rich, juicy citrus spreads throughout the mouth. Left at room temperature for two and a half months it becomes better balanced. After nine months, the texture becomes round and smooth with nice acidity. There are nuances of dried citrus peel, Rice Krispies Treats and honey with melon lurking in the background. Some sakes get better with time. This is one of them.

**Recommended pairings:** Onion soup goes well with this junmai before aging. After home aging, try roasted chicken with a miso sauce. **Type:** Junmai. **Rice variety:** Gohya-kumangoku (55% polishing ratio).

### Nanbu Bijin Tokubetsu Junmai

Nanbu Bijin (Ninohe, Iwate Prefecture)

★★★★☆

**Exceptional indeed**

In 2017, this Nanbu Bijin won the "Champion Sake" title at the International Wine Challenge, taking its place as the best sake in the world. Not bad for a brew that's widely available and reasonably priced—in Japan, at least.

Chilled to 54°F (12°C), the texture is soft on the tongue with thin acidity wrapped in a melty sweetness. Fruity aromas of winter melon and lychee rise up through the nose, giving way to rice nuances. Bitterness and astringency bring a firm and sharp finish. The aftertaste is rather strong with lingering melon. Warmed to 108°F (42°C), a gentle texture and enhanced sweetness are made even more pleasant with melon and orange hints. A hint of rice and bitter pepper linger. Serve chilled or slightly warmed.

**Recommended pairings**: When chilled, prosciutto, six-month aged Comté cheese or roast beef are good. Warmed, try pot-au-feu or daikon radish in a dashi broth. **Type:** Tokubetsu junmai. **Rice variety**: Gin Otome and unspecified (55% polishing ratio).

### Hakurakusei Junmai Ginjo

Niizawa Jozoten (Osaki, Miyagi Prefecture)

★★★★☆

**Local, refreshing and excellent**

The Niizawa Jozoten brewery sourced local Kuranohana rice for this excellent and refreshing junmai ginjo. For more on this brewery, see pages 50–51.

This is a slightly chewy sake. On arrival, there's a hint of powdered sugar and good acidity. Strawberry, milk and green, floral notes follow. The finish is sharp, with a hint of lingering astringency. When warmed to 104°F (40°C), the texture becomes even softer, with the milky nuances becoming more apparent. In the background, there's a lingering citrus peel. Drink chilled or warmed.

**Recommended pairings:** Vegetable dishes complement this junmai ginjo's green, floral notes. It's good with shellfish, too. Overall, Hakurakusei highlights savory flavors. **Type:** Junmai ginjo. **Rice variety:** Kuranohana (55% polishing ratio).

### Denshu Tokubetsu Junmai

Nishida Shuzoten (Aomori, Aomori Prefecture)

★★★★⯪

**Rice-field sake**

The brand name Denshu, which means "rice-field sake," indicates the importance of rice and the rich flavor derived from it. Denshu is one of those sakes that won't wear out its welcome, even after the third or fourth cup.

This brew is well defined. Sweet notes of banana, melon and lychee accompany mellow and soft texture. It also has aromas of citrus, sour cream and green elements of cider leaves. Intense sweetness is accompanied with a hint of granulated sugar. Milky notes linger in the finish. Serve slightly chilled at around 59°F (15°C). It's also excellent warmed to 104°F (40°C).

**Recommended pairings:** Prosciutto, bacon, grilled salted pork, vegetable tempura, vegetable stew and roast beef are nice companions. **Type:** Tokubetsu junmai. **Rice variety:** Hanafubuki (55% polishing ratio).

### Yuki no Bosha Yamahai Junmai

Saiya Shuzoten (Yurihonjo, Akita Prefecture)

★★★★⯪

**Transparent and elegant**

Yuki no Bosha is one of Akita's great breweries. Its sakes are straightforward and well made. The brewery has worked with the new generation of younger *kuramoto-toji* to offer advice and expertise. Chilled to 50°F (10°C), this yamahai has a mild bouquet of apricot, melon, mint, condensed milk and yogurt. It's rather elegant with good mouthfeel. The finish is crisp, with milky notes returning. This is underscored by a pleasing bitterness and savory umami. Warmed to 104°F (40°C), it becomes softer. There are still apricot notes, but a rice-flour scent becomes noticeable. In the background, there are subtle yet rough leafy nuances. This yamahai is slightly less balanced when warm, but the drink's composition becomes more clearly defined. Recommended either chilled or warmed.

**Recommended pairings:** Prosciutto, melon and salt-and-pepper grilled chicken. **Type:** Junmai, yamahai. **Rice variety:** Not specified.

### Nami Junmai Daiginjo 40

Sakecul SA de CV (Culiacán, Sinaloa State, Mexico)

★★★★☆

**Made in Mexico**

The Sakecul sake brewery was founded in 2016 in Culiacán, Mexico. As it specializes in junmai-shu, no brewer's alcohol is added. Also, it is not cut with water before bottling. The brewery's brand name, Nami, means "wave" in Japanese. Junmai Ginjo 40 is the high-end release, made from US-grown Yamada Nishiki rice. The result is quite good. The initial intense sweetness is pleasant and accompanied by strong acidity and subtle bitterness. This isn't a heavy sake, but it's not a lightweight. It has good body. Aromas are fruity and floral: tart green apple, lychee and fragrant lilies. There are also yogurty notes and hints of cacao. The finish is somewhat short and lacks the signature bitterness of a classic daiginjo, but it has enough to please regular daiginjo drinkers. Serve chilled.

**Recommended pairings:** Fatty tuna or raw king salmon. And, yes, Mexican food. Anything with cheese and spice. **Type:** Junmai daiginjo. **Rice variety:** US-grown Yamada Nishiki (40% polishing ratio).

## MEDIUM BODIED

### g Joy Saké Junmai Ginjo Genshu

SakéOne (Forest Grove, Oregon, United States)

★★★★⯪

**Well balanced and well made**

Straight out of the fridge at 54°F (12°C), this junmai genshu from Oregon's SakéOne is golden yellow with aromas of fresh cream and apricot. On the palate, a mellow yet sturdy sweetness and an elegant acidity are followed by milky aromas. Next come notes of hay, cacao and honey. While there is some sharpness when chilled, at room temperature it softens and its sweetness becomes more rounded. Heated to 113°F (45°C), things get mellow with syrupy and sugary apricot notes. At 131°F (55°C), it becomes chewier than at room temperature—it's actually rather unpleasant. But at 140°F (60°C), it's excellent, with a mellow, silkiness reminiscent of milk chocolate. The peppery finish keeps things balanced. Drink chilled, slightly heated or piping hot.

**Recommended pairings:** When chilled, dim sum, teriyaki pork, or grilled salmon. Aged Comté pairs well. **Type:** Junmai ginjo. **Rice variety:** Calrose (55% polishing ratio).

### Sakura Masamune Yukimare Kyokai Yeast No. 1

Sakura Masamune (Higashi-nada, Kobe, Hyogo Prefecture)

★★★★⯪

**A classic rice-flavored sake born to be warmed**

The yeast used in this junmai was isolated from the Sakura Masamune brewery's moromi in 1906 and distributed to breweries all over this country as assocation yeast No. 1, which was thought to have been lost during the chaos of World War II. This sake is brewed with that rediscovered yeast. Chilled, this junmai is off-kilter, but warmed to 113°F (45°C), this is a superbly balanced and sublimely soft sake. The rice flavor is nuanced and elegant, with a range of aromas coming through on arrival: evaporated milk, chocolate, citrus and rice. The finish is quite long with loads of umami. This is the sake equivalent of a traditional ink-brush painting: modest, well balanced and expertly done. Serve warmed.

**Recommended pairings:** Grilled or fried fish seasoned with salt. **Type:** Junmai, kimoto. **Rice variety:** Not specified (80% polishing ratio).

### Sanshoraku Junmai

Sanshoraku Shuzo (Nanto, Toyama Prefecture).

★★★⯪☆

**Juicy chilled, ricey when warmed**

The Sanshoraku Shuzo brewery is in Toyama Prefecture, with snow accumulating over six feet in winter. That snow filters the air and also provides excellent brewing water. This is a perfect spot to make sake. Here they mostly brew with locally grown Gohyakumangoku sake rice, a product of the local climate.

When this junmai is chilled to 50°F (10°C), there are fruity notes of melon, Asian pear and orange, followed by green herbal aromas. The finish is crisp. The lingering orange and melon are pleasant. At room temperature sweet, round aromas of rice dominate, punctuated by a peppery aftertaste. To drink warmed, I recommend it at around 140°F (60°C). At first, you might feel overwhelmed by the heat, but milky richness and rice nuances with a light and smooth texture soon become apparent. Umami and citrus peel linger.

**Recommended pairings:** Prosciutto, roast pork (sweet and sour pork, too!), cream cheese or shiitake mushrooms. **Type:** Junmai. **Rice variety:** Gohyakumangoku (65% polishing ratio).

### Sentoku Junmai

Sentoku Shuzo (Nobeoka, Miyazaki Prefecture)

★★★⯪☆

**Ideal for southern weather**

Miyazaki Prefecture, on Japan's southern island of Kyushu, is famous for shochu, a distilled beverage made from sweet potato, rice, barley or other grains. Generally, the prefecture isn't ideal for brewing sake due to its warm climate. Yet there are two breweries that do make sake. Sentoku Shuzo is the one that mainly brews it.

When this sake is chilled to 54°F (12°C), modest fruity-sweet bouquets of white peach and rice flour appear. Rice sticks around in the afternotes. Warmed to 108°F (42°C), this sake shines. In addition to the fruity notes that appear when chilled, there's the aroma of orange. The finish is crisp with lingering rice notes.

**Recommended pairings:** Sweet and sour pork or teriyaki chicken are standouts. **Type:** Junmai. **Rice variety:** Unspecified (60% polishing ratio).

### Iwakigo Matabee Junmai

Shike Shuzoten (Iwaki, Fukushima Prefecture)

★★★★☆

**Carefully prepared traditional craft**

Brewery founder Matabee Shike's enthusiasm for sake developed into a full-blown brewing business in 1845. This sake was named after him.

This well-balanced sake begins smooth, but suddenly, alcohol tingles the tongue. On the palate, there is sweet rice and moderate fruity acidity. Nuances of hay, condensed milk and cooked rice spread throughout the mouth. The flavors and aromas are on the traditional side. Forgo glassware and drink this sake in a ceramic cup. It's best at either room temperature or at 113°F (45°C).

**Recommended pairings:** Tempura, tofu and dashi broth are all excellent companions. Miso-flavored dishes, salty cheese and vinegar-seasoned foods also pair well. **Type:** Junmai. **Rice variety:** Not specified (60% polishing ratio).

### Daiten Shiragiku Junmai Ginjo

Shiragiku Shuzo (Takahashi, Okayama Prefecture)

★★★★☆

**Ginjo with discreet aroma**

Ginjo sakes are famous for their aroma. Over the past few years, the aroma for many premium brews has become even more pronounced and fragrant. But in Okayama, ginjo sakes are typically more discreet. They're not looking to make a flashy first impression. This does have the typical melon aromas of ginjo, along with grapefruit peel. But while the aromas are restrained, this sake with tongue-tingling spice lands with a thud on the palate. It is smooth and sweet, masking any protruding sharpness. Melon returns in the finish, with condensed milk. Warming to 113°C (45°C) brings out a silky sweetness with notes of rice, milk chocolate and cashew nuts. Warm is recommended.

**Recommended pairings:** Bitter chocolate, cream cheese and crème brûlée. Also good with vegetable soup. **Type:** Junmai ginjo. **Rice variety:** Asahi-mai (Okayama) (55% polishing ratio).

## MEDIUM BODIED

### Juyondai Honmaru Hiden Tamakaeshi

Takagi Shuzo (Murayama, Yamagata Prefecture)

★★★★☆

**Rich, elegant and substantial**

In 1993, Akitsuna Takagi took over his family's brewery in Yamagata while still in his 20s. Takagi and his brew Jyuyondai (meaning "14th generation"), named after his father, caused a shift in sake flavor, inspired young brewers across the country and won him a cult following. When this sake is swirled around in a glass, it's translucent with only a slight viscosity. Upon tasting, the first impression is that overall, this is an elegant, well-thought-out sake. A refreshing acidity with a lovely sweetness and nuance of rice blossoms and spreads throughout the mouth. The finish is fairly lush, with aromas of melon, orange peel and grapefruit. Buttery honeyed sugar is present, too. Some sharpness in the finish adds complexity, with melon once again returning. In the aftertaste, acidic flavors, a slight sweetness and some savoriness linger. Serve chilled.

**Recommended pairings:** Prosciutto or grilled tuna. Sashimi is good too. **Type:** Honjozo. **Rice variety:** Hattan Nishiki (55% polishing ratio).

### Takarayama Rice Bag Label Shinnosuke

Takarayama (Niigata, Niigata Prefecture)

★★★★☆

**Brewed with a new table rice**

Shinnosuke table rice, released in 2017, is less sticky than Japan's favorite table rice Koshihikari, making sake brewing easier. Based in Niigata, Takarayama brewery has access to high-quality sake rice; however, they brew this sake with table rice grown in a rice field next to the brewery. It's a novel take on regionality: local table rice over high-quality sake rice brought in from elsewhere. At 50°F (10°C) in a standard wine glass, this light brew is pleasant with refreshing acidity, and green citrus and elegant ricey notes. It is also enjoyable at room temperature, which makes the texture softer and gives the sake the impression of flower nectar. Warming slightly to around 108°F (42°C) makes it somewhat sturdier and better balanced. In the finish, there are lingering peppery afternotes with a spritz of pear juice.

**Recommended pairings:** Beef jerky, anchovies, pancetta, hard Italian cheeses and modestly seasoned white fish. **Type:** Not specified. **Rice variety:** Shinnosuke (polishing ratio unspecified).

### Chuwu Junmai Ginjo Gold Label

Wufeng Farmers' Association (Wufeng, Taichung, Taiwan)

★★★★☆

**A taste of Taiwan**

The flavor profile is very smooth and very sweet. There are rich, evocative aromas of tree bark, dried dates, raisins and yogurt. It's an intense experience, but not overpowering. The finish is short with fig and dark fruit flavors. There is a slight bitterness. When warmed to 104°F (40°C), Gold Label becomes tremendously good. The earthy aroma of local rice is readily apparent, lingering on the nose.

Wufeng Farmers' Association uses a Taiwanese fragrant rice known as Ichuan Hsiangmi, which adds complexity and layers to this sake that simply are not found in sake made with Japanese rice. It's a fascinating and alluring brew.

**Recommended pairings:** Spicy foods work well with this ginjo's intense flavors. When warmed, try it with savory and salty stews and meats. **Type:** Junmai ginjo. **Rice variety:** Ichuan Hsiangmi (60% polishing ratio).

### Kaze no Mori Tsuyubakaze Junmai Shiboribana

Yucho Shuzo (Gose, Nara Prefecture)

★★★★☆

**Fresh and light, like fruit juice made from rice**

When the Yucho Shuzo brewery stopped selling its sake to be rebottled and rebranded by other, larger breweries, it decided to concentrate on unpasteurized sake, nama-zake. Hi-tech brewing is essential to keeping *nama-zake* fresh. This brewery has developed an array of in-house techniques to do that year-round.

Brewed from hard water, this unpasteurized brew seems light at first. Intense bubbles produced by the sake yeast follow. It's fruit-juice fresh with a light sweetness that's accented with acidity, umami and a bold bitterness. There are aromas of melon, cashew nuts and a slight hint of steamed rice. When heated, milky nuances appear. The finish is long, with a pleasant bitterness. Best served chilled in a glass.

**Recommended pairings:** Tempura as well as the Italian dish carpaccio work well with this sake's freshness and fruity acidity. **Type:** Junmai, nama. **Rice variety:** Tsuyubakaze (80% polishing ratio).

### Yamahai Okushika

Akishika Shuzo (Nose, Osaka Prefecture)

★★★★☆

**Well balanced with a silky texture**

The Akishika brewery in Osaka Prefecture grows a percentage of its brewing rice, including the Yamada Nishiki which is used to make Yamahai Okushika. Akishika's sakes are good freshly pressed, but are even better aged. This yamahai is matured for five years, and like many of Akishika's brews, it's very good hot. It was tasted at 140°F (60°C). The soft and silky mouthfeel leads to a rising crescendo of acidity, sweetness and umami. All of this is punctuated with aromas of cooked rice, fine flour, milk and citrus peel. Those ricey aromas and zesty notes return in the crisp, somewhat biting finish. When the hot sake cools down (a phenomenon called *kanzamashi* in Japanese), acidity is still present, but its sweetness rounds out with a balance reminiscent of orange juice.

**Recommended pairings:** Soups pair well with this sake, especially vegetable or oxtail soup. **Type:** Junmai, yamahai **Rice variety:** Yamada Nishiki (60% polishing ratio).

### Komeso Kimoto Yumeginka Perfect Fermentation Junmai

Aoki Shuzo (Aisai, Aichi Prefecture)

★★★½☆

**Like autumn at room temperature, visions of spring when heated**

The first impression is bold, thanks to full-bodied, intense acidity. Roasted sugar, evaporated milk and almond coat the mouth. There's a particular vegetable-like bitterness in the finish. This isn't a balanced sake, and there is a roughness—like the rustling of dried leaves. At room temperature, it's late autumn in a glass. But warmed to 122°F (50°C), the sake becomes better balanced. The acidity remains, but the aged aromas dissipate, and the vegetable notes are more pleasant. The effect is a nice day in late spring, when the rice goes from sprouts to stalks.

**Recommended pairings:** Nuts, chocolate and vanilla wafers are good companions, especially at room temperature. When warmed, this sake pairs well with vegetable soup, which harmonizes with the brew's veggie notes and savory umami. **Type:** Junmai, kimoto **Rice variety:** Yumeginka (70% polishing ratio).

## FULL BODIED

### Emishiki Tokubetsu Junmai Sensation Blue Label Nama

Emishiki Sake Brewery (Koga, Shiga Prefecture)

★★★★☆

**If rice were citrus, you'd squeeze this sake**

This full-bodied sweet sake leaves a fresh impression. A good-looking sake with a bright golden yellow hue, it has a lively and strong arrival followed by thick sweetness and acidity. There are aromas of orange juice, cashew nuts and citrus peel and an agreeable bitterness. The finish is long and coated with grapefruit flavors. Best served chilled or warmed to 104°F (40°C).

**Recommended pairings**: Roast beef and duck suit this sake's orange flavors. Savory (not sweet) fritters will hold their own against the full-bodied taste. Fermented foods are also good and really bring out this nama junmai's nutty and citrus notes. **Type:** Tokubetsu junmai, nama. **Rice variety**: Not specified (50% polishing ratio).

### Hanahato Kijoshu 8-Year

Enoki Shuzo (Kure, Hiroshima Prefecture)

★★★★⯪

**Sweet and complex**

In 1974, this brewery released the first modern *kijoshu*, which was based on a description in an early 10th-century text. Kijoshu is a style that substitutes an addition of sake for water in the last step of the brewing process. The result is an intensely sweet, yet highly acidic sake, which makes it a rather flexible brew that can be paired with main dishes and desserts. But the brewery also decided to mature this very sweet kijoshu. It has also been aged at least eight years. Taking a sip of the brew is like cutting a piece of cake: it's thick, and there's layer after layer. It's very sweet! Aromas of honey, tea, butterscotch and coffee fill the senses. But the finish is crisp and bitter with lingering notes of Darjeeling tea.

**Recommended pairings:** Blue cheese, goat's cheese, or even Stilton won't overwhelm this sake. Grilled-cheese sandwiches and Mexican food are good, too. **Type:** Junmai, kijoshu, koshu. **Rice variety**: Nakate Shinsenbon (65% polishing ratio).

### Shinryo Yamahai Junmai Daiginjo

Henmi Shuzo (Sado, Niigata Prefecture)

★★★★☆

**An island sake**

Niigata sakes are typically stereo-typed as dry, crisp and clear. This brew couldn't be more different. It's a wonderful golden yellow that you don't traditionally see in Niigata sakes. One reason why Henmi Shuzo's sakes are so different from typical Niigata brews is that the brewery is located on Sado Island, off the coast from the Niigata mainland. Another reason is that it uses medium-hard water. A sip reveals a round sweetness and an intense acidity. Then flavors and aromas coming rushing forth: cooked rice, orange, lemon peel, honey and rice candy. Milky notes dominate. It has an astringent finish, with a lingering afternotes of rice. Warming to 140°F (60°C), will smooth out many of the blips; it has more body, and the acidity is more palatable.

**Recommended pairings:** Stewed pork, teriyaki chicken and Kansas City–style BBQ ribs. Savory-sweet foods with delicious fat pair well. **Type:** Junmai daiginjo, yamahai. **Rice variety:** Not specified (50% polishing ratio).

## Ichinokura Madena

Ichinokura (Osaki, Miyagi Prefecture)

★★★★☆

**Fortified sake that echoes sherry**

The Ichinokura Brewery adapted the Portuguese method of fortifying Madeira wine by adding alcohol to stop fermentation, leaving a high sugar content. Madeira wine is akin to sherry or port but has a unique maturation process that involves heating the wine. Here, Ichinokura dunked this sake in hot springs to achieve that effect. Served chilled, this is a very flavorful, smooth and easy-to-drink sake whose mellow sweetness is complemented by a tangy acidity. Sherry, port and brandy drinkers should feel at home. Aromas of dried fruit, ripe apple and subtle mushrooms add complexity. There are notes of distilled alcohol in the finish. While the rice and cacao aromas are more pronounced at room temperature, this is best chilled to enjoy with light eats. For pairing with a meal, try it warmed to 131°F (55°C).

**Recommended pairings:** Chilled, this sake pairs well with nuts, dried fruits or mature Gruyère cheese. Warmed, go spicy. Japanese- or Indian-style curry is good. **Type:** Unspecified. **Rice variety:** Toyo Nishiki (65% polishing ratio).

## Izumibashi Tokubetsu Junmai

Izumibashi Sake Brewery (Ebina, Kanagawa Prefecture)

★★★☆☆

**Reminiscent of a rice field**

Serving this sake in a glass shows off its light amber hue. Many sake drinkers, especially in Japan, prefer clear brews, but the beautiful color of this junmai is something to behold.

Even slightly chilled, the acidity is strong. On the palate, it's sharp and dry with some mineral notes. Aromas of marshmallow, cream cheese and yogurt are complemented by fruity bouquets of apple and Asian pear. Refreshing scents of spearmint and mature aromas of cacao, mushroom and caramel linger. Warmed to around 108°F (42°C), the rice flavors expand with a silky texture and pleasant sweetness, making pairing easy.

**Recommended pairings:** Grilled oysters, fried tofu in dashi broth and apple pie are all delicious with this sake. **Type:** Tokubetsu junmai **Rice variety:** Not specified (polishing ratio not specified).

## Daisen Tokubetsu Junmai Tomizu

Kato Kihachiro Shuzo (Tsuruoka, Yamagata Prefecture)

★★★☆☆

**Lively, fruity and complex**

A full-bodied sake, this junmai arrives with a boom on the palate when chilled to 50°F (10°C). Sweetness spreads throughout the mouth, with a tinge of fresh acidity. It's fruity, with aromas of melon. However, notes of freshly snipped herbs, finely grained flour and roasted sugar add complexity. Bitterness in the finish leads to citrus afternotes. Warmed to 122°F (50°C), the sweetness dims and the acidity is even more apparent. It's best chilled.

The Kato Kihachiro Shuzo brewery uses the *tomizu jikomi* style of brewing, with equal parts water and rice. This was a common style of brewing in the Edo period (1603–1868) and results in a robust sake.

**Recommended pairings:** With crackers and cream cheese, the sake acts like jam, bringing an acidic fruitiness. **Type:** Tokubetsu junmai. **Rice variety:** Haenuki (60% polishing ratio).

## FULL BODIED

### Junmai Koshu Yamahida Genshu 2002

Kawashiri Shuzoujou (Takayama, Gifu Prefecture)

★★★⯪☆

**A harmony of mature elements**

This is a 17-year-old genshu, pressed in the 2002 brewing year, and aged, and bottled in 2019. This brewery has focused on aged sake since the 1970s, brewing small batches to mature.

On arrival, this golden-hued sake is intense, with pepper and bitterness giving way to mellow and thick flavors. There are notes of hay, dried grapefruit peel, almond, mushrooms and honey, like an autumn harvest. Warmed to 108°F (42°C), pleasant acidity appears, giving this brew a good backbone. Warmed to 113°F (45°C), there are milk chocolate, honey, cashew nut and dried mushroom notes. At 131°F (55°C), matured ricey flavors become apparent, and acidity, sweetness and umami are balanced. Warmed, the sake is still syrupy thick, so cut with water. Diluting by 10–15% brings out white lilies, plus sweetness and acidity. It's smoother and easier to drink. Good chilled or warmed.

**Recommended pairings:** Goes well with pound cake, dried fruit or nuts. **Type:** Junmai, koshu. **Rice variety:** Unspecified (70% polishing ratio).

### Kawatsuru Sanshu Oidemai Junmai Genshu

Kawatsuru Sake Brewing (Kan-onji, Kagawa)

★★★★☆

**Full bodied and sweet**

Oidemai is a relatively new rice variety, developed in 2002 in Kagawa as a variety that could still thrive during climate change. While it is a table rice, several brewers, including Kawatsuru Shuzo, are using oidemai to make sake because the rice has a favorably low protein content, like Yamada Nishiki.

The result is a full-bodied brew with honey-like sweetness and rich rice aromas. The softness coats the tongue. Aromas of roasted sugar, citrus peel, melon, sweetened milk and banana follow. The finish just keeps going and going, punctuated by bitterness and peppery notes.

**Recommended pairings:** Foie gras, Gruyère cheese or anything with umami and salty flavors. **Type:** Junmai. **Rice variety:** Oidemai (70% polishing ratio).

### Kidoizumi Junmai AFS Nama

Kidoizumi Shuzo (Isumi, Chiba Prefecture)

★★★★⯪

**Suitable for summer**

This sake is made with the "hot yamahai" method, in which the brewery adds lactobacillus to the starter mix, which is kept at a high temperature. In most sakes, rice is added as part of the three-step fermentation process, but for AFS the rice is added all at once. The result is a highly acidic yet nuanced brew. Upon tasting, the first impression is strong acidity. There is abundant texture that progressively gets smoother and lighter. White grape and slight grassy aromas prevail in this wonderfully balanced sake. The combination of acidity and fruity sweetness are reminiscent of white wine. The finish is crisp with a tinge of bitter citrus peel. To fully appreciate this refreshing brew, drink it in a glass. Adding carbonated water makes this sake drier, like a dry sparkling wine. It is less sweet, but the acidity and bitterness are nearly the same.

**Recommended pairings:** Cheese, especially cream cheese. **Type:** Junmai, yamahai. **Rice variety:** Fusanomai (65% polishing ratio).

### Junmai-shu Kimoto Zukuri Maruto

Kurosawa Sake Brewery (Sakuho, Nagano Prefecture)

★★★★☆

**Rice stalk attached to the bottle**

The Kurosawa Shuzo brewery is located 2,625 feet (800 meters) above sea level in the Nagano foothills. Sixty percent of what it makes is kimoto. One hundred percent of what it brews is made with local rice.

This isn't a very sweet sake, but it is highly acidic. At room temperature, there are aromas of melon, banana, cooked rice and rice bran. The acidic finish is crisp with banana notes. While the acidity is agreeable, there isn't much complexity and the flavors are a bit thin. Warming to 113°F (45°C) does soften and mellow the sake, but the flavors don't open up as hoped. The added heat does enhance the cooked rice nuances. Drink warm.

**Recommended pairings:** Marinated fish, pickled veggies, and lemon chicken are all winners. **Type:** Junmai, kimoto. **Rice variety:** Miyama Nishiki (65% polishing ratio).

### Fusotsuru Junmai Ginjo Omachi

Kuwabara Sakaba (Masuda, Shimane Prefecture)

★★★★☆

**Wild and crisp**

Many Shimane breweries use Omachi rice for their sake. The grain can offer lots of body and flavor, especially when aged. What's so interesting about this brew from Kuwabara Sakaba is that, yes, it uses Omachi, but the result is acidic, green and crisp.

Warmed to 122°F (50°C), this junmai ginjo is full bodied with strong acidity. The nose offers steamed rice and dried citrus peel. The astringency is strong and reminiscent of wild greens. The crisp finish is rich in umami with lingering milk and strawberry flavors. Recommended warm in a thick, earthenware sake cup.

**Recommended pairings:** Umami-rich foods like grilled oysters work best. The acidity in the sake underscores the taste of the oysters. **Type:** Junmai ginjo. **Rice variety:** Omachi (55% polishing ratio).

### Akatsuki L'aube 2017 Brewing Year

Les Larmes du Levant (Pélussin, France)

★★★★☆

**Made in France**

After Grégoire Boeuf fell in love with sake during a trip to Japan, he learned as much as he could about the drink, even working at the Umetsu sake brewery in Tottori for a year. In 2017, he founded Les Larmes du Levant in Pélussin, France, near Lyon. The initial batches were made from imported Japanese-grown Yamada Nishiki, but the brewery plans to grow its own sake rice in France. The water is from Mont Pilat, and is quite soft by French standard. The bouquet is wonderfully floral and fruity. It's good at room temperature but even better warmed. At around 104°F (40°C), the sake's intense sweetness and acidity are well balanced. There are notes of dried grapefruit, honey, sweet rice and vegetable broth. The finish is lingering, bitter and astringent.

**Recommended pairings:** Vegetable dishes, soups and Camembert are all solid choices. **Type:** Junmai. **Rice variety:** Yamada Nishiki (70% polishing ratio).

## FULL BODIED

### Tsuki no Katsura Junmai Daiginjo Nigori

Masuda Tokubee Shoten (Fushimi, Kyoto Prefecture)

★★★★☆

**A nice companion for spicy foods**

Tsuki no Katsura is a pioneer of nigorizake, having first introduced the cloudy brew in 1964. This is not doburoku, as it is filtered (and thus technically categorized as *seishu*, or "refined sake"). However, nigori sakes like this are filtered so as to allow sediment to pass through, resulting in a cloudy sake.

This brew is made with a Kyoto heirloom rice variety, Iwai. Chilled, it's a relatively dry drink with refreshing aromas of lactic-acid beverages. Elegant hints of rice flour lurk in the background. The finish is crisp and bitter. A refreshing fragrance of green citrus lingers. At 108°F (42°C), it's quite delicious. Don't drink it at room temperature, but rather chilled or slightly warmed.

**Recommended pairings:** This creamy sake is good with spicy food, like Thai curry, Szechuan cuisine or southern Indian cuisine. It's also delicious with *ikura* (cured salmon roe). **Type:** Junmai daiginjo. **Rice variety:** Iwai (50% polishing ratio).

### Suifu Jiman No. 10 Junmai

Meiri Shurui (Mito, Ibaraki Prefecture)

★★★★½

**Fruity without high acidity**

The Brewing Society of Japan's No. 10 yeast is known for creating fragrant apple and pear aromas and low acidity. As expected, this junmai is fruity and juicy. On the palate, it's round and refreshing. There is complexity, with nuances of melon, grapefruit, apricot, condensed milk and subtle herbal notes. The finish is long, with more apricot and melon, plus some added bitterness. This sake is excellent at room temperature. Full bodied and chewy, it also has a strong sweetness and acidity. Warmed to 113°F (45°C), it's still chewy but it softens and the acidity becomes mellow. There's a pleasant afternote of candied apple and savory umami. At 140°F (60°C), things become lighter with agreeable bitterness, a smooth texture and a little bit of chewiness remaining. Nuances of citrus also appear.

**Recommended pairings:** Parmigiano Reggiano, matured Gouda cheese or anchovies, sweet-and-sour pork and foie gras. **Type:** Junmai. **Rice variety:** Gohyakumangoku (66% polishing ratio).

### Hanatomoe Mizumoto x Mizumoto Muroka Nama Genshu

Miyoshino (Yoshino, Nara Prefecture)

★★★★½

**Rice flavors in the background**

Toji Hiroaki Hashimoto has made a mizumoto (bodaimoto) brew in which, in an atypical move, mizumoto sake was added once again in the final brewing stage in lieu of water. The result is a highly acidic sake.

Taking a sip, intense sweetness balances out the acidity. Chilled, it's meaty with a crisp finish. The grassy harshness isn't offputting, and the acidity adds a much-needed backbone. The bitter, fruity astringency is pleasant. Aromas are complex: Darjeeling tea, cacao nib, Gouda cheese, rice candy and cooked rice. Acidity lingers, with apple jam, preserved orange peel, yogurt and cheese. Warmed to 113°F (45°C), it's almost like country-style lemonade, with bouquets of cacao nib and bitter chocolate in the afternotes. At 140°F (60°C), the acidity is noticeable, with the pleasant bitterness of orange peel.

**Recommended pairings:** Spicy Szechuan cuisine; aged Comté; cherry pie. **Type:** Junmai, mizumoto (bodaimoto). **Rice variety:** Unspecified (70% polishing ratio).

### Ine Mankai

Mukai Shuzo (Ine, Kyoto Prefecture)

★★★★☆

**Distinctive rosé-wine appearance**

Made with an ancient variety of dark rice, Ine Mankai looks more like a bottle of rosé than sake. On the palate, the texture is light with a hint of freshness. The aromas mainly consist of cranberry, blueberry and cassis. The overwhelming berry notes certainly are surprising for a beverage made from rice. However, these fragrances are generated during fermentation from polyphenols in the ancient-rice hulls. Good acidity and slight bitterness make this sake seem less sweet than it actually is. At 108°F (42°C), the acidity stands out, and this sake is almost like drinking sweet tea. However, drink it chilled to around 50°F (10°C).

**Recommended pairings:** Ine Mankai's berry flavor marries well with bitter chocolate. Try it with New York–style cheesecake. **Type:** Tokubetsu junmai. **Rice variety:** Not specified (65% polishing ratio).

### Mizubasho Pure

Nagai Sake (Kawaba, Gunma Prefecture)

★★★★☆

**Sparkling sake, years in the making**

It was a daunting task. The Nagai Shuzo brewery set out to make a sparkling sake with a second in-bottle fermentation à la champagne. The result, after years of trial and error, was Mizubasho Pure.

Just looking at the glass, you'd swear this was a sparkling wine. But upon arrival, the traditional flavor of sake makes sure you know exactly what you're drinking. That gap between appearance and flavor is what makes Mizubasho Pure interesting. This isn't a super-sweet sake; it's dry. Apple and Asian pear aromas are joined with rice nuances. The subtle astringency helps define the sake's flavors, leading up to a long, fine rice finish. Serve chilled.

**Recommended pairings:** The fruity flavors of this sake work well with Camembert cheese. **Type:** Sparkling. **Rice variety:** Yamada Nishiki (polishing ratio not specified).

### Kozaemon Tokubetsu Junmai Miyama Nishiki Kimoto Shiboritate

Nakashima Sake Brewing (Mizunami, Gifu Prefecture)

★★★★☆

**Like a dancer, graceful and strong**

Nakashima Sake Brewing is a small brewery in the mountains of Gifu with access to excellent soft water. Their sakes are made with various rice varieties from all over Japan, purchased directly from farmers. This brew uses Miyama Nishiki, the third-most-grown sake rice. The initial impression is of a delicate flower. The sweetness is reminiscent of granulated sugar and the acidity has a hint of grapefruit. Aromas of lemon peel pickled in honey are followed by citrus juice. Afternotes of grapefruit and pear compote linger.

This is a sturdy sake, with heft. It's like a dancer: agile and graceful, but strong and powerful. The balance between these factors makes for a terrific brew. Serve chilled.

**Recommended pairings:** Cream cheese goes extremely well with this sake. Fruit, especially served as compote, is outstanding. This would also be a good dessert sake. **Type:** Tokubetsu junmai, kimoto. **Rice variety:** Shinano Miyama Nishiki (55% polishing ratio).

## FULL BODIED

### Niida Shizenshu Junmai Genshu

Niida Honke (Koriyama, Fukushima Prefecture)

★★★★☆

**A harmonious, complex gift from nature**

*Shizenshu* means "natural sake." This junmai is made without added yeast or lactic acid. On arrival, the first impression is that this sake is intense with a thick and smooth texture. There are sweet notes reminiscent of warm apple cider, winter melon and honey. The depth is impressive, with roasted sugar, Rice Krispies Treats, malted barley, jasmine tea and fresh green grass. All of these complex aromas and flavors are elegantly balanced. Warming to 122°F (50°C) brings out more umami and a candy-coated sweetness, with an acidic finish and lingering sweet rice and black tea nuances.

**Recommended pairings:** Try it chilled with apple pie. **Type:** Junmai. **Rice variety:** Unspecified (80% polishing ratio).

### Niseko Ginpu Tokubetsu Junmai

Niseko Shuzo (Kutchan, Hokkaido Prefecture)

★★★★☆

**Warming releases profound and mature characteristics**

Located in a region of Hokkaido that's famous for skiing, the Niseko Shuzo brewery makes full use of the local climate to brew with a lower-temperature fermentation method. The brewery also sources local rice, including the Hokkaido sake rice Ginpu. Japan's northernmost prefecture is known for hefty sakes, but this one is uncharacteristically soft. At room temperature, rice flavors give way to high acidity and lingering milky afternotes. Warming the brew to 113°F (45°C) brings out a round sweetness and the aroma of candied apple. Further warming to 131°F (55°C) unleashes a variety of aromas such as rice, hay and citrus peel. Fantastic stuff!

**Recommended pairings:** Grilled salted fish works well with this sake's firm acidity and rice aromas. It's also good with teriyaki-flavored dishes. **Type:** Tokubetsu junmai. **Rice variety:** Ginpu (60% polishing ratio).

### Shizengo Cuvée 18 2009

Ooki Daikichi Honten (Yabuki, Fukushima Prefecture)

★★★★☆

**The aromas of oak**

Ooki Daikichi Honten is one of the few sake breweries that ages its stuff in oak casks. Wine and whisky are matured in oak, but sake is typically aged in glass bottles or in stainless steel or enamel tanks. Amazingly, this yamahai hasn't been overwhelmed by the cask. The result is a sake with a strong *yamabuki-iro* or golden-yellow hue. There's a tangy amino acid explosion on arrival, with the no-ticeable—and rather unusual for sake—fragrance of oak. Surprisingly, the acidity and sweetness are fairly balanced. Citrus peel, honey and black tea flavors are followed by dried oranges and wood in the long finish. Recommended warmed to bring out those oak notes even more. It's also terrific at room temperature.

**Recommended pairings:** Spicy Chinese, Thai and Mexican food. It can also be enjoyed on its own. **Type:** Junmai, yamahai. **Rice variety:** Not specified.

### Yamahai Junmai Okuharima

Shimomura Shuzoten (Himeji, Hyogo Prefecture)

★★★★☆

**Born to be warmed**

The Shimomura Shuzoten brewery is located in modern-day Himeji, but the area used to be called Harima. According to the 8th-century text *Harima no kuni fudoki* (*Harima Fudoki: A Record of Ancient Japan*), it was in this region that sake was first brewed from koji. The area is now home to excellent breweries like Shimomura Shuzoten, as well as to fertile fields growing some of the best rice in Japan.

At 131°F (55°C), the sweetness is strong, while the acidity and umami are well balanced. The umami, though, is intense and reminiscent of a savory broth. Aromas of fruity melon, orange peel, caramel and honey round things out. The peppery finish has notes of melon and ice-cream wafers.

**Recommended pairings:** Tofu, prosciutto or sweet-and-sour pork make for good pairings. **Type:** Junmai, yamahai. **Rice variety:** Hyogo Yumenishiki (55% polishing ratio).

### Shinkame Junmai Seishu

Shinkame Shuzo (Hasuda, Saitama Prefecture)

★★★★★

**Reminiscent of the rice harvest**

In 1987, Shinkame Shuzo became Japan's first junmai-only brewery. It wasn't the first to revive junmai, but it was the first to entirely ditch brewer's alcohol for all its sake.

Warming to around 131°F (55°C) brings out aromas of cooked rice, condensed milk and the sake's distinctive lactic acid notes. There's acidity, followed by tastes of dry citrus peel and dried leaves and then a bitterness and a milky sweet aroma reminiscent of rice. The long afternote evokes steamed rice, rice pudding, cashew nuts and almonds. This junmai-shu is like spending a sunny autumn day sprawled out on cut rice straw. I always have a bottle of this at home.

**Recommended pairings:** Umami-rich dishes like grilled oysters are an excellent choice. The acidity and the sweet rice aromas of this sake wrap themselves around savory flavors. **Type:** Junmai. **Rice variety:** Not specified (60% polishing ratio).

### Hachi Hachi 88 Junmai

Shodoshima Shuzo (Shodoshima, Kagawa Prefecture)

★★★★☆

**An unorthodox polishing method**

The Morikuni Shuzo brewery, which was renamed Shodoshima Shuzo in 2019, decided to make this brew using local island rice. But the only rice-polishing machine they have available is for table rice, which is only able to grind away less than 10 percent of the grain. The brewery found that if it polished the rice twice, it could reach a polishing ratio of 88 percent. In Japanese, *hachi* means "eight," hence the sake's name. And what a beautiful-looking drink it is! The golden-yellow color, called *yamabuki-iro*, is that of rice straw after the harvest. Aromas of roasted rice, candied rice, roasted sugar and cashew nuts further underscore the harvest notes. There is a hint of a floral aroma—lily, to be exact. Not overly sweet, the sake does have an intense bitterness and strong astringency. The finish is sharp with rice nuances and a hint of sweetness. Try it at room temperature or hot.

**Recommended pairings:** Gumbo and cured smoked meats. It's also good with Camembert. **Type:** Junmai. **Rice variety:** Oseto (88% polishing ratio).

243

## FULL BODIED

### Harushika Kioke Yamahai Junmai Genshu Tsuyubakaze

S.Imanishi (Nara, Nara Prefecture)

★★★★☆

**A full-bodied and well-balanced sake**

One of Nara's most famous breweries, Imanishi Seibei Shoten revived its *kioke* wooden cask brewing back in 2005. At 54°F (12°C), the first impression of this junmai is that its sweetness, acidity, bitterness and umami are all intense and well balanced. This is followed by aromas of yogurt, cheese, rice and cashew nuts. The texture has a high viscosity, but the finish is crisp, with pleasant astringency. Recommended chilled for full appreciation of the freshness of this sake, but try it warmed to around 104°F (40°C) to enjoy the soft texture and rice scents. This is a very good all-round sake.

**Recommended pairings:** Thai food, especially dishes with sweet chili sauce. **Type:** Junmai, yamahai. **Rice variety:** Tsuyubakaze (70% polishing ratio).

### Suginishiki Tempo 13

Sugii Shuzo (Fujieda, Shizuoka Prefecture)

★★★★★

**Elegant but powerful**

The name of this sake, Tempo 13, refers to the equivalent year in the Japanese imperial calendar (1843 in the West), when the brewery was established. Crafted by the Sugii Shuzo brewery in Shizuoka, this sake was conceived as a modern take on the heavy junmai-shu made before World War II. This brew is made from the locally grown rices Hitomebore and Aichi no Kaori.

The result is a soft and classy sake that has a noticeable pleasing acidity. At room temperature, the texture is gentle, and while the acidity is intense, it doesn't overwhelm. There's good body with aromas of citrus peel and Rice Krispies Treats. The finish is decisive and sharp, with lime peel in the aftertaste. Drink it warm.

**Recommended pairings:** Umami-rich sashimi brings out the rice nuances. It's very good with carbonara pasta, too. **Type:** Junmai, yamahai. **Rice variety:** Hitomebore and Aichi no Kaori (koji-mai 70%, kake-mai 78% polishing ratio).

### Shoki Tokubetsu Junmai

Syoki Sake Brewery (Shiojiri, Nagano Prefecture)

★★★★☆

**This regional sake is the real deal**

*Jizake* (regional sake) is a buzz-word. You see it at breweries and at liquor stores across Japan. But a lot of jizake is designed for Tokyo consumers to satisfy the latest trends instead of reflecting local character. *Toji* Takayuki Morikawa wanted to brew sake that reflected his hometown of Shiojiri in Nagano. The only way to make real jizake was to allow the weather to influence the sake. While this means the results are often uneven, the variation is part of the appeal. Chilled to 59°F (15°C), this junmai is mellow with a fruity bouquet and a hint of sweet rice. There are also wood and honeyed nuances. A round sweetness and strong acidity carry through the long finish that punctuated with rice and savory vegetables. Warmed to 131°F (55°C), the rice flavors are more pronounced. Serve warmed.

**Recommended pairings:** Savory and salty foods; any soy sauce or miso-based dish. **Type:** Tokubetsu junmai. **Rice variety:** Not specified (70% polishing ratio).

### Iwao Gohyakumangoku Hitogokochi Shiboritate Tokubetsu Junmai

Takai (Fujioka, Gunma Prefecture)

★★★★☆

**Candied fruit in a sake cup**

Many of the sake, miso and soy sauce breweries established in the northern Kanto region were founded in the 18th century by merchants from Ohmi (modern-day Shiga Prefecture). The Ohmi merchants were savvy business-men, still known for their famous credo, *sanpo yoshi*, which means, "for the benefit of three sides: the customer, the seller, and society." This brewery was established by one of those legendary merchants.

The sweet and mellow texture of this junmai is immediately apparent, and is soon punctuated by acidity. Aromas of dried candied melon, fruit Jell-O, honey taffy and malted milk follow. The finish is short, with notes of half-ripe fruit and green papaya. That distinct semi-ripe note might put some off, while others might find it oddly appealing. Serve chilled.

**Recommended pairings:** Pistachios complement the unripe and honey notes. The same is true for almond and walnuts. **Type:** Tokubetsu junmai. **Rice variety:** Gohyakumangoku and Hitogokochi (55% polishing ratio).

### Taketsuru Junmai Seishu Hiden

Taketsuru Shuzo (Takehara, Hiroshima Prefecture)

★★★★½

**A warm cup of umami**

The Taketsuru name is well known to fans of Nikka Whisky. But long before that, it was known for tasty sake, especially in Hiroshima. The brewery makes savory, rich brews. This is a classic example.

At room temperature, it's soft, but weighty. There is Taketsuru's signature robustness balanced with excellent bitterness. Warmed to 140°F (60°C), sweetness is pronounced on arrival, followed by acidity, rice aromas, ice-cream wafers, milk chocolate and skim milk. The finish sure packs a punch! On the tongue, it's bitter and minerally with aromas of sweet rice and milk. This sake is like slipping into a warm bath.

**Recommended pairings:** Pork liver, duck and roast beef. **Type:** Junmai. **Rice variety:** Not specified (70% polishing ratio).

### Tamazakura Kimoto Jikomi Junmai Yamada Nishiki 70

Tamazakura Shuzo (Ohnan, Shimane Prefecture)

★★★★½

**Warmed and with food**

Shimane breweries tend to make sakes that are best warmed and with food. Tamazakura is not an exception. Brewed in the kimoto style with locally grown Yamada Nishiki, the sake is aged for about a year. During pressing, this brewery doesn't leave many sake lees behind, the idea being to use as much of the grain as possible.

Warmed to around 122°F (50°C), the pronounced acidity and rich flavors and aromas are impressive. Cooked rice, dried citrus peel, hay and a drizzle of honey add complexity. There's a crisp finish with afternotes of rice.

**Recommended pairings:** Lamb sauté with spicy seasonings (for example, cumin), Szechuan-style dishes and chicken vindaloo also pair nicely. **Type:** Junmai, kimoto. **Rice variety:** Yamada Nishiki (70% polishing ratio).

## FULL BODIED

### Kasen Tokubetsu Junmai Tokyo Wajo

Tamura Shuzojo (Fussa, Tokyo Prefecture)

★★★★☆

**Very Tokyo**

The word *wajo* is taken from a well-known saying in the world of sake, *wajo ryoshu*, which means "Brewing in harmony results in good sake," and also implies that the reverse is true: good sake creates harmony.

This junmai is well balanced and full bodied. Chilled at around 59°F (15°C), its sharp and transparent texture is followed by a slight bouquet of early spring, along with fruity aromas of Asian pear, orange, milk candy and chrysanthemum. Lingering nuances of rice and orange peel are joined by a pleasant bitterness and umami, punctuated by a nice peppery sharpness. Warmed to 122°F (50°C), chrysanthemum and steamed rice appear. Although lovely warmed, it is best served chilled.

**Recommended pairings:** Sweet-and-sour pork or chicken. Noodles seasoned with vinegar and sesame oil also pairs well. **Type:** Tokubetsu junmai. **Rice variety:** Gin Ginga and Yama Sake No. 4 (60% polishing ratio).

### Daigo no Shizuku

Terada Honke (Kanzaki, Chiba Prefecture)

★★★★★

**A natural sake with an ancient brewing method**

Here's one of the few bodaimoto sakes brewed outside Nara. (For more on bodaimoto, see page 24). Brewery Terada Honke used to make sake laced with additives, until former owner Keisuke Terada switched to natural and organic brewing. He regarded this bodaimoto as a high-quality fermented food rather than an alcoholic beverage.

Admiring the brew in a glass, the yellow cloudy hue is reminiscent of the harvest. Made from organic Koshihikari table rice, this sake's bouquet smells of said rice, yogurt whey and Parmigiano Reggiano cheese. Acidity dominates, but a smooth sweetness follows. Fizzy gas produced by the still-living yeast makes this brew refreshing. There are lingering notes of citrus juice, soy sauce, cheese and savory vegetable umami. It's best served chilled, but it's also good at room temperature or slightly warmed.

**Recommended pairings:** Pickles, smoked cheese and pulled BBQ pork. **Type:** Junmai, bodaimoto. **Rice variety:** Koshihikari (90% polishing ratio).

### Tamagawa Shizen Jikomi Junmai Yamahai

Kinoshita Shuzo (Kyotango, Kyoto Prefecture)

★★★★★

**If you like cheese, you'll love this**

Sake from *toji* Philip Harper (see page 127) packs a wallop. This one is especially powerful, with aromas and flavors of rice, cream cheese, evaporated milk, cashew nuts and even butter. On arrival, there's the sharpness of alcohol and strong acidity. The finish is long, with lingering savory umami, buttery afternotes and echoes of Parmigiano Reggiano cheese. This is fantastic stuff! Harper's sake is often best warmed to 113°F (45°C), but it's also incredibly versatile. Try this in simple cocktails: a one-to-one mix with chilled soda makes for a lovely summery drink, while a 1:1 mix with milk (hot or cold, you pick) results in a cocktail reminiscent of almond-milk liqueur. Part of the fun of this sake is just how adaptable it can be.

**Recommended pairings:** The strong flavors in Pecorino Romano cheese harmonize with the cheese aromas in the sake. **Type:** Junmai, yamahai. **Rice variety:** Hyogo Kita Nishiki (66% polishing ratio).

### Tsukasabotan Yama Yuzu Shibori Yuzu no Sake

Tsukasabotan Shuzo (Sagawa, Kochi Prefecture)

★★★⯪☆

**A sake liqueur with local citrus flavor**

This is a sake-based liqueur flavored with the Japanese citrus yuzu. Kochi Prefecture, where this sake is made, is famous for its yuzu citrus. Thus, the Shikoku-based Tsukasabotan brewery sources local, high quality yuzu for a unique liqueur that uses only sake, yuzu and sugar. No other additives are used.

Tasted chilled (around 50°F [10°C]), this sake is smooth with refreshing acidity, strong sweetness and good bitterness. It goes well down the throat. In the background, there are pleasing rice nuances. When warmed to 149°F (65°C), it's even smoother on arrival, with the citrus aromas floating up through the nose. The first thing that comes to mind is hot lemon juice. Yet those rice nuances remain. Serve chilled as an aperitif, but warmed on a chilly winter night.

**Recommended pairings:** When warmed, it's actually better with California roll sushi than traditional sushi. Chilled, drink solo. **Type:** Liqueur with junmai. **Rice variety:** Not specified.

### Furosen Yamahai Junmai Ginjo Kioke Shikomi Tamasakae

Uehara Shuzo (Takashima, Shiga Prefecture)

★★★★⯪

**Brewed in wood**

This an excellent full-bodied sake made with yamahai starter and ambient yeast. This sake is brewed in a *kioke* wooden tub using the local Tamasakae rice variety.

Nosing the glass, the rice bouquet has hints of sweetness. Taking a sip, the arrival is strong and the sake's texture is lucid. The milky flavor is typical for Furosen. The sweetness is subdued, but the acidity and bitterness are intense. Soft and sweet rice aromas are followed by cottage cheese and a pinch of chives. There is a strong bitterness in the aftertaste as well as green citrus. The Furosen brand has always been a little rough around the edges (and delightfully so), but this expression is a more polished and grown-up version. It's best at room temperature.

**Recommended pairings:** This sake brings out the umami of grilled bacon or roast beef. **Type:** Junmai ginjo, yamahai, nama. **Rice variety:** Yamada Nishiki (starter), Tamasakae (main mash) (55% polishing ratio).

### Soma no Tengu Junmai Ginjo Nama Genshu

Uehara Shuzo (Takashima, Shiga Prefecture)

★★★★⯪

**Richer than your typical sokujo**

*Soma no Tengu* means "long-nosed goblin of the timber clearing." This sake is brewed with locally cultivated Yamada Nishiki. This is *usu-nigori* (slightly cloudy) sake and it has a subtle golden hue.

This well-executed, full-bodied sake evokes a mountain landscape and Japan's goblin legends. Even though it's a sokujo brew, it has the deep, nuanced flavors also found in this brewery's yamahai sakes. Chilled to 59°F (15°C), it's chewy yet elegant with a noticeable rice profile. Complex aromas of whey, rice candy, cotton candy and citrus peel appear as if stacked in layers. The lingering citrus acidity, bitterness and milky notes are sublime. Warmed to around 113°F (45°C), the gentle, soft texture is enhanced with hints of rice and wax, followed by rice candy with subtle notes of Darjeeling tea. Best chilled or lightly warmed.

**Recommended pairings:** Chicken, sweet and sour pork. Sushi and marinated sardines are also good. **Type:** Junmai ginjo, nama. **Rice variety:** Yamada Nishiki (59% polishing ratio).

## FULL BODIED

### Tokubetsu Junmai Shikisakura Hana no En

Utsunomiya Shuzo (Utsunomiya, Tochigi Prefecture)

★★★★☆

**Bitter stuff**

The brand name *shikisakura* translates to "the four seasons of sakura," while "hana no en" means "flower party." Made with association yeast No. 10, this junmai is best warmed. At room temperature, it has strong milky flavors of mascarpone as well as fruity apricot notes. But, lurking deeper is the sweetness of dried rice, savory umami and lactic acid. There is a noticeable bitterness.

The finish is long, with savory umami notes, daikon radish and cream cheese. Heated to 122°F (50°C), the milk nuances become softer and the bitterness is masked. Milk chocolate and umami become more pronounced. Try it either at room temperature or warmed.

**Recommended pairings:** Teriyaki chicken, roast beef and candied orange peel. **Type:** Tokubetsu junmai. **Rice variety:** Gohyakuman-goku (60% polishing ratio).

### Hiokizakura Fukkoku Label Junmai 27BY

Yamane Shuzojo (Tottori, Tottori Prefecture)

★★★★½

**Umami synergy, warm it up**

This brewery only makes sake with rice grown by local farmers. Following the mantra, "Brewing is agriculture," Yamane Shuzojo greatly respects rice. It not only adjusts the brewing process according to rice quality, but also by trying to bring out the characteristics of the grain that result from the local climate and the skill of the farmers.

Here's a junmai designed to warm the soul during snow-covered winters. This brew has a lovely yellow hue reminiscent of the rice harvest. It's an older style of sake: soft with pleasant acidity. Aromas of honey, cooked rice and dried citrus peel evoke winter evenings. This sake is best warmed to 122°F (50°C), leaving lingering notes of honey and subtle acidity as you fill your next cup. It's also delicious at room temperature.

**Recommended pairings:** Salty, savory and smoked food complement this sake's sweetness. **Type:** Junmai. **Rice variety:** Yamada Nishiki, Nihonbare (60% polishing ratio).

### Katanozakura Yamahai Junmai Muroka Nama Genshu

Yamano Shuzo (Katano, Osaka Prefecture).

★★★★☆

**Savory food's best friend**

Located in Osaka, the Yamano Shuzo brewery specializes in genshu (undiluted sake). Around 40 percent of its output is genshu. This is an unusually high number. This is an unusual brewery.

Unfiltered, unpasteurized and not watered down, this yamahai brew is big, bold and flavorful. On arrival, the acidity is firm and distinct. Yogurty flavors dominate. The finish is peppery and the aftertaste is rife with bitterness and the sharpness of alcohol.

Osaka is famous for its savory soul food, so it's no surprise that Yamano Shuzo brews robust sake like this.

**Recommended pairings:** Savory food is good. Salty food is good. Even strong-smelling food like anchovies don't overwhelm this brew! But do try it with smoked cheese, which brings out the sake's softness and milky nuances. **Type:** Junmai, yamahai. **Rice variety:** Omachi (65% polishing ratio).

### Nihonbashi Edo no Utage

Yokota Shuzo (Gyoda, Saitama Prefecture)

★★★★☆

**A taste of Old Tokyo**

With this sake, Yokota Shuzo has reproduced the sake of the Edo era (1603–1868). Using the oldest isolated sake yeast *Saccharomyces sake*, the brewery referred to centuries-old sake-making recipes. The result is Edo no Utage, which means "a party in Edo," a full-bodied brew with intense sweetness and acidity. The historical records referenced in making this sake do not describe the brewing methods in great detail. This sake is the fruit of the efforts and imagination of the toji.

A beautiful light amber, this is one good-looking sake. At room temp, it's surprisingly tasty with milky rice notes. On arrival it's soft yet dense. Twinkling acidity sparkles. Scents of cooked rice, yogurt, dry grass, honey and dark cacao come forth. Warming the sake to 86°F (30°C) produces honey orange. The finish brings vivid flavors of cacao, ice-cream wafers and creamy milk. It's best at room temperature.

**Recommended pairings:** Savory broths such as onion soup. Chicken piccata is also good. **Type:** Junmai. **Rice variety:** Asa no Hikari (70% polishing ratio).

### Chikubushima Hana Arashi

Yoshida Shuzo (Takashima, Shiga Prefecture)

★★★★★

**A sake that blossoms**

The Yoshida Shuzo brewery has been working with a nearby farmer for decades to secure suitable local sake rice. *Hana arashi* means "flower storm," a typical sight in spring when gusts of wind dislodge cherry blossom petals.

Nosing the sake, there are apple and intense tangerine aromas, followed by rice and sweet milky notes. This is a full-bodied attack with a viscous texture that makes its arrival clearly known the moment it hits the palate. There's a medium finish with some slight sweetness and umami. In the background, a pleasant acidity reverberates. When warmed, this sake blossoms, bringing out its true character. It is also suitable for aging.

**Recommended pairings:** Fermented dishes as well as food with strong acidity and intense umami. It also goes well with fried chicken or tempura and salad with simple olive oil dressing. Try it with Camembert. **Type:** Junmai daiginjo. **Rice variety:** Yamada Nishiki (50% polishing ratio).

### Takacho Bodaimoto Junmai

Yucho Shuzo (Gose, Nara Prefecture)

★★★★☆

**The prayers of Buddhist monks**

Each January, a handful of Nara brewers gather at Shoryakuji Temple, where the bodaimoto fermentation starter was previously formalized (see page 162). Yucho Shuzo is one of the breweries that participates and it brews a bodaimoto for its Takacho brand.

Taking a sip at room temperature, it's full bodied with a syrup-like texture. There are distinctive bodaimoto-typical aromas of aged Gruyère cheese, banana and vanilla. The pronounced sweetness and acidity are reminiscent of tropical fruit. Lingering, strong aromas of cheese and milk come through in the finish. Drinking this brew brings back memories of watching Buddhist monks say prayers over the batches of bodaimoto on a cold and wet January afternoon. Good chilled or warmed.

**Recommended pairings:** Salt and pepper grilled chicken or white fish like cod, flounder or halibut. **Type:** Junmai, bodaimoto. **Rice variety:** Hinohikari (70% polishing ratio).

# GLOSSARY OF JAPANESE TERMS

**aki-agari** Literally "rising autumn," this describes how brewed sake improves and matures over the summer for delicious bottlings in the fall.

**amakuchi** Sweet flavored.

**bodaimoto** A type of highly acidic yeast starter made by Buddhist monks. It is also called *mizumoto*.

**choko** *see* **ochoko**

**daiginjo** or **daiginjo-shu** Literally "big" or "great" ginjo. This sake is made from rice with a 50 percent polishing ratio.

**doburoku** Unfiltered sake.

**futsu-shu** Literally "regular sake," but typically translated as "table sake." It contains additives like sugar and typically, brewer's alcohol.

**genshu** Sake that has not been cut with water.

**ginjo** or **ginjo-shu** This sake is made from rice with a 60 percent polishing ratio. Unless it's junmai ginjo, it contains added brewer's alcohol.

**guinomi** A sake cup that is typically larger than an ochoko cup, but those terms are used interchangeably. Guinomi might take its meaning from *guitto nomu* or "bottoms-up drinking."

**hi-ire** Pasteurization.

**hiya** Room-temperature sake. The term *jouon* refers generally to room temperature and can be used to refer to sake.

**honjozo** or **honjozo-shu** Literally "true brewed sake." It is made with a limited amount of added alcohol, and rice polished to 70 percent or less.

**jouon** *see* **hiya**

**junmai** or **junmai-shu** "Pure-rice sake." Made with water, rice, koji and yeast. It does not have added brewer's alcohol.

**junmai daiginjo** or **junmai daiginjo-shu** Daiginjo sake that is made without brewer's alcohol.

**junmai ginjo** or **junmai ginjo-shu** Ginjo sake made without brewer's alcohol.

**kai-ire** The technique of mixing with the kai stirring tool.

**kake-mai** Steamed rice is either used to make koji (*koji-mai*), or added directly to the mash (*kake-mai*). *Kake* means "pour" and *mai* means "rice."

**karakuchi** Dry flavored.

**kasu** Sake lees left over after pressing.

**kimoto** A yeast sake in which natural lactic acid bacteria is cultivated. In the kimoto method, brewers ram tubs of rice and water with

poles. It takes about four weeks to make this yeast starter.

**kioke** Traditional wooden fermentation and storage tubs.

**kobo** Yeast.

**koji** Sweet, mold-covered rice that has been inoculated with the koji-kin spores.

**koji-kin** Microorganisms that are key in making sake, shochu, miso and more. It's a cornerstone of Japanese fermentation and food production.

**koji-mai** The steamed rice set aside for koji making.

**koshiki** The tub used for steaming rice. In the past, it was traditionally made from Japanese cedar.

**koshu** Old sake. While there is no legal definition, technically any sake over a year old is koshu. If sake is over three years old, it can be called *jukusei koshu* (matured koshu).

**kura** Brewery.

**kurabito** Brewer. Literally, it means "brewery person."

**kuramoto** Brewery owner.

**kyokai kobo** Association yeast.

**moromi** The main mash.

**moto** The yeast starter. Also known as shubo.

**muroka** Unfiltered.

**nama** Unpasteurized.

**nama-zake** Unpasteurized sake.

**nihonshu** Japanese sake.

**ochoko** Sake cup. Tends to be smaller than the guinomi, but these terms are used interchangeably. It often comes with a matching tokkuri sake flask.

**reishu** Cold sake.

**sakabune** Old-style sake press in which bags filled with sake are laid upon each other and then pressure is put on top of the press to squeeze out sake.

**sandan jikomi** Three-step brewing process to make sake.

**seimaibuai** Rice-polishing ratio.

**shibori** This word refers to the pressing of sake. *Shiboritate* means "just pressed."

**shinpaku** The starchy white core found in certain types of rice, such as Yamada Nishiki.

**shinshu** "New sake." The sake made in the current brewing year.

**shubo** Literally "the mother of sake," this is the sake yeast starter used in brewing. It's also known as moto.

**shuki** Sake vessels or sake set. It includes the tokkuri (flask) and cups.

**shuzo** Brewery. Many Japanese sake makers have the word "*shuzo*" as part of their name. *Jozo*, which means "brewing,"

and *jozoten*, meaning "brewing shop," are also common.

**sokujo** or **sokujo-moto** The "quick start" yeast starter in which lactic acid is added to the mix.

**sugidama** "Japanese cedar ball." The iconic sake symbol hung outside breweries. It's also known as sakabayashi.

**tanrei** Crisp and clean.

**tanrei karakuchi** Light bodied and dry.

**taru** Cask. Taruzake is sake that has been aged in sake casks, typically for a quick finish.

**toji** Master brewer.

**tokkuri** Sake flask.

**tokubetsu** Special. In sake, it's used to denote special care given to a brew (i.e., tokubetsu junmai). There is no standard, legal definition in the sake industry for what this really means.

**umami** One of the five basic flavors. It is sometimes described as "savory."

**Yabuta** This is a brand name for the most popular and commonly found automatic accordion press.

**yamahai** A style of yeast starter in which the kimoto pole-mashing step is omitted.

**yama-oroshi** Technique of mashing rice and koki with oar-like poles in small tubs.

# SAKE RESOURCES

**Sake Speciality Stores**
An increasing number of liquor stores abroad carry high-quality sake, but here are some online and bricks-and-mortar sake specialty shops:

**MM Sake** (online only): mmsake.com

**Sake 36**: sake36.com

**The Sake Shop** (Honolulu, HI): sakeshophawaii com

**Sake Social** (online only): sakesocial.com

**Saketora** (online only): saketora.com

**Tippsy Sake** (online only): tippsysake.com

**Sakaya** (New York, NY): sakayanyc.com

**True Sake** (San Francisco, CA): truesake.com

**Sake Associations**
**American Sake Association**: americansakeassociation.org

**Japan Sake and Shochu Makers Association**: japansake.or.jp/sake/english

**Sake Education**
The organizations below offer various kinds of training.

**Sake Sommelier Association**: sakesommelierassociation.com

**J.S.A. Sake Diploma: Japan Sommelier Association**: sommelier.jp/exam/sake_en.html

**Japan Sake and Shochu Makers Association**: sakebunka.jp/academy

**The Sake Education Council**: sakeeducationcouncil.org

# PHOTO CREDITS

# INDEX

# ACKNOWLEDGMENTS

This book would not have been possible without the cooperation, insights and support of many. Thank you to Mototsune Aikawa, Matt Alt, Isao Aramaki, Asano Nihonshuten, Association for Long Term Aged Sake, Atelier Entaku, Awakura Onsen Motoyu, Mitsuhiro Ban, Bishu Tachinomi Melon, Grégoire Boeuf, Roberto Casillas, Chang Chin Cheng, Aoi Chao, Suzy Cho, Marcus Consolini, Yasutaka Daimon, Blaise DeAngelo, Atsushi Deguchi, Rio Domae, Doshisha University Library, Brandon Doughan, Yoshiyuki Endo, Masatsugu Fujino, Hisashi Fukuda, Kazuhiro Fukumoto, Fukunishiki Sake Brewing, Fushimi Sakezo's Bar, John Gauntner, Takuma Goda, Ozanne Guillaume, Gotoshi, Hakko Shokudo Kamoshika, Hana Sake Bar, Norihide Harada, Yumi Harada, Margarida Haraguchi, Philip Harper, Ryuji Hashimoto, Tadakazu Hashimoto, Teruaki Hashimoto, Yoshihiro Hashimoto, Shunsuke Hayakawa, Toshihito Hayakawa, Gordon Heady, Chiyoko Higashi, Akitsu City Library Higashihiroshima, Koichi Higuchi, Shu Hirata, Yoko Hiraoka, Kiyoo Hirooka, Hirotsugu Hisada, Ryusuke Honda, Aki Ikeda, Masayuki Imanishi, Chiso Inaseya, Hiroya Ishida, Keizo Ishida, Tatehiro Ishiguro, Yuichiro Ishii, Kadzuo Ishikura, Koichi Itogawa, Satoko Iwai, Takashi Iwai, Izakaya Issa, Izakaya Matsu, David Joll, Teruyuki Kamachi, Noriko Kamei, Saori Kasai, Isonobu Kawasaki, Yasushi Kawasaki, Yuji Kawasaki, Eriko Kikkawa, Genki Kimura, Hisato Kimura, Shikou Kimura, Kinkonkan, Kinoshita (São Paulo), Yukihiro Kitagawa, Tamami Kiyono, Tadahiko Kobayashi, Kyoto Brighton Hotel, Mads Kleppe, Takeshi Kodera, Tatsuya Kojima, Dai Komai, Hiroyuki Konno, Arve Krognes, Hironobu Kubota, Takahisa Kusaka, Lee Cheng Yen, Machiya Studio (Kyoto Research Park), Tsuneo Maruyama, Natori Masanori, Marc Matsumoto, Tadayuki Matsuse, Kazuma Matsuzawa, Masakazu Minatomoto, Tony Mitchell, Shokichi Mitsui, Fumiya Miura, Daisuke Miyauchi, Masashi Mizogaki, Nobuo Mori, Takayuki Morikawa, Izumi Motai, Mari Motoda, Kuniko Mukai, Shigeru Mukuda, Yoshihiko Murai, Satoshi Murayama, Jake Myrick, Ayako Nakamura, Tomohiro Nakamura, Nami Bar, National Diet Library, Misayo Nihei, Iwao Niizawa, Michitaka Nishimura, Tsukasa Nishida, Naohiko Noguchi, Noma, Shunsuke Ogino, Tetsuo Ohara, Hideharu Ohta, Hiroshi Oishi, Hiroaki Oku, Kotaro Oku, Mariko Oku, Osaka University Library, Maho Otsuka, Hideyuki Ozaki, Jeff Pash, Ernesto Reyes, Kazuhiro Sakai, Yashiro, Sakasyo Kumazawa, Sake Story, Hiroshi Sakurai, Kazuhiro Sakurai, Takanobu Sato, Yusuke Sato, Akira Shimmyo, Jiro Shinoda, Yumi Shintani, Masataka Shirakasi, Butch Smith, Joslyn Hernandez Smith, Kinnosuke Sugii, Sugawara Saketen Standing Bar, Tachinomi Jack and Matilda, Takuma Sugimoto, Toshinari Takahashi, Yukichi Takamatsu, Atsunori Takeshima, Ryuji Takahashi, Mr. and Mrs. Saburo Takeshita, Toshio Taketsuru, Tamba Toji Museum, Takeshi Tamura, Akira Tanaka, Hisatomo Tanaka, Yosuke Tanaka, Yuuya Tanaka, Naruaki Tanda, Yoshifumi Tashima, Ti-da in A new+clear structure on-da building, Yasunobu Tomita, Rodrigo David Ortigosa Torres, Ben Turner, Isao Uehara, Naoko Ueta, Hiroshi Ujita, Umasake Kamunabi, Yuki Urabe, Kazuki Usui, Jesus Ernesto Reyes Valenzuela, Wakka Shinsaibashi, Washu Bar AGI, Waura Sakaba, Kunihiro Yamauchi, Hironomi Yamada, Tasuku Yamada, Toshiharu Yamamoto, Kunihiro Yamauchi, Yuji Yamauchi, Michihiro Yamamura, Yuuko Yamaji, Shohei Yamane, Sonia Yuki Yamane, Kazuhiko Yanase, Kenny Yang, Yoshiaki Yano, Taiji Yasuda, Robert Yellin, Masayuki Yokomoto, Yasuo Yokosaka, Yasuyoshi Yokota, Hajime Yoshida, Sumio Yoshida and all the breweries we visited but were unable to feature.

Brian Ashcraft would also like to thank his wife, three sons, his mother, and extended family as well as Cathy Layne and Eric Oey at Tuttle. He dedicates this book to his father, who taught him the value of hard work.

Takashi Eguchi would like to thank his wife and daughter, brother, parents, sake friends and workshop participants, Cathy Layne and Eric Oey.

Published in 2020 by Tuttle Publishing, an imprint of Periplus Editions (HK) Ltd.

**www.tuttlepublishing.com**

ISBN 978-4-8053-1505-7

Distributed by
**North America, Latin America & Europe**
Tuttle Publishing
364 Innovation Drive
North Clarendon, VT 05759-9436 U.S.A.
Tel: (802) 773-8930 | Fax: (802) 773-6993
info@tuttlepublishing.com | www.tuttlepublishing.com

**Japan**
Tuttle Publishing
Yaekari Building, 3rd Floor
5-4-12 Osaki
Shinagawa-ku
Tokyo 141 0032
Tel: (81) 3 5437-0171 | Fax: (81) 3 5437-0755
sales@tuttle.co.jp | www.tuttle.co.jp

**Asia Pacific**
Berkeley Books Pte. Ltd.
3 Kallang Sector #04-01/02,
Singapore 349278
Tel: (65) 6741-2178 | Fax: (65) 6741-2179
inquiries@periplus.com.sg | www.tuttlepublishing.com

Printed in Malaysia    2309VP
27  26  25  24  23    6  5  4  3

## "Books to Span the East and West"

**Tuttle Publishing** was founded in 1832 in the small New England town of Rutland, Vermont [USA]. Our core values remain as strong today as they were then—to publish best-in-class books which bring people together one page at a time. In 1948, we established a publishing outpost in Japan—and Tuttle is now a leader in publishing English-language books about the arts, languages and cultures of Asia. The world has become a much smaller place today and Asia's economic and cultural influence has grown. Yet the need for meaningful dialogue and information about this diverse region has never been greater. Over the past seven decades, Tuttle has published thousands of books on subjects ranging from martial arts and paper crafts to language learning and literature—and our talented authors, illustrators, designers and photographers have won many prestigious awards. We welcome you to explore the wealth of information available on Asia at **www.tuttlepublishing.com.**